Geography of Growth

Geography of Growth
Spatial Economics and Competitiveness

Raj Nallari, Breda Griffith, and Shahid Yusuf

THE WORLD BANK
Washington, D.C.

1 2 3 4 15 14 13 12

ISBN (paper): 978-0-8213-9486-1
ISBN (electronic): 978-0-8213-9487-8
DOI: 10.1596/978-0-8213-9486-1

Library of Congress Cataloging-in-Publication Data
Nallari, Raj, 1955-
Geography of growth : spatial economics and competitiveness / by Raj Nallari, Breda Griffith, and Shahid Yusuf.
  p. cm.
Includes bibliographical references.
  ISBN 978-0-8213-9486-1—ISBN 978-0-8213-9487-8 (electronic)
1. Space in economics. 2. Urban economics. 3. Economic geography. I. Griffith, Breda. II. Yusuf, Shahid, 1949- III. World Bank. IV. Title.
  HT388.N36 2012
  330.9173'2 — dc23
                                                                                2012008450

Cover photo: view of Sofia, Bulgaria by Boris Balabanov/World Bank.

Contents

Preface   *xi*
About the Authors   *xiii*
Abbreviations   *xv*

Chapter 1   **Frameworks for Spatial Analysis**   1
                  The Form of Urbanization   2
                  Agglomeration Economies   8
                  Conclusion   11
                  Notes   12
                  References   12

Chapter 2   **Urbanization as a Typology of Space**   15
                  Urbanization and Space   16
                  Classification of Cities   18
                  Size of Cities across Developing and
                      Developed Regions   20
                  Criticism of the Data and Suggested Alternatives   23
                  Conclusion   26
                  Notes   27
                  References   28

Chapter 3	**Urban Transition and Growth**	**29**
	Urbanization and Development	30
	Urbanization in Developing Countries	38
	Key Features of Cities in Developing Countries	43
	Conclusion	46
	Notes	47
	References	48
Chapter 4	**Spatial Concentration and Specialization**	**51**
	Specialization of Cities	52
	Knowledge Cities	54
	The Creative City	65
	The Global City	73
	Green Cities/Eco Cities	76
	Conclusion	81
	Notes	82
	References	83
Chapter 5	**The Attributes and Role of "Smart Cities"**	**89**
	Growth and Technology-Intensive Subsectors	91
	What Makes Cities Smart	99
	Toward an Urban Innovation Strategy	108
	Policy Measures That Facilitate Technological Upgrading and Innovation	112
	Identifying and Promoting Smart Cities	117
	Annex: Technology Capability and Innovation Criteria	118
	Notes	120
	References	122
Chapter 6	**Globalization, Urban Regions, and Cluster Development**	**127**
	A Holistic Approach to Development	128
	The Role of Clusters	128
	Policies to Support Clusters	130
	Sustaining Clusters	130
	Conclusion	132
	Notes	134
	References	134

Chapter 7	Urban Development and Growth	**137**
	Urbanization: From Canter to Gallop	139
	The Metropolitan Powerhouse	143
	Metropolitan Challenges	146
	Wealth of Cities and National Policies	147
	Notes	149
	References	153
Chapter 8	Elements for Future Success of Metropolitan Regions	**157**
	The Industrial Matrix	159
	Connectivity	163
	The Smarter Metropolis	167
	Governing the Metropolitan Center	169
	The Resilience Imperative	170
	Metropolitan Futures	174
	Annex: City Rankings	176
	Notes	178
	References	181

Box

| 4.1 | Indexes Used in the Global City Indicators Program | 76 |

Figures

1.1	Primacy and Economic Development, 1965–95	4
1.2	Concentration of Economic Activity in the United States	6
2.1	Total Population, by City Size, 1995, 2009, and 2025	19
2.2	Distribution of the World Urban Population, by Region, 1950, 2009, and 2050	22
2.3	Key Indicators of the Agglomeration Index	25
2.4	Agglomeration Index and UN Estimates of Urban Population, by Region, 2000	25
2.5	Sensitivity to Indicators Used: Example of Minimum Population Size of Large Cities	27
3.1	Relationship between GDP and Spatial Concentration	32
3.2	Density and GDP per Capita in Selected Countries, by Phase of Urbanization	34
3.3	Rural-Urban Disparities in GDP per Capita	35

3.4   Rural-Urban Disparities and Density in the Philippines,
        China, and India, Various Years   36
3.5   Change in Urban Population with and without
        China and India, 1985–2005   38
4.1   GCIF Membership in 2010, by Population Category   77
5.1   Shanghai R&D Public Service Platform   115
6.1   Ranking of Metropolitan Cities   133
7.1   Strong Correlates of Urban Productivity
        (City GDP per Capita) in China, 2007   142
7.2   Exposure of People to Cyclones and Earthquakes,
        2000 and by 2050   144
7.3   Coastal Population of Selected Countries That Are
        Highly Vulnerable to Sea Level Rise   145
8.1   Industry Contributions to Productivity Growth in the
        United States, 1960–2007   160
8.2   R&D Intensity, by Industry Averaged across 10 OECD
        Countries   161
8.3   Contributions to Productivity Growth in the
        United States, by Industry, 1960–2007   163
8.4   Industry Contributions to Productivity in the
        United States, 1960–2007   164

Tables

1.1   Regional Development Policies Calibrated to Integrate
        Countries, by Density of Population   9
2.1   Population and Average Annual Rate of Change,
        by Group and Selected Years, 1950–2050   17
2.2   Number of Cities and Percentage of Total Population,
        by Size of City, 2009 and 2025   19
2.3   Size of Cities, by Region, Number of Inhabitants, and
        Share of Population, Selected Years, 1975, 2009, 2025   20
2.4   Percentage of Population Living in Urban Areas
        by Region, Selected Years, 1950–2050   21
2.5   Average Annual Rate of Change in Urban Population,
        1950–2025   23
2.6   National and UN Data on Urbanization
        in Selected Countries   24
3.1   Regional Differences in Urbanization   39
3.2   A Dozen Economies of Scale   44

4.1   Manufacturing and Business Services in the
       United States, by Size of City, 1910 and 1995   53
4.2   Share of New York County (Manhattan)
       in Total Private Employment in the United States, 1997   54
4.3   Dimensions of Knowledge Base: Measures and Results   56
4.4   The Knowledge Base and Economic Performance
       in Select Cities   57
4.5   Metropolitan Area Regressions   59
4.6   Underpinnings of Knowledge Cities   63
4.7   Creativity Rankings in the United States,
       by City Size   67
4.8   Creative Class Occupations, Ranked
       by Percentage Change   69
4.9   Creative Workers: Consumers and Producers   71
4.10   Global City Indicators: City Services   75
4.11   Global City Indicators: Quality of Life   75
4.12   Role of Standardized Indicators for Cities   77
4.13   Summary of Results on Carbon Emissions
       per Home, 2006   78
5.1   Sources of GDP Growth in China, 1978–2004   92
5.2   Sources of GDP Growth in the Industrial
       and Services Sectors in China, 1978–2004   92
5.3   Fastest-Growing Manufactured Exports Worldwide,
       1997–2007   93
5.4   Fastest-Growing Manufactured Exports from Asia,
       1997–2007   94
5.5   Fastest-Growing Manufacturing Industries in China,
       1996–2003   95
5.6   Top 10 Exports from China, 2006   95
5.7   Imports to China, 2002, 2005, 2008   96
5.8   Imports of High-Tech Products as a Percentage
       of Total Imports in China, 2002, 2005, 2008   96
5.9   Top USPTO Patents Worldwide, 2005–09   97
5.10   Share of WIPO Patents, by Sector, 2007–09   98
5.11   Top Five Patenting Industries in the United States, 2006 98
5.12   Top Five Industries Contributing to TFP Growth
       in the United States, 1960–2005   99
5.13   Science and Technology Occupations
       in the United States   103

5.14	S&T Jobs in Select High-Tech Industries in the United States, 1997	104
5.15	High-Tech Jobs in Select Cities in the United States, 1997	104
5.16	IT Jobs in Select Cities in the United States, 1997	105
5.17	Key High-Tech Sectors in Seattle	105
7.1	Contribution of Manufacturing and Services to GDP, 1980–2008	140
8A.1	Mercer Quality of Living Ranking of Cities Worldwide, 2010	176
8A.2	Ranking of Creative Cities in the United States, by Arts Employees per Capita, 2008	177
8A.3	Ranking of Innovative Cities in the United States, 2008	177
8A.4	Top 10 Innovation Cities in the World, 2010	177
8A.5	Ranking of Innovation Cities in the Americas, 2010	178

Preface

Economists have emphasized the importance of geography in growth and competitiveness, yet rarely has there been literature that identifies the cause of growth in some cities but not in others. Why was the city of Bangalore more attractive for industries than Karachi? What are the defining characteristics of successful cities? This book seeks to answer these questions through multiple consultations with leading experts and in-depth research on urban centers.

Geography of Growth has been written for academics and practitioners; it combines the theoretical background on urban centers with concrete recommendations. The eight chapters move from providing background on the various models of urban centers to hypothesizing why growth and development are more prominent in some cities than in others.

Chapter 1 addresses two questions: How has spatial concentration evolved with growth and development, and what are the efficiency implications of too much or too little spatial concentration? This chapter summarizes the various models that analyze growth by geographic concentration and sets the foundation for concepts discussed in later chapters.

Chapter 2 focuses on urbanization in geographies. There is pressure to effectively measure the urban population, which is expected to grow by

84 percent within the next 40 years. This chapter discusses how UN data measures growth, as well as the criticisms on the metrics used.

Chapter 3 correlates urban presence with economic density in developed and developing countries. It initially focuses on how urban transition and growth are blurring the rural-urban divide and the unprecedented volume of people who are moving to urban areas. The second part examines regional trends in urban growth for the developing countries, then discusses some key features of cities in developing regions.

Chapter 4 discusses how different industries inhabit and impact various urban sectors. For example, the chapter opens by describing how small and medium cities in Japan, the Republic of Korea, and the United States are highly specialized because of the requirements and influences of the types of industry there. This chapter expands on the economic correlations mentioned in chapter 3.

Chapter 5 contextualizes urban growth in the current technological landscape as innovation, particularly in information technology, has become critical to increasing productivity and consequently growth. This chapter provides examples of "smart cities" and identifies common attributes that contribute to their success. This chapter also provides policy recommendations for practitioners on how to make cities "smarter."

Chapter 6 further analyzes urbanization in the current global context, specifically, the impact of globalization and industry clusters on urbanization. By citing examples of how globalization has had spillover effects in the urban sector, the chapter demonstrates the importance of globalization and the relevance of the growth of industry clusters in places such as Bangalore and Shenzhen. It segues to chapter 7.

Chapter 7 addresses a current fundamental global trend: Why has urbanization been growing rapidly since the 1950s? Some theories suggest that it is industry that spurs urbanization and consequently growth in infrastructure, however this is not the case. Instead—the chapter concludes by looking at data across regions and cities—the municipalities are pivotal in influencing infrastructure development and growth in urban centers.

Finally, chapter 8 deciphers why some cities are more successful than others. Why do Karachi and São Paulo have the human capital that qualifies them as urban centers but not as thriving cities? By citing examples of successful cities, this chapter provides policy recommendations on how to make a city competitive in today's economy.

The authors would like to thank the policy experts and academics who helped identify key data, as well the administrative and publishing staff for helping in the successful production of this book.

About the Authors

Raj Nallari is the sector manager for the Growth and Competitiveness Practice at the World Bank Institute (WBI). He has worked at the World Bank for more than 20 years in various departments. Previously he worked at the International Monetary Fund. Raj has published on various topics, including growth adjustment systems, the labor market and gender, and macroeconomics. He has also edited several volumes of *Development Outreach*. He holds a PhD in economics from the University of Texas at Austin.

Breda Griffith has worked as a consultant with WBI since 2005 in the areas of growth, poverty, gender, development, and labor markets. Her experience is deep and wide-ranging with publications in refereed journals on development and language maintenance, entrepreneurship, and small business. Breda has also co-authored books on economic growth, poverty, gender and macroeconomic policy, new directions in development, and labor markets in developing countries. She holds a PhD in economics from Trinity College Dublin, Ireland and an MA in economics from the National University of Ireland.

Shahid Yusuf joined the World Bank in 1974 as a Young Professional; while at the Bank, he spent more than 35 years tackling issues confronting developing countries. He has written extensively on development issues, with a special focus on East Asia, and has also published widely in various academic journals. Shahid is currently Chief Economist for the Growth Dialogue at the George Washington University School of Business. He holds a PhD in economics from Harvard University and a BA in economics from Cambridge University.

Abbreviations

AI	agglomeration index
FDI	foreign direct investment
GCIF	Global Cities Indicators Facility
GCIP	Global Cities Indicators Program
GDP	gross domestic product
GHG	greenhouse gas
GVIO	gross value of industrial output
ICT	information and communications technology
IT	information technology
MNC	multinational corporation
MSA	metropolitan statistical area
OECD	Organisation for Economic Co-operation and Development
PMSA	primary metropolitan statistical area
R&D	research and development
SAR	Special Administrative Region
SME	small and medium enterprise
S&T	science and technology
TFP	total factor productivity
UN	United Nations
USPTO	U.S. Patent and Trademark Office
WIPO	World Intellectual Property Organization

CHAPTER 1

Frameworks for Spatial Analysis

Since the 1990s, the new economic geography has received a lot of atten-tion, as mainstream economists such as Krugman (1991a, 1991b) and others began to focus on where economic activity occurs and why. While economic geography has always been central to such questions, it has often been ignored, given the difficulties with modeling some of the relationships—for example, increasing returns and imperfect competition at the regional and urban levels. Using models to analyze industrial orga-nization, international trade, and growth theory has helped to spur the use of economic geography, which seeks to explain concentrations of population, economic activity, or both, such as agricultural areas, indus-trial areas, cities, and industry clusters. These concentrations of popula-tion or economic activity are subject to agglomeration economies and are thus self-reinforcing. The new economic geography seeks to understand why such concentrations arise and why they are self-reinforcing.[1] Our concern here is not with the new economic geography per se but rather with the forces that give rise to spatial concentration of population and economic activity: How has spatial concentration evolved with growth and development, and what are the efficiency implications of too much or too little spatial concentration?

The Form of Urbanization

Urbanization is a transitory process (Henderson 2003) exemplified by movements of population from rural to urban areas predicated on the marginal product of labor being higher in the urban area. The Harris and Todaro (1970) model, the workhorse for most development economists, deals with issues concerning rural-urban migration, where workers decide to migrate or not based on expected income differentials between rural and urban areas rather than just wage differentials. Here, we assume that agriculture is the traditional sector, with low productivity, low wages, and no unemployment, as labor is perfectly competitive and mobile. This implies that rural-urban migration in a context of high urban unemployment can be economically rational if expected urban income (defined as actual wages adjusted for the unemployment rate) exceeds expected rural income. In equilibrium, the expected urban wage is equal to the marginal product of an agricultural worker, and there is no migration.

However, economic activity began to concentrate in certain places, leading to uneven growth and development. The assumption of constant returns to scale as in the Harris-Todaro model could not explain the unevenness or "spikes in economic maps." Regional and urban development seemed to be better explained by monopolistic competition and increasing returns to scale of production, and this meant that the assumption of perfect competition in models of spatial economics had to be dropped. Around this time, Dixit and Stiglitz (1977) developed a model of monopolistic competition, and this proved useful in several fields, including spatial economics, new trade theory, and new growth theory: monopolistic competition gives rise to economic power, which in turn can lead to increasing returns.

Henderson (2003) acknowledges the contribution that these dual-economy models make but points out critical defects. First, the dual starting point is assumed and not modeled. Second, there are no forces for agglomeration where we would expect to see industrial concentration in the urban sector. And third, there is little mention of spatial aspects of the economy. The core-periphery models, especially those configured in an economic growth context, and Krugman's 1991 interpretation attempt to address these three issues. Core-periphery models are "more about urban concentration" (Henderson 2003, 5).

Urban Concentration

Urbanization involves the movement out of rural areas and into urban areas, and government policy can have an effect on this transition and on the sectoral composition of national output. For example, central government policies that promote labor mobility, develop infrastructure, and remove impediments to internal trade will affect the mix of urban-rural population. Other policies of local governments such as the provision of public goods and amenities also get reflected in the urban cost-of-living curve and may influence the population mix. At initial and middle stages of development, government policies—through tariffs, price controls, and subsidies—directly affect the national composition of output and indirectly affect urbanization.

Urban concentration is usually predicated on the existence of urban primacy and its robustness over time. For example, the convergence-divergence debate in the economic growth literature has also been applied to urban primacy—that is, it asks, Do the other urban centers converge on the primary city over time? What are the economic policies hindering or helping such a process? The models assume a dual-economy approach: the primary city and other urban places. Primacy is the simplest measure of urban concentration, and a common expression is the ratio of the population of the largest metro area to all of the urban population in the country (Henderson 2003).[2] Results from the empirical studies suggest that there is an inverted U-shape relationship, where relative concentration first peaks and then declines with economic development (figure 1.1). The U shape is more relevant in earlier (1965–75) than in later (1985–95) periods (Henderson 2003).

Optimal primacy is the level that maximizes national productivity growth, with large deviations in primacy strongly affecting productivity growth.[3] Henderson notes a tendency toward primacy in Algeria, Argentina, Chile, Mexico, Peru, and Thailand. Political economy and government policies can be complicit in fostering excessive concentration and favoring a primary city (usually the national capital) over other cities. Favored cities tend to draw in enormous populations that create an "extremely congested high cost-of-living metro area" (Henderson 2003, 10). Local government can help to preempt this unsustainable situation, and Henderson notes previous efforts in China that did limit internal migration. Democratization and fiscal decentralization tend to disfavor the existence of primary cities. Ades and Glaeser (1995) find that if the primary city is a national capital, it is 45 percent larger; if the country is a dictatorship, then the primary city is 40–45 percent larger. Davis and Henderson (2003), using panel data from 1960–95 with instrumental variable estimation, find that moving from the extreme of most to least centralized government reduces primacy by 5 percent. Moving from the extreme of least to most democratic form of government reduces primacy by 8 percent (Henderson 2003).

Figure 1.1   Primacy and Economic Development, 1965–95

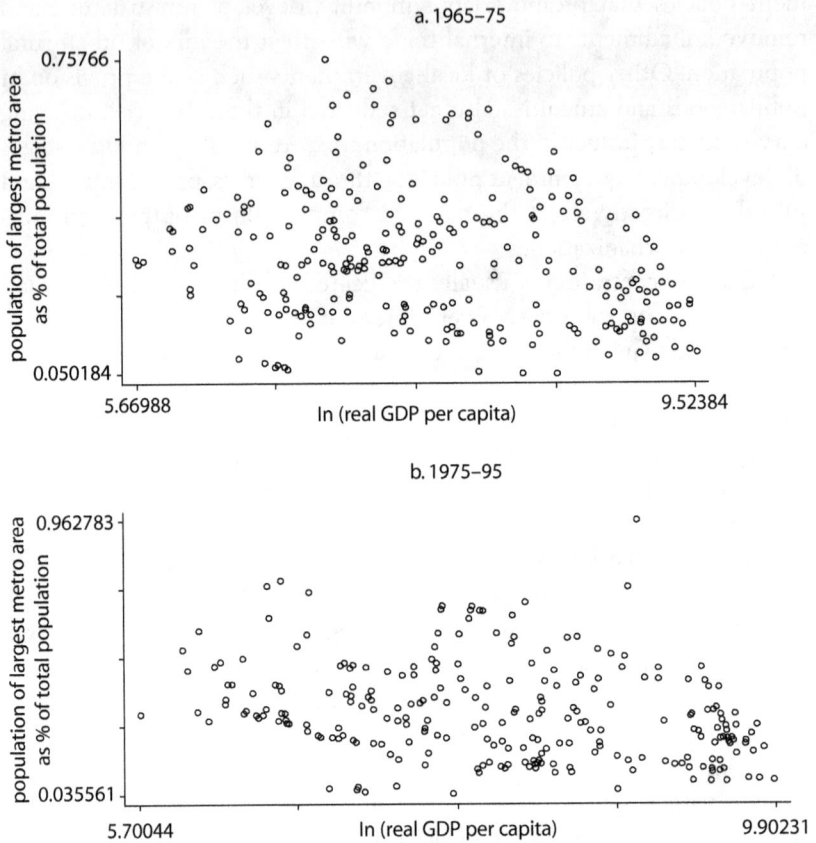

a. 1965–75

b. 1975–95

Source: Henderson 2003.
Note: GDP = gross domestic product.

Urban infrastructure (roads, airports, well-functioning rental markets) can reinforce productive efficiency and reduce primacy. Increasing the amount of roads per square kilometer of national land or the amount of navigable inland waterways per square kilometer, ceteris paribus, by one standard deviation reduces urban primacy by 10 percent. Urban policy making in developing countries often has the twin objectives of making cities better by improving the delivery of local public goods, such as garbage collection, sewerage, and public transport and by limiting urbanization, which implies limiting the inflow of people from rural areas to crowded cities. Cities bring efficiency gains and, therefore, economic benefits that are derived largely from between- and within-city allocation of resources. Therefore, limiting urbanization entails losses. The policy objective should be to deal with imbalances (slums, congestion) rather than to stop the influx of people. The bottom line is to avoid concentrating resources in one place, which implies that governments should ensure competition in all markets and secure well-defined property rights and land markets if they want healthy urban areas.

During the past few decades, the costs of transport and communication have been reduced dramatically, and space as an impediment has been minimized. For example, lower transport and communication costs have enabled firms and their workers to compete globally across both developed and developing countries. Local markets, regional markets, and international markets are now seen as seamless "world markets" and open for competition. As such, all markets have to beat the "China price of low wage," and this requires firms to innovate constantly to stay ahead of their competitors. Thus, China, Japan, and the Republic of Korea are able to produce steel in areas that are not known to have iron and coal mines. Locations now compete on the basis of providing secure property rights and law and order rather than strategic location or proximity to a seaport. Location becomes redundant for many services, as communications have become increasingly more accessible and mobile. Thus, numerous low-skill service jobs have begun to migrate from high-wage locations to low-cost locations overseas in places as diverse as Brazil or India or Ireland. Closeness and connectivity are important and concentrate goods and workers in the center.

Core-Periphery Models

The core-periphery models focus on the effect of transportation costs on spatial concentration. Krugman (1991a) introduces a basic trade model of "core-periphery" with two goods (agriculture and manufacturing) in two regions with two types of labor (farmers and workers), where increasing returns at the firm level interact with transport costs, and factor mobility can cause spatial economic structures to emerge and change.

Using an approach originally suggested by Alan Turing (1952) for the analysis of morphogenesis in biology yields surprisingly clear results about this two-region economy. For instance, Krugman (1996) outlines a "racetrack economy" with 12 regions around the circumference of a circle, like a clock, in which goods must be transported along the circumference. When one starts with any initial distribution of economic activity nearly equal across all space, the simulation always ends with all manufacturing agglomerated in just two regions, which are located on the exact opposite side of each other. This self-organizing central place of activity can also be derived using Turing's model, which is also called the reaction diffusion model.

International trade and spatial economics are also linked. While trade theory deals with the immobility of factors of production (land and labor) between locations and the mobility of output or commodities, spatial economics is concerned about the mobility of factors (labor and capital) and the implications for the concentration of economic activity. The approach introduces the possibility that labor can move between agriculture and manufacturing and assumes that manufacturing firms use each other's outputs as intermediate inputs. This yields backward and forward linkages, as in the core-periphery model, but here it causes international inequalities in wages and could explain why some nations prosper while others decline. If there were no countries in the world, just one continuous space across the globe, this framework could be used to show the emergence of regions of specialization in a borderless world with continuous space.

At one extreme lies the core-periphery dichotomy at the global scale. In 2000, for example, the North American Free Trade Agreement yielded 35 percent of world gross domestic product (GDP), the European Union (15 countries) yielded 25 percent, and East Asia yielded 23 percent; thus, 83 percent of world GDP was concentrated in three regions. Furthermore, the concentration of world GDP in these three regions has been intensifying since 1980. At a national scale, about 50 percent of the output in the United States is produced on less than 2 percent of the country's land (figure 1.2). Output is concentrated in a few counties such as the area along the Boston–New York–Washington, DC, corridor, in the state of Florida, in and around Galveston-Houston, in Silicon Valley in California,

Figure 1.2   Concentration of Economic Activity in the United States

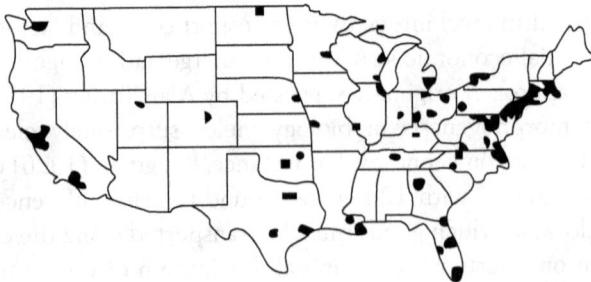

Source: Easterly and Levine 2002.
Note: Counties shown in black take up 2 percent of U.S. land area but account for half of U.S. GDP.

and in a few other places. A similar pattern is observed within cities such as Washington, DC, where rich neighborhoods are concentrated in the northwest of the city and poor neighborhoods are concentrated in the southeast.

Economic maps of France, Germany, India, Japan, Poland, and most other countries show a similar pattern, with "spiky" economic density (GDP per square kilometer). Maps of economic density indicate that some areas are lagging in relation to others—for example, Bihar, Orissa, and Rajasthan in India. The existence of lagging regions motivates policy and the commitment of large amounts of resources in the form of taxes and subsidies to these regions.

Several concerns arise from such uneven growth and development. First, at the local level, people are concentrated in cities, and this trend threatens to outstrip the concentration of economic activity. As a result, a billion people live in the world's slums, and this problem has to be dealt with in policy and planning. At the national level, spatial disparities in living standards widen as economic mass concentrates in leading provinces and lagging regions are left behind: a billion people are now marginalized in remote and lagging areas of the world. At the global level, poor people are trapped in isolated countries that are not developing at all (Paul Collier calls them the "bottom billion").

Should rural labor move to jobs, which are more likely to be in cities and leading regions, or should jobs be provided in remote parts of a country? The general policy advice is that governments should remove impediments to the flow of capital and labor and reinforce agglomeration economies by abolishing national minimum wages, reducing unemployment and social benefits, and abolishing rent control to increase the supply of housing, among other policies.

Do agglomeration economies accrue at the plant, industry, city, or regional level? Krugman (2010) believes that they accrue at the plant level, whereby firms are located in a single area nearer to consumer demand (in large cities with large populations), which minimizes transport costs. In contrast, Michael Porter (1990) is of the view that intraindustry economies lead to clusters. This debate has implications for policy: Should governments target industrial policy to facilitate individual firms or to facilitate a whole industry?

The *World Development Report 2009* (World Bank 2009) emphasizes that the most potent instruments for integrating leading and lagging regions are spatially blind improvements in institutions or, put more simply, the provision of essential services such as education, health, and public security. The main findings of research on economic growth are that (a) growth will remain unbalanced and, to try to spread out economic activity—too much, too far, or too soon—will discourage it (Gill 2010), and (b) development can still be inclusive, in that even people who start their lives far from economic opportunity can benefit from the growing concentration of economic activity in a few places. The way to get both the benefits of uneven growth and inclusive development is through economic integration and mobility of labor and capital to fast-growing areas, so (c) leading and lagging regions need to be connected not only by infrastructure that connects places but also by institutions (for example, political and fiscal decentralization, property rights for land, financial integration, education and training, and assured product markets) that connect people (table 1.1).

Agglomeration Economies

Agglomeration or clustering of activities (shops, restaurants, movie theaters) can happen when a new road or a new factory is built. Agglomeration occurs at many geographic levels and can take many forms. It is most intense at the level of the city, where close spatial proximity makes the prospect of agglomeration spillovers—both scale externalities and knowledge economies—most relevant and a factor in promoting economic growth (Henderson 2003).

Important forces affect geographic concentration and dispersion of economic activity. These are the centripetal forces, such as backward and forward linkages, thickness of markets, and knowledge spillovers. They are countered by or opposed to agglomeration by centrifugal forces such as immobile factors, transport costs, land rents, congestion, pollution, and other pure diseconomies. External effects are exerted on both centripetal and centrifugal forces, creating market failures that abound in urban economics. These forces determine the size of the city—in other words, the agglomeration may be too big.

Alfred Marshall ([1890] 1920) suggested over a century ago a threefold classification of the reasons for industrial concentration. Concentration arises because of (a) knowledge spillovers, (b) the advantages of thick markets for specialized skills, and (c) the backward and forward linkages associated with large local markets.[4] Most of the theoretical and empirical work has focused on the backward and forward linkages. These linkages lead to increasing returns to production at the level of the individual firm. Increasing returns introduce self-reinforcing and multiplier effects and

Table 1.1　Regional Development Policies Calibrated to Integrate Countries, by Density of Population

Indicator	Sparsely populated lagging regions	Densely populated lagging regions in united countries	Densely populated lagging regions in divided countries
Example (countries)	Chile, China, Ghana, Honduras, Pakistan, Peru, Russian Federation, Sri Lanka, Uganda, Vietnam	Bangladesh, Brazil, Colombia, Arab Rep. of Egypt, Mexico, Thailand, Turkey	India, Nigeria
Dimensions of the integration challenge	Economic distance	Economic distance; high population densities in lagging areas	Economic distance; high population densities; internal divisions
What policies should facilitate	Labor and capital mobility	Labor and capital mobility; market integration for goods and services	Labor and capital mobility; market integration for goods and services; selected economic activities in lagging areas
Policy priorities			
Spatially blind institutions	Fluid land and labor markets; security; education and health programs; safe water and sanitation	Fluid land and labor markets; security; education and health programs; safe water and sanitation	Fluid land and labor markets; security; education and health programs; safe water and sanitation
Spatially connective infrastructure		Interregional transport infrastructure; information and communication services	Interregional transport infrastructure; information and communication services
Spatially targeted incentives			Incentives to agriculture and agro-based industry; irrigation systems; workforce training; local roads

Source: World Bank 2009.

Note: Countries are classified based on a typology outlined in World Bank (2009). Three types of countries are identified: those with sparsely populated lagging regions; those with densely populated lagging regions that are united based on ethnolinguistic and little or no political fragmentation; and those with densely populated lagging regions and within-country divisions such as ethnolinguistic differences and political fragmentation.

coexist with imperfect competition, which has implications for how firms set prices and wages. von Thünen's model (1826) explained the economic effects of falling "space-bridging" costs. Owners of mobile factors of production, such as capital and technical knowledge, need to be paid the same return whether their assets are employed in the center of market activity or in the periphery. Otherwise there is an incentive to engage in "locational arbitrage." For example, in a city or region, real estate rents drop as the distance from the center of activity grows. In the center, enterprises use a lot of capital to build high-rises, thus saving on land costs, and only space-saving offices are located there. Cheap land on the periphery is devoted to space-intensive uses, such as manufacturing plants, logistics centers, and dumps. If landowners on the periphery were to raise their rents, they would soon be out of business.

Why do certain cities such as Detroit for automobiles, Hollywood for movies, and Silicon Valley for high technology specialize in a narrow range of industries? A small modification of Von Thünen's model shifts the focus from agglomeration of resources to the geographic concentration of particular industries. When production is vertically integrated, with both upstream and downstream sectors producing inputs for each other, and when both sectors have higher returns and transport costs, there are both backward and forward linkages, and production could be in a single location because both have an incentive to be closest to the largest markets for each other.

What happens to spatial concentration if manufacturing is more dynamic and mobile, but agriculture is immobile? What happens to economic mass if both manufacturing and agriculture are mobile? A model that combines a von Thünen–style explanation of land rent with a linkage explanation of manufacturing concentration can show how a spatial pattern in which a single city is surrounded by an agricultural hinterland can be self-sustaining as long as the urban population is not too large. If the population does become too large, it will be in the interest of a small group of workers to move to some other location; by using the criterion of sustainability, it is possible to develop a model of the emergence of new cities and hence a multicity structure. If several manufacturing industries exist with different costs of transportation or economies of scale, the process of city formation can yield a hierarchy of cities of different types and sizes.

A larger city allows for a more efficient *sharing* of indivisible facilities (such as local infrastructure), risks, and the gains from variety and specialization. Furthermore, a larger city also allows for a better *matching* between employers and employees, buyers and suppliers, and entrepreneurs and financiers. Finally, a larger city can facilitate *learning* about new technologies, market evolutions, or new forms of organization. More frequent direct interactions between economic agents in a city can thus favor the creation, diffusion, and accumulation of knowledge. Hence, many different mechanisms can generate increasing urban returns. Moreover, sources of increasing urban returns may also be sources of urban inefficiencies.

The wage in a city increases with the size of the urban labor force, reflecting the existence of urban agglomeration externalities. The intensity of increasing urban returns is measured by the slope of the wage curve. Since the nature and intensity of increasing returns are expected to differ across activities, so will the exact shape of the wage curve. This upward-sloping wage curve stands in sharp contrast to "neoclassical" wage curves that slope downward. Increasing urban returns have received a considerable amount of theoretical attention.

The wage curve masks the many distortions beneath it. For example, most developing countries distort agricultural prices (rural) and manufacturing prices (urban). The "urban bias" of most developing countries is well documented, as reflected in higher urban wages and thus a higher wage curve. In turn, this bias should lead to larger cities. More generally, national technology and public policies are reflected in the wage curve of any particular city, affecting its level and, sometimes, its slope.

The cost-of-living curve in urban areas is linked to the wage curve and traffic congestion, among other determinants. Governments can address many components of the cost-of-living curve, from sewerage to public transport, and thus reduce the costs.

Conclusion

The spatial economy was given new impetus in the 1990s with the work on the new economic geography, which provided economists with new tools to examine why and where population or economic activity is located. It also tied in with the theoretical and empirical work of the new economic growth literature at that time. The chapter has discussed the two principal ways in which urbanization is organized at a spatial scale. Central to this are the study of urban concentration and the study of agglomeration economies.

Notes

1. "By modeling the sources of increasing returns to spatial concentration, we learn something about how and when these returns may change—and then explore how the economy's behavior will change with them" (Fujita, Krugman, and Venables 1999, 4).

2. Henderson (2003) cites the empirical work of Ades and Glaeser (1995), Junius (1999), and Davis and Henderson (2003).

3. "A 33 percent increase or decrease in primacy from a typical best level of 0.3 reduces productivity growth by 3 percent over five years" (Henderson 2003, 9).

4. Concentration minimizes transport costs, but also creates other externalities, such as congestion and overcrowding.

References

Ades, Alberto F., and Edward L. Glaeser. 1995. "Trade and Circuses: Explaining Urban Giants." *Quarterly Journal of Economics* 110 (1): 195–227.

Collier, P. 2007).*The Bottom Billion. Why the Poorest Countries are Failing and What Can Be Done About It*. Oxford, England: Oxford University Press.

Davis, James, and J. Vernon Henderson. 2003. "Evidence on the Political Economy of the Urbanization Process." *Journal of Urban Economics* 53 (1, January): 98–125.

Dixit, Avinash K., and Joseph E. Stiglitz. 1977. "Monopolistic Competition and Optimum Product Diversity." *American Economic Review* 67 (3): 297–308.

Easterly, William, and Ross Levine. 2002. "It's Not Factor Accumulation: Stylized Facts and Growth Models." In *Economic Growth: Sources, Trends, and Cycles*, ed. Norman Loayza and Raimundo Soto, 61–114. Santiago: Central Bank of Chile.

Fujita, Masahisa, Paul Krugman, and Anthony J. Venables. 1999. *The Spatial Economy: Cities, Regions, and International Trade*. Cambridge, MA: MIT Press.

Gill, Indermit. 2010. "Regional Development Policies: Place-Based or People-Centred?" Vox.org, October 9. http://www.voxeu.org/index.php?q=node /5644.

Harris, John R., and Michael P. Todaro. 1970. "Migration, Unemployment, and Development: A Two-Sector Analysis." *American Economic Review* 60 (1): 126–42.

Henderson, J. Vernon. 2003. *Urbanization, Economic Geography, and Growth*. Providence, RI: Brown University Press.

Junius, Karsten. 1999. "Primacy and Economic Development: Bell Shaped or Parallel Growth of Cities?" *Journal of Economic Development* 24 (1): 1–22.

Krugman, Paul. 1991a. *Geography and Trade.* Cambridge, MA: MIT Press.

———. 1991b. "Increasing Returns and Economic Geography." *Journal of Political Economy* 99 (3, January): 483–99.

———. 1996. *Self-Organizing Economy.* Cambridge, MA: Blackwell.

———. 2010. "The New Economic Geography, Now Middle-Aged." Presentation for the Association of American Geographers, April 16.

Marshall, Alfred. [1890] 1920. *Principles of Economics: An Introductory Volume,* 8th ed. London: Macmillan.

Porter, Michael E. 1990. *The Competitive Advantage of Nations.* New York: Macmillan.

Turing, Alan. 1952. "The Chemical Basis of Morphogenesis." *Philosophical Transactions of the Royal Society of London, Series B* 237 (641): 37–72.

von Thünen, J. H. 1826. *Der Isolierte Staat in Beziehung auf Landtschaft und Nationalökonomie.* Hamburg: Perthes. English translation: *von Thünen's Isolated State,* trans. C. M. Wartenberg. Oxford: Pergamon Press, 1966.

World Bank. 2009. *World Development Report 2009: Reshaping Economic Geography.* Washington, DC: World Bank.

CHAPTER 2

Urbanization as a Typology of Space

World urban population is expected to increase 84 percent by 2050, rising from 3.4 billion in 2009 to 6.3 billion in 2050. Almost all of this increase will take place in the developing regions. By 2050, the rate of urbanization is expected to reach 66 percent (from 45 percent currently) in the less developed regions and 86 percent (from 75 percent currently) in the more developed regions.

The developing countries are experiencing rapid urbanization and are expected to become predominantly urban societies over the coming four decades. The transformation of the urban system has rendered obsolete the distinction between rural and urban areas, and the advances in transportation and telecommunications have facilitated this. Settlement systems have increased in complexity. An example is the change from a monocentric system of cities to a polycentric one, whereby clusters of smaller cities surround a larger one—in effect, a form of territorial specialization.

The chapter begins by examining the data on urbanization and projections over the coming four decades, primarily using urbanization data from the United Nations (UN). The remainder of the chapter discusses the main criticism of these data and suggests an alternative measure of urbanization that provides a more robust measure of spatial concentration.

Urbanization and Space

Classifying cities by population size is a comprehensive way of identifying various types of cities. The UN compiles data on urban population and its share of total national population for various countries. The countries report the data to the UN, and as a result, there is no standard definition, which makes cross-country comparisons problematic. The most recent UN publication on urbanization suggests the following:

- Half of the world's 6.7 billion people will live in urban areas by 2010.
- Not all of the world's regions are equally urbanized.
- Asia and Africa are the least urbanized regions but account for most of the urban population.
- Asia's urban population, currently 1.6 billion, is expected to double over the coming four decades, adding another 1.8 billion persons by 2050.
- China is expected to become 70 percent urban (from 40 percent presently), accounting for 1 billion people by 2050.
- India is expected to urbanize the least over the coming four decades. Currently, 30 percent of its population live in urban areas, a rate that is expected to reach 55 percent by 2050, or 900 million people.
- Dhaka, Karachi, and Lahore are expected to grow the fastest and will acquire megacity status—cities with more than 10 million inhabitants—by 2050.
- Africa's urban population is likely to triple over the next 40 years, increasing from 340 million to more than 900 million.
- The fastest-growing cities in Africa are not yet megacities, but Kinshasa and Lagos are expected to surpass 10 million inhabitants by 2050.
- Urbanization in Latin America and the developed world will remain largely the same over the coming four decades.
- Natural increase accounts for the majority of urban growth, some 60 percent. An exception is China, where increases in urbanization are primarily due to changes in the number of areas considered urban and to migration.

Projections to 2050 depend on a continuing decline in the fertility rate in the developing world. If fertility rates continue at their current levels and urbanization continues at the predicted pace, the global urban population will reach 8.1 billion by 2050 instead of the projected 6.3 billion.

Table 2.1 illustrates these points. The world's urban population is expected to reach 6.3 billion by 2050, with growth coming from the urban areas in the less developed regions. While rural population in the

Table 2.1 Population and Average Annual Rate of Change, by Group and Selected Years, 1950–2050

Group	Population (billions)					Average annual rate of change (%)			
	1950	1975	2009	2025	2050	1950–75	1975–2009	2009–25	2025–50
Total population									
World	2.53	4.06	6.83	8.01	9.15	1.89	1.53	1.00	0.53
More developed regions	0.81	1.05	1.23	1.28	1.28	1.02	0.48	0.22	–0.01
Less developed regions	1.72	3.01	5.60	6.73	7.87	2.25	1.82	1.16	0.63
Urban population									
World	0.73	1.51	3.42	4.54	6.29	2.91	2.40	1.76	1.31
More developed regions	0.43	0.70	0.92	1.01	1.10	1.97	0.82	0.58	0.33
Less developed regions	0.30	0.81	2.50	3.52	5.19	3.96	3.30	2.15	1.55
Rural population									
World	1.80	2.55	3.41	3.48	2.86	1.39	0.85	0.12	–0.77
More developed regions	0.39	0.35	0.31	0.26	0.18	–0.39	–0.35	–1.01	–1.62
Less developed regions	1.41	2.20	3.10	3.21	2.69	1.77	1.01	0.22	–0.71

Source: UN 2010.

more developed regions has been declining for some time, rural population in the developing regions is expected to continue increasing until 2025, when it will begin to contract. Urban population growth at the global level is slowing down. Between 1950 and 2009, urban population grew at an annual average rate of 2.6 percent, increasing from 0.7 billion to 3.4 billion (UN 2010). Contraction of the rural population and sustained increase of the urban population will result in increasing proportions of the global population living in urban areas.

Classification of Cities

The United Nations classifies various types of cities by the size of their population. Cities with less than 1 million people are classified as small cities, and those with greater than 1 million but less than 5 million are classified as medium-size cities. Large cities are those with populations between 5 million and 10 million, and megacities have a population of 10 million or greater. Figure 2.1 shows total urban population by size of city for 1995, 2009, and 2025.

Figure 2.1 illustrates the uneven distribution of world population among cities of different sizes. Almost 52 percent of urban occupants live in cities of less than half a million people. These small cities are expected to account for 45 percent of the projected increase in the world's urban population up to 2025. Small cities with less than half a million people account for 53.2 percent of the urban population in the more developed regions, marginally higher than the share in the less developed regions: 51.4 percent (UN 2010).

At the other end of the spectrum are the megacities, often comprising urban agglomerations of "several cities or urban localities that are functionally linked" (UN 2010, 6). The largest megacity, Tokyo, the capital of Japan, with an estimated population of 36.5 million in 2009, comprises 87 surrounding cities and towns, including Chiba, Kawasaki, and Yokohama. There were just three megacities in 1975—Mexico City, New York, and Tokyo. By 2009, 21 cities had attained this size, and 8 more are expected to become megacities by 2025, all in developing countries (table 2.2).[1]

Large cities, or those with a population of between 5 million and 10 million, numbered 32 in 2009 and are expected to number 46 by 2025. They accounted for 6.6 percent of the total population in 2009. Three-quarters of these large cities are "megacities in waiting" and are located in the developing regions (UN 2010, 8). Large cities account for a greater proportion of the urban population in the less developed

Figure 2.1   Total Population, by City Size, 1995, 2009, and 2025

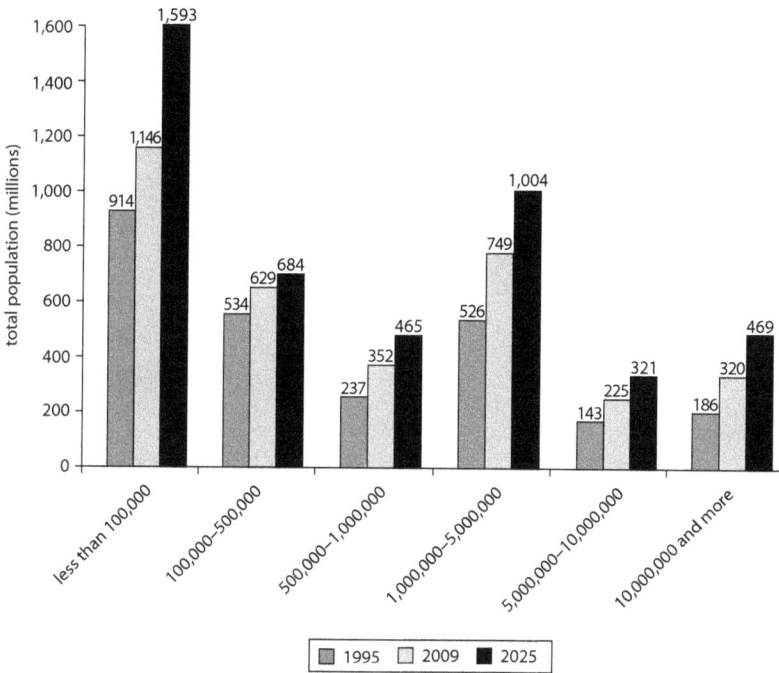

Source: UN 2010.

Table 2.2   Number of Cities and Percentage of Total Population, by Size of City, 2009 and 2025

Size of city	Number of cities		Urban population (% of total population)	
	2009	2025[a]	2009	2025[a]
Mega	21	29	9.4	10.3
Large	32	46	6.6	7.1
Medium	374	506	21.9	22.1
Small	509	667	10.3	10.3

Source: UN 2010.
Note: Megacities = more than 10 million; large cities = between 5 million and 10 million; medium-size cities = between 1 million and 5 million; small cities = between 500,000 and 1 million.
a. Projection.

regions, 8.8 percent in 2009, than in the more developed regions, 4.9 percent in 2009 (table 2.3).

Medium-size cities, with more than 1 million inhabitants but fewer than 5 million, are numerous—374 in 2009, rising to 506 in 2025 (table 2.2).

Table 2.3   Size of Cities, by Region, Number of Inhabitants, and Share of Population, Selected Years, 1975, 2009, 2025

Region and size of urban settlement	Population (millions)			Percentage distribution		
	1975	2009	2025	1975	2009	2025
World						
Total urban area	1,511	3,421	4,536	100.0	100.0	100.0
Mega	53	320	469	3.5	9.4	10.3
Large	109	225	321	7.2	6.6	7.1
Medium	292	749	1,004	19.3	21.9	22.1
Small	157	352	465	10.4	10.3	10.3
Very small	900	1,775	2,277	59.6	51.9	50.2
More developed region						
Total urban area	698	924	1,014	100.0	100.0	100.0
Mega	42	101	104	6.1	10.9	10.3
Large	50	45	70	7.1	4.9	6.9
Medium	137	202	207	19.6	21.9	20.4
Small	73	84	92	10.5	9.1	9.0
Very small	396	491	541	56.7	53.2	53.4
Less developed region						
Total urban area	814	2,497	3,522	100.0	100.0	100.0
Mega	11	219	365	1.3	8.8	10.4
Large	60	180	251	7.3	7.2	7.1
Medium	155	546	797	19.1	21.9	22.6
Small	83	268	374	10.3	10.7	10.6
Very small	505	1,284	1,736	62.0	51.4	49.3

Source: UN 2010.
Note: Megacities = more than 10 million; large cities = between 5 million and 10 million; medium-size cities = between 1 million and 5 million; small cities = between 500,000 and 1 million; very small-size cities = less than 500,000.

They account for 22 percent of the urban population. Medium-size cities in the less developed and more developed regions account for the same percentage of the urban population—21.9 percent in 2009 (table 2.3).

The number of small cities, those with a population between 500,000 and 1 million, was 509 in 2009, increasing to 667 by 2025. These smaller cities account for just 10.3 percent of the urban population (table 2.2).

Size of Cities across Developing and Developed Regions

Across the regions, city size varies tremendously. Roughly 67 percent of the urban population in Europe reside in cities with less than 500,000 inhabitants, while just 8 percent live in cities of 5 million or greater. The urban distribution by city size is similar in Africa—58 percent of urban inhabitants live in smaller cities and 9 percent live in cities of 5 million or more. Roughly one in five people lives in a large city in Asia, Latin America and the Caribbean, and North America. The proportion of people living in smaller cities is 49 percent in Asia, 48 percent in Latin America and the Caribbean, and 37 percent in North America. Oceania is a special case, as none of its cities is larger than 5 million people and relatively few—38 percent—of its inhabitants live in cities with fewer than half a million people (UN 2010).

Table 2.4 shows the rapid urbanization that has taken place since 1950 and is expected to continue. The process began in the more developed regions, which were approximately 30 percent urban in 1920. By 1950, more than half of the population was living in an urban area. North America, Australia, and New Zealand led the group in 1950, with more than 60 percent of the population living in an urban area, while Europe was the least urbanized,[2] with more than 50 percent living in an urban area (UN 2010). The ranking is expected to hold until 2050, when more than 90 percent of North America, New Zealand, and Australia and 84 percent of Europe will be urban (UN 2010).

Latin America and the Caribbean has a high level of urbanization, surpassing Europe in 2009 and expected to increase until 2050, when 89 percent of its inhabitants will reside in urban areas. By contrast, Asia and Africa are mostly rural, with only 42 and 40 percent, respectively, of the population living in urban areas in 2009. These regions are expected to urbanize rapidly over the coming four decades, when 65 and 62 percent of the population, respectively, will reside in urban areas (table 2.4).

As a whole, in 2009, Asia was home to more than half of the world's urban population (figure 2.2). Together with Africa, Asia will experience

Table 2.4   Percentage of Population Living in Urban Areas by Region, Selected Years, 1950–2050

Major area	1950	1975	2009	2025	2050
World	28.2	37.2	50.1	56.6	68.7
More developed regions	52.6	66.7	74.9	79.4	86.2
Less developed regions	17.6	27.0	44.6	52.3	65.9
Africa	14.4	25.7	39.6	47.2	61.6
Asia	16.3	24.0	41.7	49.9	64.7
Europe	51.3	65.3	72.5	76.9	84.3
Latin America and the Caribbean	41.4	60.7	79.3	83.8	88.8
North America	63.9	73.8	81.9	85.7	90.1
Oceania	62.0	71.5	70.2	70.8	74.8

Source: UN 2010.

Figure 2.2   Distribution of the World Urban Population, by Region, 1950, 2009, and 2050

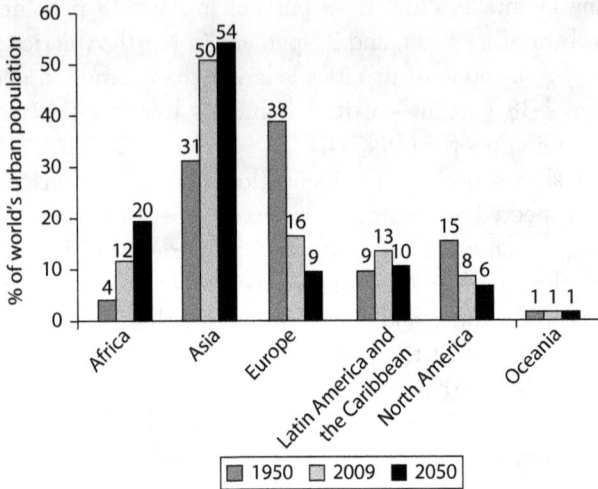

Source: UN 2010.

a significant increase in its urban population over the coming four decades. By 2050, roughly 54 percent of the global urban population will reside in Asia, and 20 percent will reside in Africa.

The world's urban population is highly concentrated, with roughly 75 percent of the 3.4 billion urban dwellers worldwide living in 25 countries. Urban population in these countries ranges from 31 million in South Africa to 620 million in China. Together, China, India, and North America account for 36 percent of the global urban population.

Furthermore, the increase in world urban population is concentrated in a few countries. China and India are expected to account for roughly one-third of the total increase in urban population over the coming four decades, with nine additional countries expected to contribute 26 percent of the urban increase. These countries, which will increase their urban population between 15 million and 51 million, are the Democratic Republic of Congo and Nigeria in Africa; Bangladesh, Indonesia, Pakistan, and the Philippines in Asia; Brazil and Mexico in Latin America; and the United States in North America. Table 2.5 shows the urban growth rates for the world regions. The rates in Africa and Asia are of particular note—a projected 3 and 2 percent a year, respectively, between 2009 and 2025.

Table 2.5   Average Annual Rate of Change in Urban Population, 1950–2025
average annual rate of change (%)

Major area	1950–75	1975–2009	2009–25
Africa	4.77	3.85	3.14
Asia	3.66	3.24	2.04
Europe	1.81	0.55	0.34
Latin America and the Caribbean	4.17	2.51	1.22
North America	1.96	1.37	1.11
Oceania	2.60	1.44	1.20

Source: UN 2010.

Criticism of the Data and Suggested Alternatives

The main criticism of the UN data on population is the subjectivity in their compilation. Each participating country reports on the level of urbanization in the country according to its classification system, which may change over time. The national classification system does not always coincide with that used by the UN. Uchida and Nelson (2008) cite several examples of where and how country-level data on urbanization differ from the official data reported by the UN (table 2.6).

Differing country classifications of urbanization make cross-country analyses difficult, if not impossible. For example, Sweden defines urban as settlements of 200 inhabitants, whereas Nigeria and Syria define urban as settlements of 15,000 (Uchida and Nelson 2008). Furthermore, the concept of "urban" is becoming more difficult to classify in an environment where improvements in transportation systems and communications render obsolete the traditional divide between urban and rural.

The literature on the form of urbanization has thus moved away from the simple urban-rural dichotomy to embrace a more dynamic form that explores the relationship between urbanization and economic development (see Cohen 2004, 2006). Dichotomy has been expressed in the core-periphery models, two-region models, dual-economy models, and urban primacy models. Theoretical and empirical studies examine the evolution of spatial concentration with development and the efficiency implications of too much or too little spatial concentration. Focusing on spatial concentration as opposed to a simple dichotomy emphasizes problems in the measurement of urban concentration.

Various methods are used to measure urban concentration, including the Hirschman-Herfindahl index of concentration, the Pareto parameter, and primacy.[3] All of these measures depend on how a city and an urban

Table 2.6   National and UN Data on Urbanization in Selected Countries
% of population living in urban areas

Country and year	National data	UN data	Note
India, 1991	39	26.0	National data suggest a higher rate of urbanization and include 113 million inhabitants residing in areas with populations of 5,000 and more.
Mauritius, 2000	66	42.7	Reclassifying the population residing in settlements of between 5,000 and 20,000 inhabitants suggests a much higher rate of urbanization than reported by the UN.
Mexico, 2000	67	74.4	UN data suggest a higher rate of urbanization when settlements of 2,500 are included.

Source: Compiled from Uchida and Nelson 2008.

area are defined, and, given the vagaries across time and space, the measures may not be systematic or consistent.

Uchida and Nelson (2008) suggest an alternative measure of urban concentration, which they term an agglomeration index (AI). Their agglomeration index consists of population density, the size of population in a "large" urban center, and travel time to that urban center. They define their index for 2000 and note that it "creates a global definition of settlement concentration that could be used to conduct cross-country comparative analyses" (Uchida and Nelson 2008, 2) (figure 2.3). Locations that satisfy all three indicators are included in the agglomeration index and are delineated by them. The concept of the AI is, as a result, more fluid and transcends discrete entities (cities, administrative boundaries, and rural and urban space [see Uchida and Nelson 2008]). The AI is not influenced by country definitions of urban. Furthermore, a key advantage of the index is that population counts are not used to calculate it but serve instead to define and locate cities for the purposes of measuring travel time. For this reason, the accuracy of population counts is far less important here than in the primacy measure (Uchida and Nelson 2008).

Uchida and Nelson (2008) compare their agglomeration index, which uses a minimum threshold of 150 people per square kilometer for density, a maximum travel time of 60 minutes, and a minimum of 50,000 inhabitants to define a large city, with the UN estimate for the share of urban population in world regions (figure 2.4).

Figure 2.3   Key Indicators of the Agglomeration Index

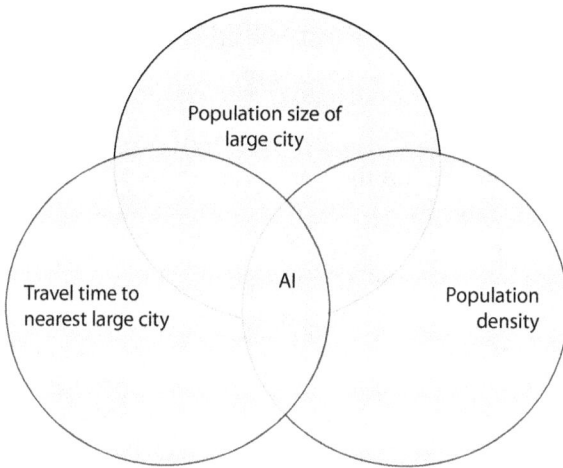

Population size of
large city

Travel time to
nearest large city

AI

Population
density

Source: Uchida and Nelson 2008.

**Figure 2.4   Agglomeration Index and UN Estimates of Urban Population,
by Region, 2000**

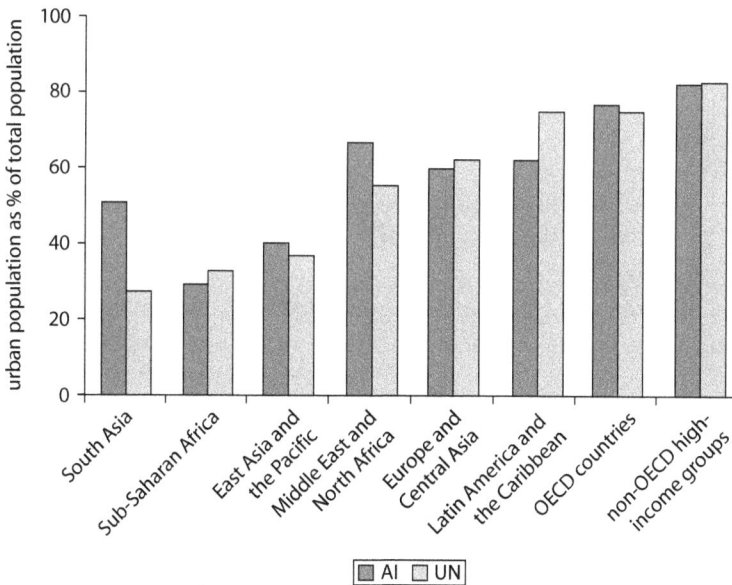

AI UN

Source: Uchida and Nelson 2008.
Note: OECD = Organisation for Economic Co-operation and Development. The agglomeration index defines urban as a minimum threshold of 150 people per square kilometer for density, a maximum of 60 minutes travel time, and a minimum of 50,000 inhabitants.

The index and the UN estimate differ markedly for South Asia, Middle East and North Africa, and Latin America and the Caribbean, where the agglomeration index indicates a higher urban concentration in the first two regions and the UN estimates indicate a higher share in the third region. Uchida and Nelson (2008) suggest that the higher AI share in South Asia is picking up the higher density of population in that region and that Latin America and the Caribbean may not be as heavily urbanized as originally thought.

The results are, however, dependent on the threshold levels chosen, and it is therefore important to have good justification for those levels. Uchida and Nelson (2008) find that the results are quite robust when considering changes in the population density threshold—that is, from 150 in the base case to 300 and 500 people per square kilometer. However, the results change remarkably when considering differences in travel time, from 30 minutes in the base case to 60 and 90 minutes, respectively. According to Uchida and Nelson (2008), with a moderate increase in the threshold (from 60 to 90 minutes), the AI for South Asia rises to 60.8 percent, more than double the UN figure. Similarly, a change in the minimum size for classification as a city from 50,000 in the base case to 100,000 and 500,000, respectively, alters the results for the AI, causing a steep drop relative to the UN estimates (figure 2.5).

The agglomeration index is a superior measure when examining issues of urbanization. Its components—density, travel time, population size—differentiate among cities of various sizes and in so doing provide greater information on urban settlements and the impact of, for example, environmental footprints, congestion, and provision of public infrastructure. The UN data alone cannot differentiate between "one city growing ever-larger and numerous small cities sprouting in what was a sparsely populated area" (Uchida and Nelson 2008, 10). While there are data difficulties in compiling the index, the authors note that developments in satellite technology make available a wide variety of data that are current and accurate, facilitating a better-informed index.

Conclusion

The chapter examined urbanization data by first focusing on the data collected by the United Nations. These data provide information on past, current, and future trends in urbanization for cities categorized by size and location. Although the UN data are the most comprehensive available, they are often criticized for not comparing cities adequately over

Figure 2.5   Sensitivity to Indicators Used: Example of Minimum Population Size of Large Cities

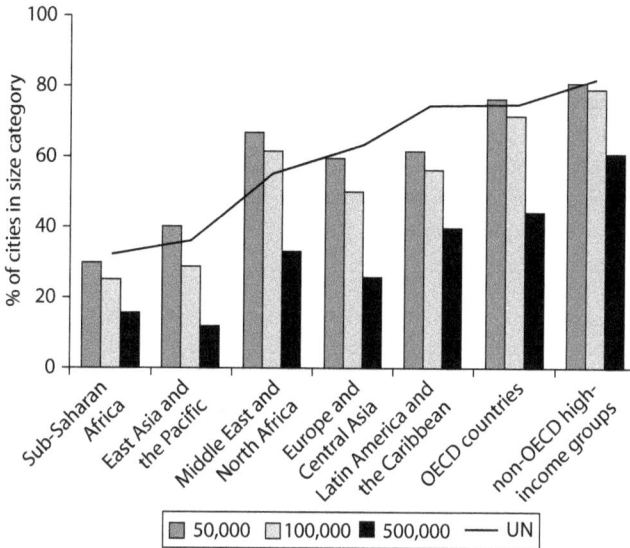

Source: Uchida and Nelson 2008.
Note: OECD = Organisation for Economic Co-operation and Development.

time and place. As urbanization continues, the traditional dichotomy between urban and rural areas is not tenable, yet the official data continue to be organized at these levels. The text considered an alternative measure of spatial concentration—an agglomeration index that takes into account population density, the amount of population in the large urban center, and travel time to that urban center. The index is sensitive to the threshold values chosen for these variables, and timely, up-to-date data availability may be an issue. Despite these caveats, the index has much to recommend it; its main advantage is that it facilitates a consistent cross-country comparison of urbanization and differentiates among different city sizes.

Notes

1. Asia is expected to gain five megacities, while Latin America is projected to gain two, and Africa is projected to gain one.
2. Oceania includes developing regions as well as the developed countries of Australia and New Zealand. Oceania includes Melanesia (Fiji, New Caledonia, Papua New Guinea, the Solomon Islands, and Vanuatu), Micronesia (Guam,

Kiribati, the Marshall Islands, the Federated States of Micronesia, Nauru, Northern Mariana Islands, and Palau), and Polynesia (American Samoa, Cook Islands, French Polynesia, Niue, Pitcairn, Samoa, Tokelau, Tonga, Tuvalu, and the Wallis and Futuna Islands).

3. The Hirschman-Herfindahl index of concentration is the sum of the square of the share of population in each city relative to the national urban population. The Pareto parameter is a measure of how cities decline in size as they move from the largest to the smallest (Uchida and Nelson 2008). Primacy is the share of the population contained in the largest city relative to the national urban population.

References

Cohen, Barney. 2004. "Urban Growth in Developing Countries: A Review of Current Trends and a Caution Regarding Existing Forecasts." *World Development* 32 (1): 23–51.

———. 2006. "Urbanization in Developing Countries: Current Trends, Future Projections, and Key Challenges for Sustainability." *Technology in Science* 28 (1): 63–80.

Uchida, Hirotsugu, and Andrew Nelson. 2008. "Agglomeration Index: Towards a New Measure of Urban Concentration." Background Paper for *World Development Report 2009: Reshaping Economic Geography*. World Bank, Washington, DC. http://siteresources.worldbank.org/ INTWDR2009/Resources/4231006-1204741572978/Hiro1.pdf.

United Nations. 2010. "World Urbanization Prospects: The 2009 Revision; Highlights." Department of Economic and Social Affairs (DESA), Population Division, United Nations, New York, March.

CHAPTER 3

Urban Transition and Growth

There is a close association between urbanization—a growing share of urban population—and economic growth and development. This association suggests various typologies that are based on population size, economic density, and territorial specialization.[1] Economic density refers to the economic mass or output generated on a unit of land. It is the defining characteristic of urban settlements. Density is measured by the value added or gross domestic product (GDP) generated per square kilometer of land and is higher the more concentrated these factors—capital and labor—are. Thus, economic density is highly correlated with employment and population density.

Economic density is examined here for developing and developed countries as a key part of urban transition and growth. Further aspects of urban transition and growth are the blurring of the rural-urban divide and the unprecedented volume of people moving to urban areas. The second part of the chapter examines regional trends in urban growth for the developing countries and concludes with a discussion of some of the key features of cities in developing regions.

Urbanization and Development

Urbanization is the pathway to development: no country has developed without the growth of its cities (World Bank 2009). The path to urbanization is not linear, and cities come in many different sizes. The economic landscape has a similar picture. The *World Development Report 2009* contrasts the economic and population density of Brussels, where an average square kilometer hosts 2,000 workers producing US$350 million of goods and services and population density is 6,000 people per square kilometer, with the agricultural areas of Belgium, where an average square kilometer hosts 7 workers producing US$330,000. In between is a continuum of density. At the head is the primary or leading city, followed by a spectrum embracing secondary cities, small urban centers, towns, and villages. In some countries, the size difference between the leading or primary city and the next city is considerable. Paris has 10 million inhabitants; Marseille, the next largest city, has just 1.5 million inhabitants. By contrast, the primary city in the United States—New York, with 22 million—is not that different from Los Angeles, with 18 million. Mumbai and New Delhi in India both have 22 million inhabitants (World Bank 2009). In addition to the continuum of density that transcends a simple rural-urban dichotomy, it is possible to identify a symbiosis of places. Cities of different sizes complement one another. The primary city forms the core of a country's metropolitan area with adjacent cities. Furthermore, secondary cities may act as regional hubs, providing economic functions for the areas around them—finance, commerce, public health, education, and culture (World Bank 2009).

Using an agglomeration index that derives from the close association between the economic and urban landscape, the *World Development Report 2009* examines the relationship between city size (a proxy for economic density) and development. The agglomeration index facilitates cross-country comparisons. Using this agglomeration index, the report identifies three main findings for developed and developing countries.

- Economic density rises with development. The proportion of inhabitants in an urban area rises rapidly as the city or town transforms from an agrarian to an industrial economy. This geographic transformation coincides with the urban area's move from low to middle income. While urbanization may slow after this, economic density continues to increase, given that services (the next transformation) are even more geographically concentrated than industry.[2]

- Rural-urban and within-urban disparities in welfare narrow with development. Rural-urban gaps in income, living standards, and poverty begin to converge as economies begin to grow and development takes hold. Within-city gaps may take longer to narrow and may kick in only at advanced stages of development.
- Neither the pace of urbanization nor its association with economic growth is unprecedented. What is unprecedented is the sheer number of inhabitants being added each year to the urban population in the developing regions (World Bank 2009).

Economic Density Rises with Development

The urban landscape at early stages of development is likely to consist of small towns and cities that evolved to fulfill various functions, such as a port city or a market town. As industrialization takes hold, urbanization takes off, with new cities emerging and current cities expanding, leading to a hierarchy of places. As cities multiply and expand, population and economic density increase. The *World Development Report 2009* identifies two transitions that lead to a transformation of the geographic landscape. First, the move from an agrarian to an industrial base coincides with urbanization and a transition from a rural to an urban economy. Second, the transition from a manufacturing to a service economy occurs at a much higher level of development and the process of urbanization is much slower. "In most countries, these transformations happen at the same time, but in different areas" (World Bank 2009, 57). The concentration of economic activity suggests that the richer the area, the more economically dense it is. Using the primary city and an area of 1° longitude by 1° latitude, the *World Development Report 2009* shows a historically rapidly rising concentration, followed by a leveling off for primary cities and cities in the densest grid cells (figure 3.1).

Dublin, London, Paris, Singapore, and Vienna ranked at the top of the densest cities in the world in 2005, with more than US$200 million in GDP per square kilometer. Tokyo-Kanagawa, New York–New Jersey, Oslo-Akershus-Vestfold, and Vienna-Mödling were the densest grid cells of 1° longitude by 1° latitude, producing GDP per square meter in excess of US$30 million (World Bank 2009).

Primary cities in both developing and developed countries account for a disproportionate share of national GDP. For example, Mexico City contributed 30 percent of Mexico's GDP in 2005 and occupied just 0.1 percent of its land. Similarly, Budapest, Casablanca, Lagos, Nairobi, and Riyadh

Figure 3.1 Relationship between GDP and Spatial Concentration

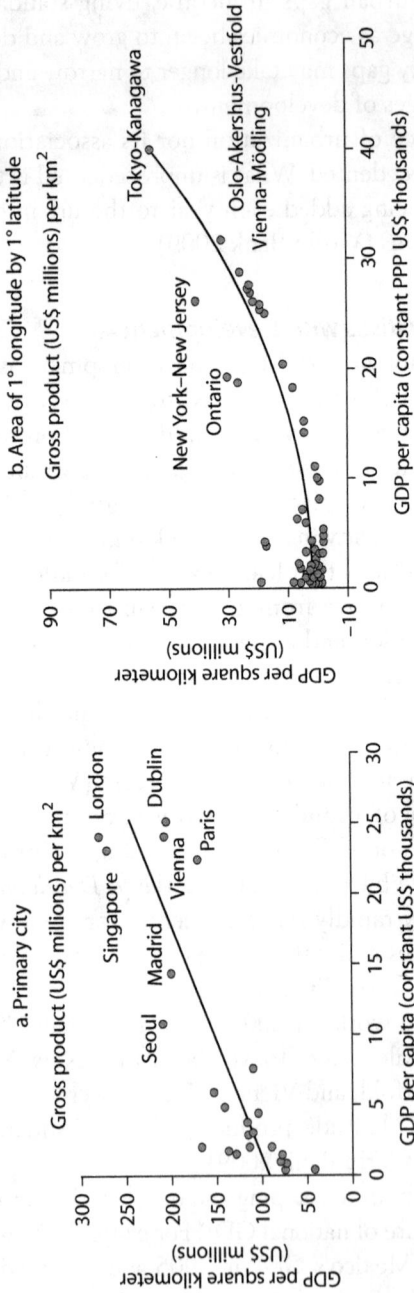

a. Primary city

b. Area of 1° longitude by 1° latitude

Source: World Bank 2009.
Note: PPP = purchasing power parity.

contributed around 20 percent of the country's GDP, while occupying less than 1 percent of its land. Faster urbanization, which occurs at early stages of development and is now taking place in the developing world, is associated with higher total GDP growth that then levels off (figure 3.2). Furthermore, the geographic concentration of population, GDP, and household consumption rises sharply with development, then levels off (World Bank 2009).

Rural-Urban Dichotomies and Development

The "bumpy" nature of the economic and urban landscape has implications for economic welfare, living standards, and poverty that become more pronounced as countries develop (World Bank 2009). Rising income inequality accompanies urbanization initially, but then declines as urbanization takes hold. Rural-urban disparities among today's developed countries have largely disappeared (figure 3.3).

However, rural-urban disparities in productivity and income are very much part of the economic landscape in developing countries, which are still in the first phase of urbanization. As occurred for the developed countries before them, the disparities in consumption, social services, and productivity diminish with urbanization. World Bank (2009, 65) notes, "Most developing countries have passed the peak in their rural-urban disparities" and have made considerable progress toward achieving the Millennium Development Goals. Convergence takes place more rapidly when the economy is more urbanized, as has occurred in China, India, and the Philippines (figure 3.4).

According to Cohen (2004, 37), "Ease of transportation and communication has blurred the distinction between urban and rural areas." In some areas of the world, this has led to the emergence of new types of settlement systems that do not belong in the rural or urban classification. An example, from Pacific Asia, is the extended metropolitan areas called *desakota*. In these settlements, the geography is rural, with much of the land under cultivation, but the income derives from nonagricultural sources;[3] for example, inhabitants are employed in nonfarm jobs or commute to the city for work. Cohen also notes that the nature of agricultural work in these regions has shifted to higher-value production. In areas that are already highly urbanized, such as countries in Latin America, there is little point in continuing to differentiate human settlement into urban and rural areas. What is needed is an appreciation of the changing spatial context in a predominantly urban environment. Cohen (2004) refers to the experience in Mexico, where a highly monocentric system of cities

Figure 3.2   Density and GDP per Capita in Selected Countries, by Phase of Urbanization

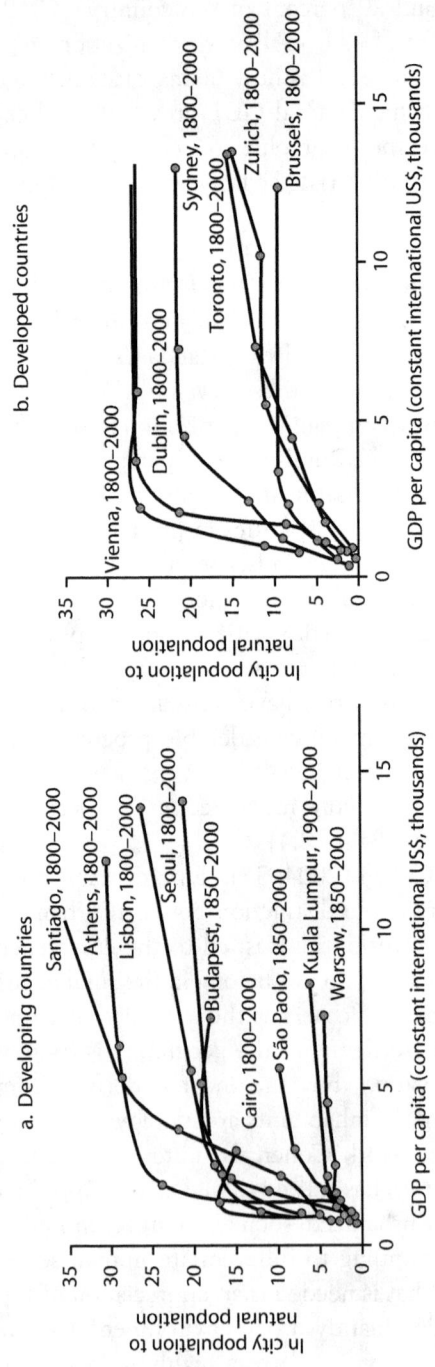

a. Developing countries

ln city population to natural population

GDP per capita (constant international US$, thousands)

Santiago, 1800–2000
Athens, 1800–2000
Lisbon, 1800–2000
Seoul, 1800–2000
Budapest, 1850–2000
Cairo, 1800–2000
São Paolo, 1850–2000
Kuala Lumpur, 1900–2000
Warsaw, 1850–2000

b. Developed countries

ln city population to natural population

GDP per capita (constant international US$, thousands)

Vienna, 1800–2000
Dublin, 1800–2000
Sydney, 1800–2000
Toronto, 1800–2000
Zurich, 1800–2000
Brussels, 1800–2000

Source: World Bank 2009.

34

Figure 3.3   Rural-Urban Disparities in GDP per Capita

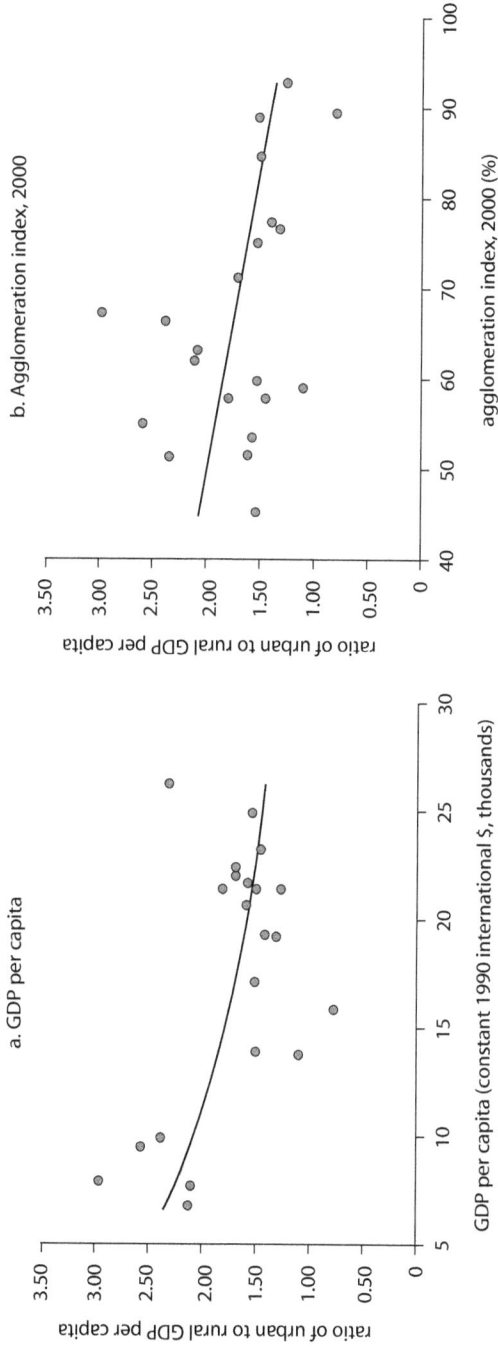

a. GDP per capita

b. Agglomeration index, 2000

Source: World Bank 2009.

Figure 3.4   Rural-Urban Disparities and Density in the Philippines, China, and India, Various Years

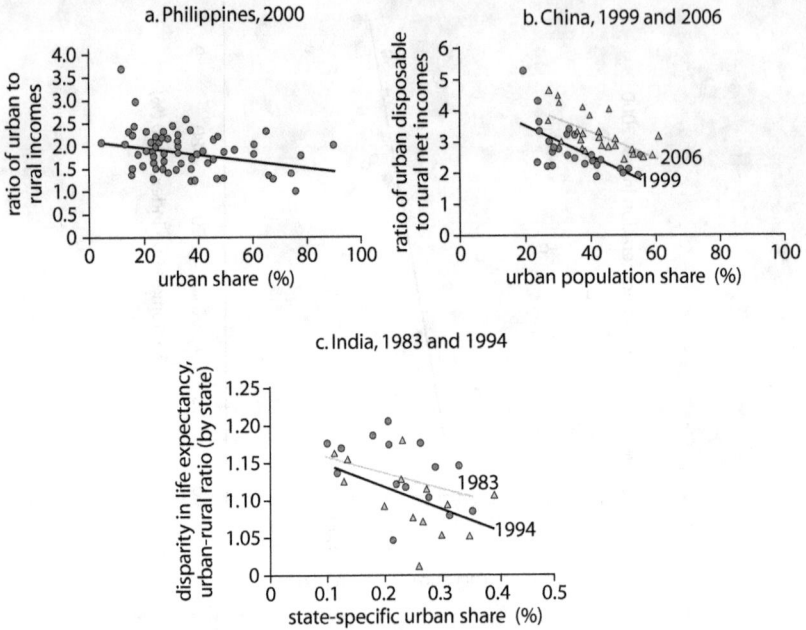

a. Philippines, 2000

b. China, 1999 and 2006

c. India, 1983 and 1994

Source: World Bank 2009.

became, over two decades between 1980 and 2000, a polycentric system with nine large metropoles. Greater use of satellites and geo-coding of census and survey data enable different conceptualizations and measurements of spatial concentration. One spatial form that has emerged over the past 20–30 years is the city-region. According to Cohen (2004, 38), "The 'city-region' can be identified loosely by the extent and nature of economic activity within an extended economic zone surrounding the city proper." Bangkok is one such example, containing more than 17 million people and expected to extend more than 200 kilometers from its center by 2010. These city-regions have evolved to house large-scale capital investments, such as airports and manufacturing plants, located on the urban fringe, and the core has become "the command center" for regional or global businesses, offering telecommunications, banking, law, financial management, information services, and management consulting services, for example (Cohen 2004).

Income disparity within a city is a phenomenon that many developing cities experience. This disparity is visible in the slums—chronically overcrowded dwellings of poor quality in underserved areas within cities (World Bank 2009).[4] Slums are a part of rapid urbanization—as labor markets expand to fulfill demand from industries and services, labor moves to cities. Underdeveloped land markets are unable to cope with increasing urbanization, and slums emerge. For many slum-dwellers, the proximity to the large city provides opportunities for economic gain. Many residents in the Dharavi slum in Mumbai started their own businesses after the state government provided limited rights over their dwellings and access to water and power (World Bank 2009). Henderson (2010) is less sanguine about the emergence of slums and suggests that the favela- or slum-style development of Latin American cities is a result of local government policy that favors certain areas by restraining inmigration.[5]

Unprecedented Volumes of Population

The take-off in urbanization originated in nineteenth-century Great Britain. The urban share of population in 1800 was 19.2 percent, increasing rapidly to 40.0 percent by 1820. Urbanization spread to the new world—Canada and United States—by the mid-nineteenth century. The pace of urbanization in Europe and North America at the end of the nineteenth century was 7.7 percentage points over the 20 years from 1880 to 1900. This was not unlike the pace of urbanization for the developing countries between 1985 and 2005, which experienced median and mean absolute increases of 7.1 and 8.0 percentage points, respectively. There are two ways in which the urbanization story for the developing world today differs from the experience of the developed world during the mid-to-late nineteenth century. The first is the sheer size of population. As one example, China added 225 million people to its towns and cities between 1985 and 2002, almost the entire population of the United States (World Bank 2009). Over the 10 years beginning in 1985, the developing world experienced an increase in its urban population of 8.3 million, close to three times the increase in population witnessed by many countries in Europe and North America in the final two decades of the nineteenth century (World Bank 2009). Furthermore, the megacities in the developing world are unprecedented in their size and number (figure 3.5). The second way in which the developing countries are experiencing a different pattern of urbanization is in public services. Cities in developing countries today are benefiting from advances in public health and medicine and improvements in water systems. Cities in developed countries at similar stages of urbanization in the nineteenth century had

Figure 3.5   Change in Urban Population with and without China and India, 1985–2005

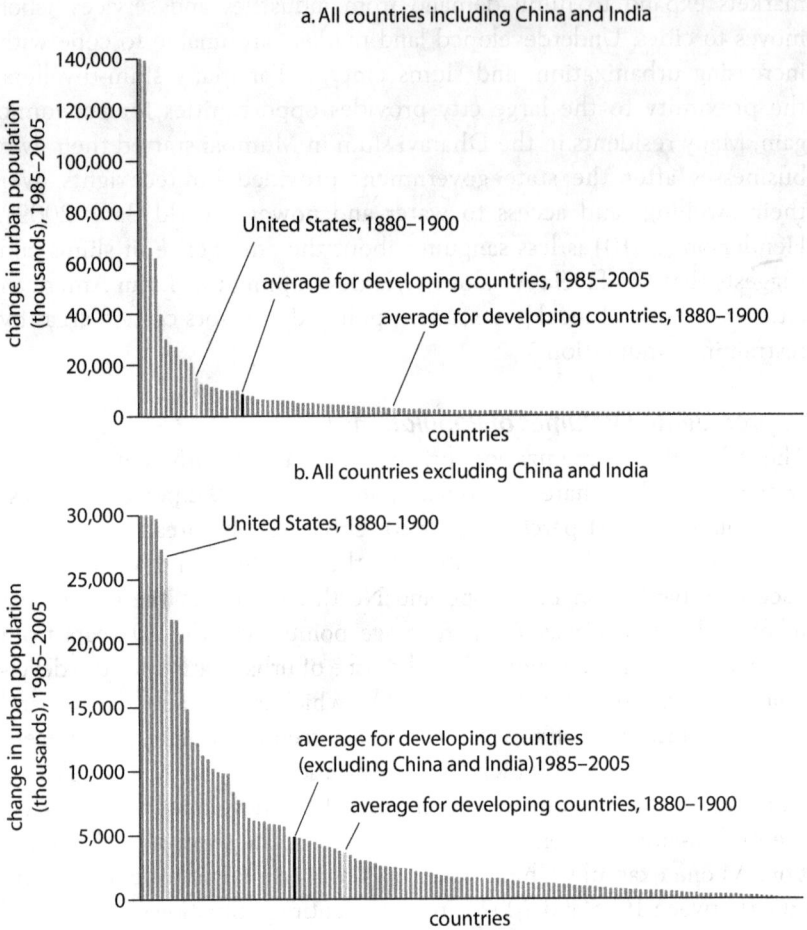

a. All countries including China and India

b. All countries excluding China and India

Source: World Bank 2009.

poorer health and lower life expectancy than rural areas (World Bank 2009).

Urbanization in Developing Countries

Cohen (2004) summarizes the major differences in urbanization experienced by the developing regions and identifies some of the challenges in the coming decades. The discussion is summarized in table 3.1. Enormous interregional and intraregional differences are evident in the pattern of

Table 3.1 Regional Differences in Urbanization

Region	Rate of urbanization (%)		Characteristics of urbanization
	1950	2000	
Latin America and the Caribbean	42	75	Urban primacy; many cities with more than 1 million people; reverse polarization; spatial polarization between rich and poor; long tradition of urbanization in some countries;[a] most Caribbean countries have a high rate of urbanization, with Haiti as an exception.
South Asia	18	27	Population becoming increasingly urban; extreme poverty and depravation, creating enormous urban management challenges; region is home to 5 of the world's 30 largest cities: Mumbai, Kolkata, and Dehli (India), Dhaka (Bangladesh), and Karachi (Pakistan); improved modes of transportation have extended the reach of urban areas and blurred the distinction between rural and urban—*desakota*; the majority of land is under cultivation, but nonfarm jobs are an important source of employment and income; region will be home to three of the world's five largest urban agglomerations;[b] most urban growth in the future will take place in smaller cities and towns.
East Asia and the Pacific	—	38	Areas that have integrated into the global economy experienced rapid urban transformation that is now being repeated in the newly industrializing economies;[c] special economic zones[d] along China's coastal regions were a catalyst for industrialization and urbanization; population projections suggest that the 1.25 billion additional people by 2030 will be absorbed into urban areas and that 54% of the population will be urban by 2030.
Former Soviet republics	—	—	Historically, government determined the nature, scale, and spatial distribution of economic activities; cities were planned in concentric circles with large industrial plants and large-scale housing estates; the end of the Cold War and collapse of the Soviet Union had huge economic, social, and demographic consequences that were most apparent in the cities.
Middle East and North Africa	27	58	Less diversity in urbanization among countries in the region compared to other regions; the need for access to water, rapid industrialization, and high levels of international labor migration to oil-rich Gulf states resulted in urban population of more than 50% and more than 85% in many countries;[e] socioeconomic and political heterogeneity within the region results in a wide variety of urban problems and challenges.

(continued next page)

Table 3.1 *(continued)*

Region	Rate of urbanization (%)		Characteristics of urbanization
	1950	2000	
Sub-Saharan Africa	15	38	Least developed and least urbanized region of the world; most cities are small by international standards; Kinshasa and Lagos are exceptions; colonialism influenced the structure and pattern of economic growth—cities displaced traditional networks of trade and influence and attracted migrants; colonial urbanization also affected the physical structure and layout of many cities into two highly uneven zones—a European space with a high level of infrastructure and an indigenous space with marginal services; postcolonial cities grew quickly as a result of high population growth and high spatial mobility; cities are economically marginalized in the new global economy;[f] challenges for urban authorities are to provide low-income housing, high-quality urban services, and employment.[g]

Source: Compiled from Cohen 2004.

Note: — = Not available.

a. Argentina, Chile, and Uruguay.

b. Delhi, Dhaka, and Mumbai.

c. Indonesia, Malaysia, Philippines, and, the Thailand.

d. For example, Shantou, Shenzhen, Xiamen, and Zhuhai, which were established as testing grounds for a more open, export-oriented development strategy.

e. Bahrain, Kuwait, Lebanon, Libya, Qatar, and Saudi Arabia. The Republic of Yemen is an exception, with just 25 percent of the population classified as urban.

f. "Since the 1970s, urban growth in Africa has been most affected by the region's economic crisis. A current list of ailments includes declining productivity in agriculture and industry, a lack of foreign exchange, increasing indebtedness, worsening balance-of-payments position, and declining real wages" (Cohen 2004, 45).

g. In addition to economic mismanagement, several countries have suffered from long civil wars, with large numbers moving to cities. Cities are growing despite poor macroeconomic performance and without significant foreign direct investment.

urbanization from the 1950s to the present. In each case, the socioeconomic and political history interacts with the geographic landscape to determine the urbanization experience and is affected by globalization, democratization, and decentralization. As each region's and, indeed, each country's socioeconomic, political, and geographic landscape is different, so too has been their path of urbanization.

Latin America and the Caribbean is primarily an urban region with a long history, at least in some countries. The overall rate of urbanization masks intraregional differences, whereby Argentina, Brazil, Chile, French Guiana, Mexico, Uruguay, the República Bolivariana de Venezuela, and several Caribbean countries or territories (Anguilla, The Bahamas, Cuba, Guadeloupe, Martinique, Puerto Rico, Trinidad and Tobago) are more than three-quarters urban, while the Dominican Republic, Guatemala, Guyana, and Jamaica are around 50 percent urban. Haiti has the lowest rate of urbanization in the region, at around 30 percent. Large-scale rural-to-urban migration, coupled with industrial policies that targeted cities and were predicated on import substitution and protection of infant industries, led to a high rate of urban primacy. Cities with more than 1 million people in the region increased from 6 in 1950 to more than 50 in 2000, and "the four largest cities—Buenos Aires, Mexico City, Rio de Janeiro, and São Paulo—have grown to previously unimaginable sizes" (Cohen 2004, 40). Rural-to-urban migration is expected to continue. However, industrial policy has shifted to favoring areas outside of the megacities. This shift, coupled with congestion costs, economic recession, and programs of structural adjustment in the 1990s, has adversely affected many Latin American cities and the megacities in particular. Urbanization will continue, but at a slower pace.

At the other end of the spectrum is Sub-Saharan Africa, one of the least urbanized regions and where urbanization has been largely predicated on demographic factors and not always for benign reasons (see the notes to table 3.1). The region's colonial past affected the manner in which the physical aspects of urban space developed, incorporating two zones—a European zone "enjoying a high level of urban infrastructure and services and an indigenous space that was marginally serviced" (Cohen 2004, 45). Data problems make it difficult to describe urban trends. And while fertility rates are falling, population momentum suggests a fast pace of urbanization, such that "before 2023, African society will become predominantly urban" (Cohen 2004, 45).

The Middle East and North Africa region is home to some of the world's oldest cities, yet urbanization was slow to take off, with just

27 percent of the population classified as urban in 1950. By 2000, there had been an eightfold increase in urban inhabitants. Cairo, Istanbul, and Tehran are among the largest urban agglomerations in the world, home to more than 7 million inhabitants each. Most countries within the region are at least 50 percent urban (Cohen 2004). The challenges for urban planners are many, given the socioeconomic and political heterogeneity within the region. For example, rural-to-urban migration and population growth in the Arab Republic of Egypt have led to many slums and housing shortages in Cairo. Urban issues in postconflict Iraq "have to do with establishing the infrastructure of urban government and other issues of rehabilitation and reconstruction" (Cohen 2004, 44).

China and India dominate the East Asia and the Pacific region, and the combined urban population in the region contains just under half of the world's urban population. The vastness of the region makes generalizations difficult. Cohen (2004) classifies countries based on their experience with economic development and urbanization (table 3.1). Some countries have opened up to the world economy, benefiting from globalization and experiencing increasing rates of urbanization. Many of the coastal cities have undergone rapid urban transformation as a result. The designation of special economic zones in China also led to rapid urban transformation in cities such as Dalian, Guangzhou, Qingdao, Shenzhen, Tianjin, and Xiamen.

The pace of urban change in South Asia has been relatively modest due largely to the more rural nature of the countries. Significant urban challenges abound in an environment with extreme poverty and inadequate physical infrastructure. Increasing industrialization has benefited urbanization, as have improved modes of transportation that have extended the reach of the urban areas, blurring the distinction between urban and rural areas. Nonfarm jobs have become a feature of the *desakota* zones around the cities, contributing positively to employment and income.

Urbanization in the former Soviet republics was dictated by government decisions relating to the nature, scale, and spatial distribution of economic activities. The absence of a land market in cities led to a large amount of unused land throughout the city. Large-scale industrial production was favored over the service or retail sectors. Moreover, many of these industrial production plants were kept in operation long after they had ceased to be profitable. The fallout once the Soviet Union collapsed was felt most strongly in the cities, with enormous declines in output, "rapid impoverishment of large sections of society, great uncertainty about the future, and a fundamental reevaluation of the location, functioning, and organization of productive activity" (Cohen 2004, 43). The social, economic, and demographic consequences were also unprecedented, with declining rates of marriage, birth, and male life expectancy.

Key Features of Cities in Developing Countries

Duranton (2008) provides a theoretical framework in which he examines the key features of cities in developing countries, first from a static efficiency perspective and then from a dynamic growth perspective. He augments the theoretical discussion with examples from the empirical literature, where relevant and where available.

The literature on cities in developing economies, although much thinner in volume, is nevertheless consistent with the more voluminous literature on cities in developed economies in supporting an upward-sloping wage curve, costs of living that rise with city size, a bell-shape net wage curve, and some labor mobility driven by net wage differentials (Duranton 2008).[6] Various studies on agglomeration economies identify both localization effects (agglomeration effects take place within sectors) and urbanization effects (agglomeration effects take place between sectors) for cities in developing countries (table 3.2).[7] Localization economies foster specialized cities, while urbanization economies foster diversified cities. However, cities in developing countries are rarely specialized, especially when compared with cities in the developed countries. Despite some caveats with regard to the data, the evidence suggests the existence of both diversified and specialized cities in the developing regions.[8]

Turning to the labor supply curve and mobility, the literature suggests that internal migration flows in developing countries are consistent with an upward-sloping labor supply curve but that mobility is not perfect (Henderson 2008). Brueckner (1990) and Ravallion and Wodon (1999) find that the direction of migration flows is consistent with existing differences in net wages. Henderson (2008) concludes that movements in the labor supply curve are driven largely by what is happening in the countryside. For example, Barrios, Bertinelli, and Strobl (2006) note that climate change that affects living standards in rural areas gives rise to mobility to the cities. Fay and Opal (1999) suggest that worsening rural conditions that lower the labor supply curve lead to urbanization without growth. These "negative correlations may explain why many developing countries attempt to restrain urbanization," yet Henderson finds "scant evidence about cities being too large in general" (Henderson 2008, 18, 19).

Table 3.2   A Dozen Economies of Scale

Type of economy of scale	Static or dynamic	Example
Internal		
1. *Pecuniary*		Firms are able to purchase intermediate inputs at volume discounts.
Technological		
2. Static technological	Static	Average costs fall because of fixed costs of operating a plant.
3. Dynamic technological	Dynamic	Firms learn to operate a plant more efficiently over time.
External or agglomeration		
Localization		
4. "Shopping"	Static	Shoppers are attracted to places where there are many sellers.
5. "Adam Smith" specialization	Static	Outsourcing allows both the upstream input suppliers and downstream firms to profit from productivity gains because of specialization.
6. "Marshall" labor pooling	Static	Workers with industry-specific skills are attracted to a location where there is greater concentration.
7. "Marshall-Arrow-Romer" learning by doing	Dynamic	Reductions in costs arise from repeated and continuous production activity over time and spill over between firms in the same place.
Urbanization		
8. "Jane Jacobs" innovation	Static	The more different things are done locally, the more opportunity there is for observing and adapting ideas from others.
9. "Marshall" labor pooling	Static	Workers in an industry bring innovations to firms in other industries; this is similar to number 6, but the benefit arises from the existence of diverse industries in one location.
10. "Adam Smith" division of labor	Static	Similar to number 5 above, the main difference being that the division of labor is made possible by the existence of many different buying industries in the same place.
11. "Romer" endogenous growth	Dynamic	The larger the market, the higher the profit; the more attractive the location to firms, the more jobs there are, the more labor pools there are, the larger the market, and so on.
12. *"Pure" agglomeration*		Fixed costs of infrastructure are spread over more taxpayers; diseconomies arise from congestion and pollution.

Source: World Bank 2009.

He refers to the strong barriers to labor mobility that have made Chinese cities too small, as examined in Au and Henderson (2006a, 2006b), but other examples are difficult to find. Henderson (2008) questions whether restrictions on labor mobility, either because of a misguided application of the Harris and Todaro (1970) model[9] or because of a policy of restrictions, may be part of a political-economy equilibrium and therefore difficult to change.

What is evident in developing economies is a large preponderance of urban primacy, where the largest city is often disproportionately bigger than the second largest city. Henderson (2008) disagrees with the trade policy arguments that have been used to explain urban primacy on the grounds of theoretical ambiguity and available empirical evidence.[10] He suggests that urban primacy is due to political and institutional factors. These factors are difficult to quantify in terms of their magnitude and direction. Ades and Glaeser (1995) and Davis and Henderson (2003) suggest a positive relationship between urban primacy and unstable and undemocratic regimes. Henderson (2008) suggests that the many regulations and permits that govern economic activity in developing countries may also favor urban primacy, as those nearer to the center of power may find it easier to obtain permits or circumvent regulations. The political economy associated with urban primacy may be very difficult to break. Henderson (2008) suggests that administrative deregulation, as in the Republic of Korea, may be an effective tool to limit primacy, but at the end of the day, the issue appears to be one of political economy.

What one also finds in some cities in developing economies is the existence of a dual housing sector. This is manifest by a division between formal housing and squatter settlements. Henderson (2008, 29) notes that in "some large developing country cities, more than half the population live in squatter settlements." In examining the reasons for squatter settlements, he concludes the following:

- If squatter settlements were simply a matter of some of the poor opting out of formal housing, policy choices would revolve around issues of redistribution and the most effective way to do this.
- Squatter settlements arise because of a lack of effective, formal property titles (which also have knock-on effects for enterprise development and female labor supply).
- Squatter settlements may be the outcome of policy distortions—for example, binding minimum lot size and rent controls.

- Squatter settlements may not be so cheap if the inhabitants have to pay high prices for necessities such as water, for example, or, in the absence of titles, have to pay for some form of protection (Henderson 2008).

Based on these points, Henderson concludes that regulatory constraints in the formal housing sector, while limiting the size of the city, will be crowded out by the growth of squatter settlements. Removing regulatory constraints is socially desirable. Titling policies are desirable, and these should be grounded in the legal and taxation system. There is a political economy of squatter settlements, with many vested interests that benefit from this undesirable status quo (Henderson 2008).

In summary, cities in developing countries would benefit from (a) eliminating primary city favoritism, (b) solving the biases that lead to squatter settlements by implementing a titling policy, and (c) not discouraging the internal migration of people. These policy suggestions also hold when examining the features of cities from a dynamic growth perspective. However, pursuing such policies is demanding,[11] and the political economy of these issues may be difficult to address (Henderson 2008).

Conclusion

Urbanization—the movement of people into cities—has implications for the economic development of the land area that this population will occupy or inhabit. The chapter examined several features of urbanization associated with economic development. Economic density—the output produced per unit of land—is a principal feature of urban transition and growth. It rises with urbanization and becomes ever more concentrated as the structure of output changes from manufacturing to services. The economic landscape is bumpy, with some areas exhibiting higher rates of economic density. This has implications for economic welfare, living standards, and poverty. Initially, inequality rises with economic density and urbanization, but over time, convergence occurs between the rural and urban areas, blurring the dichotomy between them. Urbanization in the developing world differs from that in the developed. First, it differs in its history: the volume of people moving into cities in the developing world today is unprecedented. Furthermore, advances in security, health, and sanitation suggest that the experience is different than what occurred in the developed world when urbanization was beginning to take place. The chapter also examined regional differences in urbanization for the developing countries and noted some of the facets of urbanization—primacy, squatter settlements, discouragement of city growth—that characterize many developing cities today.

Notes

1. The population size of cities is examined in chapter 2. Chapter 4 examines territorial specialization of cities.

2. One may argue that developments in transportation and in information and communication technology dispute this claim. However, the raison d'être of cities and urban areas is the face-to-face communication they facilitate.

3. Remittances from family members working in the city also constitute income to the *deskota* (Cohen 2004).

4. Examples include Dharavi in Mumbai, Kibra and Huruma in Nairobi, Washington in Abidjan, Majboor Nagar and Kanchan Puri in Delhi, San Fernando in Buenos Aires, and Rocinha in Rio de Janeiro (World Bank 2009).

5. China provides an example. An explicit policy limits migration to certain key cities by making living conditions unpleasant for migrants. This supersedes a less explicit policy that used the *hukou* (the system of household registration) to constrain rural people to live in rural areas but take industrial jobs and controlled migrants to ensure that urbanization was localized and diffuse (Henderson 2010).

6. Empirical studies on the cost-of-living and bell-shape net wage curve for developing economy cities are scant and not examined here.

7. Duranton (2008) cites Henderson (1988) for localization economies in Brazil; Henderson, Lee, and Lee (2001) for localization economies for Korean industries, particularly traditional industries; Lall, Shalizi, and Deichmann (2004) for India; and Deichmann et al. (2005) for Indonesia. Henderson (2009) also finds urbanization economies for advanced sectors in Korea. Furthermore, Lall, Funderburg, and Yepes (2004) find evidence, albeit weak, of urbanization economies in India, while Lall, Koo, and Chakravorty (2003) find stronger evidence for India. Deichmann et al. (2005) find mild evidence of urbanization effects for several sectors in Indonesia, and Au and Henderson (2006a, 2006b) find both urbanization and localization effects for several cities in China. Henderson (2005) and Overman and Venables (2005) review the literature on agglomeration economies in developing countries.

8. Duranton (2008, 17) suggests two main criticisms. First, the presence of agglomeration economies may reflect the sorting of "more productive workers in bigger and more specialized cities, rather than true agglomeration

economies." Second, the data represent the formal sector. Case study evidence suggests that the informal sector is a strong contributor to agglomeration economies.

9. The argument for dual labor markets "was first developed by Harris and Todaro (1970) and has been extremely influential in policy circles." Workers in the formal sector are paid higher wages in urban than in rural areas. "The initial earnings gap between the rural and formal urban sector causes workers to move to the city" (Henderson 2008, 27).

10. Trade liberalization does reduce urban primacy in the model of Krugman and Livas Elizondo (1996), in which all cities are able to import differentiated goods. This equalization of market potential reduces the tendency for agglomeration of manufacturing in a single core city. Henderson (2008) questions the assumption of equalization and suggests that trade liberalization is more likely to benefit cities in coastal regions or cities close to trading partners, thus reinforcing their dominance. Empirical studies find weak evidence for urban primacy and are beleaguered by other variables that are correlated with trade. According to Henderson (2008, 20), "Ades and Glaeser (1995); Nitsch (2006) suggest that trade plays no systematic role with respect to urban primacy."

11. Henderson (2008, 44) writes, "Such an agenda is rather demanding since it includes raising the efficiency of public good provision, lowering barriers to mobility, improving market access to allow secondary cities to develop, and so forth."

References

Ades, Alberto F., and Edward L. Glaeser. 1995. "Trade and Circuses: Explaining Urban Giants." *Quarterly Journal of Economics* 110 (1): 195–227.

Au, Chun-Chung, and J. Vernon Henderson. 2006a. "Are Chinese Cities Too Small?" *Review of Economic Studies* 73 (3): 549–76.

———. 2006b. "How Migration Restrictions Limit Agglomeration and Productivity in China." *Journal of Development Economics* 80 (2): 350–88.

Barrios, Salvador, Luisito Bertinelli, and Eric Strobl. 2006. "Climatic Change and Rural Urban Migration: The Case of Sub-Saharan Africa." *Journal of Urban Economics* 60 (3): 357–71.

Brueckner, Jan K. 1990. "Analyzing Third World Urbanization: A Model with Empirical Evidence." *Economic Development and Cultural Change* 38 (3): 587–610.

Cohen, Barney. 2004. "Urban Growth in Developing Countries: A Review of Current Trends and a Caution Regarding Existing Forecasts." *World Development* 32 (1): 23–51.

Davis, James C., and J. Vernon Henderson. 2003. "Evidence on the Political Economy of the Urbanization Process." *Journal of Urban Economics* 53 (1): 98–125.

Deichmann, Uwe, Kai Kaiser, Somik V. Lall, and Zmarak Shalizi. 2005. "Agglomeration, Transport, and Regional Development in Indonesia." Policy Research Working Paper 3477, World Bank, Washington, DC.

Duranton, Gilles. 2008. "Cities: Engines of Growth and Prosperity for Developing Countries?" Working Paper 12, World Bank, Washington, DC, on behalf of the Commission on Growth and Development.

Fay, Marianne, and Charlotte Opal. 1999. "Urbanization without Growth: A Not-So-Uncommon Phenomenon." Policy Research Working Paper 2412, World Bank, Washington, DC.

Harris, John R., and Michael P. Todaro. 1970. "Migration, Unemployment, and Development: A Two-Sector Analysis." *American Economic Review* 60 (1): 126–42.

Henderson, J. Vernon. 1988. *Urban Development: Theory, Fact, and Illusion.* Oxford: Oxford University Press.

———. 2005. "Urbanization and Growth." In *Handbook of Economic Growth*, vol. 1B, ed. Philippe Aghion and Steven N. Durlauf, 1543–91. Amsterdam: North-Holland.

———. 2008. "Cities: Engines of Growth and Prosperity for Developing Countries?" Commission on Growth and Development Working Paper 12, commissioned by the World Bank, Washington, DC.

———. 2009. "Urbanization in China: Policy Issues and Options." Report prepared for CERAP (China Economic Research and Advisory Programme). http://www.cairncrossfund.org/download/十二五项目报告/Background%20Papers/Henderson%20-%20Final_Report_2009.11.10%5BUrbanization%5D.pdf.

———. 2010. "Cities and Development." *Journal of Regional Science* 50 (1): 515–40.

Henderson, J. V., T. Lee, and Y. J. Lee. 2001. "Scale Externalities in Korea." *Journal of Urban Economics* 49 (3): 479–504.

Krugman, Paul, and Raul Livas Elizondo. 1996. "Trade Policy and the Third World Metropolis." *Journal of Development Economics* 49 (1): 137–50.

Lall, Somik V., Richard Funderburg, and Tito Yepes. 2004. "Location, Concentration, and Performance of Economic Activity in Brazil." Policy Research Working Paper 3268, World Bank, Washington, DC.

Lall, Somik V., Jun Koo, and Sanjoy Chakravorty. 2003. "Diversity Matters: The Economic Geography of Industry Location in India." Policy Research Working Paper 3072, World Bank, Washington, DC.

Lall, Somik V., Zmarak Shalizi, and Uwe Deichmann. 2004. "Agglomeration Economies and Productivity in Indian Industry." *Journal of Development Economics* 73 (3): 643–73.

Nitsch, Volker. 2006. "Trade Openness and Urban Concentration: New Evidence." *Journal of Economic Integration* 21 (2): 340–62.

Overman, Henry G., and Anthony J. Venables. 2005. "Cities in the Developing World." Report for the Department for International Development, London.

Ravallion, Martin, and Quenton Wodon. 1999. "Poor Areas, or Only Poor People?" *Journal of Regional Science* 39 (4): 689–711.

World Bank. 2009. *World Development Report 2009: Reshaping Economic Geography*. Washington, DC: World Bank.

CHAPTER 4

Spatial Concentration and Specialization

The chapter presents a further typology of space based on today's specialization of cities. Urban specialization arises from the trade-off between scale economies—internal and localized external economies that include knowledge economies[1] arising from the education level of city inhabitants—and diseconomies in own industry and in living (housing costs including rents, crime, overcrowding, land use).[2] Industries that benefit from local agglomeration economies as well as internal economies are more likely to reside in larger cities. Industries that depend on their own activity for productivity improvements are likely to locate in small, specialized cities where own industry economies of scale are maximized (Henderson 2010).[3]

Cities in developing countries tend to host many specializations. Territorial specialization has not yet taken place, as urbanization is still progressing. Furthermore, "The important inheritance of colonially created port cities, the economic necessity to concentrate the first major efforts in infrastructure, the availability of skilled labour in a situation of great skills scarcities, the dependence upon imported manufacturing inputs and services" are suggestive of why developing cities lack territorial specialization (Harris 1991, 26). The largest cities are the most accessible to foreign investors and are "incubators for new firms trying to discover the best product lines and production methods" (Henderson 2010, 524).

Cities in developed economies are highly specialized, given their advanced stage of economic development and history of urbanization. Small and medium-size cities in Japan, the Republic of Korea, the United States, and other countries are highly specialized and have been for some time (Henderson 2010). When heavy manufacturing was a major part of the economy, the typology of cities included cities producing steel, textiles, automobiles, ships, aircraft, pulp and paper, and petrochemicals. Henderson (1974), using data from the United States, estimates that between 50 and 60 percent of the urban labor force lies in the nontraded sector (wholesale, retail, personal services, construction, utilities), with the remaining share engaged in the traded sector.[4] In current times, small cities have become specialized in consumer service activities such as retirement, health, and insurance services (Henderson 2010). Very little research has yet been carried out on the scale economies arising from service activities.

Specialization of Cities

Cities have specialized in certain activities since the fourteenth century, and early writers in urban hierarchy have classified cities based on their engagement in primary industries, secondary industries, and tertiary industries (MacKenzie 1933). Later, Ogburn (1937) classified seven types of cities based on their industrial and economic activity. These included (a) trading cities, (b) factory cities, (c) transportation cities, (d) mining cities, (e) pleasure cities, (f) health resort cities, and (g) college cities. Duncan and Reiss (1956) classified cities based on (a) regional location, (b) economic activity, (c) economic specialty, and (d) population size and growth rate. The authors noted the interdependence of cities in the urban hierarchy.

Table 4.1 shows the spatial allocation of manufacturing and business services in U.S. cities for 1910 and 1995. In 1910, manufacturing was part of the urban landscape. As urbanization and development continued, manufacturing activity was replaced by business services. Henderson (2010) cites three principal reasons cities become inefficient for standardized manufacturing:

1. Firms and industries as a whole have accomplished much learning and adoption of foreign technologies and no longer benefit so much from the learning environment of the largest cities.

Table 4.1   Manufacturing and Business Services in the United States, by Size of City, 1910 and 1995

% of employment

Metro area population	Share of employment in manufacturing	Share of employment in business services	Share of employment in consumer services
1910			
Four largest MSAs[a]	35.1	6.2	18.5
Medium-size MSAs[b]	35.3	5.1	18.2
Small MSAs[c]	30.9	4.6	20.1
Nonmetro area	25.1	4.4	24.3
National average	30.2	5.0	21.2
1995			
Over 2.5 million	14.3	21.3	23.3
1 million to 2.5 million	15.2	19.3	22.8
500,000 to 1 million	15.8	17.7	23.6
250,000 to 500,000	19.1	15.5	23.2
Under 250,000	18.8	13.3	24.6
Nonmetro area	26.9	9.1	22.6
National average	17.2	17.7	23.2

Source: Holko 1999.

Note: MSA = metropolitan statistical area.

a. Refers to the largest MSAs (private sector employment over 600,000: New York, Chicago, Boston, Philadelphia).
b. Private sector employment between 100,000 and 600,000
c. Private sector employment under 100,000.

2. Cities become very expensive locations, with high rents and labor costs. Infrastructure and skilled labor are in greater relative abundance in other locations.
3. The business service sector is expanding, demanding locations inside large cities and outbidding manufacturing for central city lands in them (Henderson 2010).

Henderson (2010) posits that territorial specialization is associated with a certain population size. Business and professional services suggest a large city by population size. Similarly, high-tech industries that undergo substantial technological progress locate in larger cities, where they also benefit from local agglomeration—for example, the aircraft industry in Los Angeles or the research and development (R&D) segment of the electronics industry in Tokyo (Henderson 2010). Cities like London and New York are global financial service cities, with a very small manufacturing sector (table 4.2 gives the example of New York). Strong institutions in the economic and legal environment contribute to

Table 4.2   Share of New York County (Manhattan) in Total Private Employment in the United States, 1997

Sector	% of private employment
All industries	1.8
Headquarters	3.0
Financial headquarters	11.7
Financial services	12.0
Security brokers	25.0
Business services	7.5
Advertising	15.0

Source: Henderson 2010.

the development and sustainability of these global cities, which are also cultural cities and attract a creative class of worker.

In between the large cities and small and medium-size cities are metro areas that are more diverse. Theoretical modeling and empirical work suggest that the share of service activity increases in line with the size of the metro area (Henderson 2010).

Cities in developed countries that have made the transition from manufacturing to services and have become specialized in various service activities represent a new typology of cities. Among this typology are knowledge cities, creative cities, global cities, and green (eco) cities. The following sections examine this typology.

Knowledge Cities

The comparative advantage of developed economies lies in their knowledge base. The generation and application of the knowledge base define an area's competitiveness and growth at the local, regional, and national levels.[5] Knowledge may take the form of investment in R&D, a qualified and skilled labor force, high-quality entrepreneurship, or all three. Knowledge enhances productivity through innovation in products, services, and processes (Lever 2002). Numerous writers attest to the association between the urban knowledge base and economic growth and development (Knight 1995; Kresl and Singh 1999; Lambooy 2000; Lever 2002). As the knowledge base of the city increases, the nature of development changes. Knowledge-based services (financial services, insurance, and communications) outgrew knowledge-based manufacturing industries (high-technology and medium-technology industries) for the Organisation for Economic Co-operation and Development (OECD) countries as a whole between 1985 and 1998 (Lever 2002).

Critical to the explanation of economic growth and development is the distinction between tacit and codified knowledge. Codified knowledge is available to all businesses and at low or zero cost. It does not impart any competitive advantage. An example is the Internet. Tacit knowledge is available to only limited contacts and is often passed through face-to-face communication. It does confer competitive advantage. Large cities, where inhabitants are in contact with one another, benefit from tacit knowledge.

Lever (2002) examines a multidimensional index of the scale of the knowledge base for European cities. This study presents a wider definition of the knowledge base and is a departure from other studies that define it as the number of R&D establishments per million inhabitants or workers (Lever 2002). Three dimensions of the knowledge base are considered: tacit knowledge, codified knowledge, and knowledge infrastructure. Knowledge infrastructure is captured by telecommunications infrastructure (table 4.3).

Using the variables listed in table 4.3, Lever (2002) develops a general index comprising seven measures: presence of corporate producer service companies in the knowledge sectors (finance, law, marketing, research), connectivity of the local airport, the hosting of commercial conferences and exhibitions, the rate of new enterprise formation, two variables for the size of the local universities (number of students and number of published academic research papers in science, computing, medicine, and technology), and the quality of local telecommunications infrastructure (Lever 2002). The index is then applied to 19 European cities that scored on at least four of the seven measures,[6] and the mean rankings are calculated. The results are shown in table 4.4.

London and Paris emerge as "world cities" and are ranked in the top three positions in all but one of the seven variables (university size). National capitals fare well as knowledge-based cities, and many other cities in Germany also fare well on the knowledge base score. This may reflect the decentralized system of government there. Furthermore, the knowledge base in London and Paris is so heavily concentrated in the finance, law, and administrative sectors that no other cities qualify for inclusion. The mean score increases as the rankings fall, and Lever (2002) suggests that this may reflect the peripheral location of these cities from the center of the European Union. London and Paris fare less well across the measures of economic success: annual percentage employment change, annual percentage change in gross value added per worker, and the shift-share residual, which standardizes for industrial structure at the

Table 4.3 Dimensions of Knowledge Base: Measures and Results

Dimensions of knowledge base and measures	Data source	Results
Tacit knowledge		
(Rank of) leading world cities in four service sectors (accountancy; advertising; banking and finance, and law)	Globalization and World Cities Research Group (Taylor and Walker 2001)	*Alpha cities* (London, Milan, Paris) *Beta cities* (Brussels, Madrid, Moscow, Zurich) *Gamma cities* (Amsterdam, Barcelona, Berlin, Budapest, Copenhagen, Dusseldorf, Geneva, Hamburg, Munich, Prague, Rome, Stockholm, Warsaw)
Airport connectivity (number of connections and change in number over a period, 1991–93)	Buursink (1994)	Amsterdam, Brussels, Copenhagen, Dusseldorf, Frankfurt, Geneva, London, Munich, Paris, Vienna, Zurich
Fairs and trade exhibitions (composite index based on local population size, rental levels, local per capita income, infrastructure, transport, and weather)	Regression study that defined the economic advantage to holding fairs and trade exhibitions (Rubalcaba-Bermejo and Cuadrado-Roura 1995)	Barcelona, Birmingham, Bologna, Cologne, Dusseldorf, Frankfurt, Hanover, London, Madrid, Milan, Munich, Paris
New enterprise formation	Registered new businesses (not cited)	Not cited
Codified knowledge		
Number of students in local universities.	Local universities (not cited)	Not cited
Volume of academic and scientific papers in refereed journals	Total number of published papers; number of papers per 1,000 inhabitants[a] (Matthiessen and Schwartz 1999)	Berlin, Cambridge, Copenhagen, Edinburgh-Glasgow, London, Madrid, Manchester-Liverpool, Moscow, Oxford-Reading, Paris, Randstadt, Stockholm
Knowledge infrastructure		
Quality of telecommunications provision	Rankings based on technical definitions of the pricing of services, the choice of physical infrastructure available, and the availability of the most advanced and sophisticated connections (Finnie 1998)	Amsterdam, Berlin, Brussels, Frankfurt, London, Madrid, Milan, Paris, Stockholm, Zurich

Source: Compiled from Lever 2002.

a. Number of papers per 1,000 inhabitants yielded the following rank: Cambridge, Oxford-Reading, Geneva, Basel, Bristol-Cardiff, Zurich, Stockholm, Helsinki, Copenhagen, Randstadt, Munich, Edinburgh-Glasgow.

Table 4.4   The Knowledge Base and Economic Performance in Selected Cities

City	Knowledge base mean score	Annual % employment change, 1985–96	Change in gross value added per worker (%), 1985–96	Shift-share residual, 1978–96
London	2.8	−0.3	2.0	−25.7
Paris	3.7	−0.1	3.3	−11.8
Frankfurt	6.0	0.2	3.1	6.5
Amsterdam	6.8	2.5	2.0	21.0
Stockholm	7.0	1.0	3.5	8.7
Milan	7.0	0.1	3.0	4.7
Cologne	7.2	0.3	2.7	4.8
Bologna	7.5	0.0	2.9	0.6
Zurich	8.0	1.7	3.3	3.0
Brussels	8.3	−0.8	2.8	−22.1
Madrid	10.0	1.5	4.1	5.5
Munich	10.0	−0.1	3.5	10.6
Copenhagen	10.0	0.2	1.6	−7.1
Dusseldorf	10.3	0.2	2.5	0.6
Barcelona	10.8	1.6	3.3	1.6
Geneva	12.0	1.7	3.0	1.0
Berlin	12.3	1.7	3.5	1.2
Rome	13.3	0.4	2.9	10.5
Vienna	14.5	0.5	2.3	−23.3

Source: Lever 2002.

start of the period. This may reflect the fact that these cities do not compete with smaller cities once their reliance on financial services, law, and administration is taken into account, and the urban agglomeration diseconomies of high rents, high living costs, and congestion outweigh the knowledge base of these cities.

Gabe et al. (2010) argue for a broader interpretation of knowledge that would combine educational achievement and skills from various occupations. Classifying knowledge in this manner identifies clusters of U.S. and Canadian metropolitan areas by similar knowledge traits. Their study focuses on six specific groupings: making regions, which are characterized by manufacturing activity; thinking regions, characterized by knowledge about the arts, humanities, information technology(IT), and commerce; comforting regions, with a high knowledge about mental health; building regions, with a high knowledge about construction and transportation; innovating regions, with a very high knowledge about information technology, arts, commerce, and engineering; and working regions, characterized by low knowledge in information technology and commerce. Using data on occupations in an area provides a broader measure of human capital than using just college attainment, because this approach captures the skills and knowledge acquired in the workplace. The authors find that this broader knowledge variable identifies clusters and is a better predictor of regional economic development than college attainment. Furthermore, in a fixed-effects regression, engineering, enterprising, and building regions have higher levels of productivity and earnings per capita. Teaching, understanding, working, and comforting regions have lower levels of economic development.

Education Level and City Growth

A significant part of the work on knowledge cities focuses on the relationship between the education level of a city's inhabitants and its growth. Education is an important ingredient in local agglomeration economies, and cities, by their nature, speed the accumulation of human capital.[7]

Cities with an educated population grow faster than cities where inhabitants have less education. Glaeser and Saiz (2004) find this statement to be true for more than a century of data in the United Kingdom and the United States. More recently, in the two decades prior to 2000, the population of metro areas in which more than 25 percent of adults held college degrees grew 45 percent. By contrast, the population in metro areas in which less than 10 percent held a college degree grew just 13 percent. In a similar vein, Shapiro (2006) finds that, during the period 1940 to 1990, a 10 percent increase in a metropolitan area's concentration of human capital is associated with an increase in that area's employment of 0.8 percent. Shapiro (2006, 324) refers to a "substantial body of literature that confirms this correlation between human capital and local area employment (or population) growth."[8] Furthermore, Glaeser, Ponzetto, and Tobio (2011) examine the relationship between education and city growth and find that, as the share of the adult population increased 5 percent in 1970, predicted growth between 1970 and 2000 increased about 8 percent. Table 4.5 examines the regression results from equation 4.1:

$$\log (Y_{2000}/Y_{1970}) = B_r{}^* \text{ Schooling}_{1970} + \text{Other Controls}, \quad (4.1)$$

where Y denotes one of three outcome variables: population, median income, and self-reported housing values. Other controls refers to the initial values of population, median income, and housing values and three region dummies (the Midwest is omitted). The equation permits the

Table 4.5 Metropolitan Area Regressions

Indicator	Log change in population, 1970–2000		Log change in median income (2000 US$), 1970–2000		Log change in median housing value (2000 US$), 1970–2000	
	(1)	(2)	(3)	(4)	(5)	(6)
Log population, 1970	−0.007	−0.007	0.003	0.003	0.056	0.057
	(0.019)	(0.019)	(0.006)	(0.006)	(0.013)**	(0.013)**
Log median income in 2000 and 1970	−0.769	−0.841	−0.391	−0.403	−0.297	−0.328
	(0.191)**	(0.191)**	(0.061)**	(0.062)**	(0.133)*	(0.135)*
Log median housing value in 2000 and 1970	0.273	0.272	0.173	0.174	−0.008	0.004
	(0.117)*	(0.115)*	(0.037)**	(0.038)**	(0.081)	(0.082)
South dummy	0.146	−0.133	−0.010	0.015	0.028	0.012
	(0.054)**	(0.122)	(0.018)	(0.040)	(0.038)	(0.087)
East dummy	−0.054	−0.077	−0.044	−0.039	0.054	0.041
	(0.057)	(0.158)	(0.016)**	(0.052)	(0.040)	(0.112)
West dummy	0.384	0.632	0.797	−0.145	0.299	0.052
	(0.051)**	(0.135)**	(0.142)**	(0.044)	(0.035)**	(0.096)
College completion among population 25 and older 1970	1.528		0.797		0.802	
	(0.445)**		(0.142)**		(0.310)*	

(continued next page)

Table 4.5 *(continued)*

Indicator	Log change in population, 1970–2000		Log change in median income (2000 US$), 1970–2000		Log change in median housing value (2000 US$), 1970–2000	
	(1)	(2)	(3)	(4)	(5)	(6)
South dummy * % BA in 1970		3.840		0.673		0.405
		(0.772)**		(0.252)**		(0.548)
East dummy * % BA in 1970		1.498		0.839		0.424
		(1.310)		(0.428)		(0.929)
West dummy * % BA in 1970		−0.573		1.364		2.257
		(0.812)		(0.265)**		(0.576)**
Midwest dummy * % BA in 1970		1.314		0.583		0.363
		(0.597)*		(0.195)**		(0.424)
Constant	5.264	6.074	2.275	2.407	2.81	3.040
	(1.576)**	(1.595)**	(0.504)**	(0.521)**	(1.100)*	(1.132)**
Number of observations	257	257	257	257	257	257
R^2	0.427	0.466	0.379	0.396	0.339	0.362

Source: Glaeser, Ponzetto, and Tobio 2011.

Note: Standard errors in parentheses. * = significant at 5 percent, ** = significant at 1 percent.

impact of education to be estimated separately by region (South, East, West, and Midwest) and is thus a departure from the approach of other studies of education and city growth. B_y interacts with four region dummies and thereby allows the impact of schooling on population, income, and housing value growth to differ by region.

The second regression in table 4.5 allows the impact of education in 1970 to differ by region. In the South, which shows the strongest effect, "a 5 percent increase in the share of the adult population with a college degree in 1970 is associated with 19 percent faster population growth" (Glaeser, Ponzetto, and Tobio 2011, 28). The results for the Midwest are also significant, and a 5.0 percent increase in the share of adults with a college degree in 1970 is associated with a 6.5 percent predicted increase in population. The Northeast shows the second largest coefficient of the group and is similar to the coefficient for the national average, but it is insignificant. The coefficient for the West is negative and insignificant.

Regressions 3 and 4 in table 4.5 examine the effect of median growth in income. Glaeser, Ponzetto, and Tobio (2011) note that mean income reverts, except perhaps in areas with high housing values, which may indicate a migration of wealthier people to areas with more amenities. Coefficients on the regional dummies, apart from the West, where income increased the least, are statistically insignificant. There is a strong association between median income and initial education levels: "As the share of population with college degrees in 1970 increased by 5 percent, median income rose by 4 percent more since then" (Glaesser, Ponzetto, and Tobio 2011, 28). Moreover, this may reflect a return to skills and the tendency of highly educated people to move to areas already rich in human capital (see also Moretti 2003). Education has a positive impact on median income growth at the regional level (regression 4). The biggest impact is in the West (0.7 log points increase for a 5 percent increase in the share of those with a college degree), and the least impact is in the Midwest (less than half that found in the West).

Regressions 5 and 6 examine the impact of education on the appreciation of median housing values. The West saw much greater appreciation in housing values compared to the other regions. In total, housing values increased about 4 percent more when the share of the population in 1970 with a college degree increased by 5 percentage points (Glaeser, Ponzetto, and Tobio 2011). Finally, turning to regression 6, the results indicate a much larger appreciation in the West: prices increased by more than 10 percent for a 5 percentage point increase in the 1970 share of population with a college degree. The results for the other regions are far lower and statistically insignificant.

Further studies examine the relationship between a city's education level and other economic variables, such as migration, wages, and sectoral employment. These studies are representative of the empirical work on knowledge cities that deal with omitted-variable bias.[9] Table 4.6 lists these variables and the studies that have used them.

The results from the empirical studies in table 4.6 show the positive impact of knowledge, measured by college education, on growth of the city or metropolitan statistical area (MSA). Controlling for other growth-inducing variables raises this positive impact at the level of the MSA. Glaeser and Saiz (2004) find little impact at the level of the city and attribute this to the high level of service employment or better weather at this spatial level. However, college education is a more powerful predictor of growth at the MSA level, becoming even stronger when other control variables are included. Moretti (2003) refers to the long-run trend of increasing education in the United States. The features of this are a wide dispersion of human capital among cities (between 1990 and 2000, the fraction of college graduates rose from about 10 percent in the least educated cities to above 40 percent in the most educated cities [Moretti 2003]) and an increasing stock of college graduates (cities with a larger stock of human capital in 1990 experienced larger increases over the next decade).

For the most part, empirical studies of the knowledge city have focused on college education. Glaeser and Saiz (2004) also include the high school dropout rate as an alternative measure. This alternative measure is a stronger (negative) correlate of education at the level of the city compared to the MSA—the correlation between the share of high school dropouts and population growth is −28 percent for cities and −18 percent for metropolitan areas. The correlations suggest that the impact of higher education may be more important at the MSA level, whereas the impact of low education is more important at the city level. Controlling for high school dropout rates and unemployment rates[10] at the city level significantly reduces the impact of higher education on city growth. Avoiding low human capital[11] matters more for smaller units of geography. Shapiro (2006) finds no evidence to indicate a growth effect for high school graduates.

The empirical studies also attempt to identify the connection between skills and growth. For the most part, productivity accounts for this connection, but some authors (Glaeser and Saiz 2004; Shapiro 2006)

Table 4.6 Underpinnings of Knowledge Cities

Source and dependent variable	Independent variable	Observations	Results
Shapiro (2006)			
Growth in employment	Initial employment; log % prime-age white males with a college degree	495 metropolitan areas, 1940–90	A 10% increase in share of college-educated residents is associated with an 0.8% increase in employment.
Growth in wages	Initial wages; log % prime-age white males with a college degree	495 metropolitan areas, 1940–90	A 10% increase in share of college-educated residents is associated with a 0.2% increase in wages.
Growth in rental price	Initial rental price; log % prime-age white males with a college degree	495 metropolitan areas, 1940–90	A 10% increase in share of college-educated residents is associated with a 0.7% increase in rental price.
Growth in house value	Initial house value; log % prime-age white males with college degree	495 metropolitan areas, 1940–90	A 10% increase in share of college-educated residents is associated with a 0.7% increase in house value.
Moretti (2003)			
Change in percent of college educated	Initial level of college; population; family income; black*; Hispanic; immigrants*; agriculture; manufacturing*; high tech; Northeast; Midwest; South; West	237 metropolitan areas, 1990–2000	Overall fraction of college graduates grew faster in cities that were larger and richer in 1990; the percentage of Hispanics is negatively correlated with changes in college share; the percentage of agricultural jobs is negatively correlated with changes in college share; the percentage of high-tech jobs is a strong predictor of change in college share; change in college share was 3.7% (northeastern cities), 3.6% (midwestern), 3.2% (western), and 2.8% (southern).
Winters (2008)			
ln in-migration	Share with a bachelor's degree	323 PMSAs/MSAs, 1995–2000	A 10% increase in share with a bachelor's degree increases inmigration by 5%.
ln out-migration	Share with a bachelor's degree	323 PMSAs/MSAs, 1995–2000	A 10% increase in share with a bachelor's degree increases outmigration by 3%.

(continued next page)

Table 4.6 *(continued)*

Source and dependent variable	Independent variable	Observations	Results
ln net migration	Share with a bachelor's degree	323 PMSAs/MSAs, 1995–2000	A 10% increase in share with a bachelor's degree increases net migration by 2%.
ln in-migration, ln out-migration, ln net migration	Share with bachelor's degree; population; median family income; manufacturing share; January temperature; July temperature; precipitation; Midwest; South; West	323 PMSAs/MSAs, 1995–2000	Adding controls raises the coefficients on share with a bachelor's degree; population and median family income have a negative effect on inmigration, outmigration, and net migration; increases in the average January daily low temperature increase both the inmigration rate and the net migration rate; increases in average July daily temperature increases net migration.
Glaeser and Saiz (2004)			
Difference in ln population between census years	Share of population with a college degree	723 cities 318 MSAs, 1970, 1980, 1990, 2000	For the MSA regressions, a 1% increase in share of adult population with a degree increases the decadal growth rate by approximately 0.5%. For the city-level regressions, a 1% increase in the share of adult population with a degree increases the decadal growth rate by approximately 0.2%.
Difference in ln population between census years	Share of population with a college degree; initial level of population; ln average precipitation; share of workers in manufacturing; share of workers in professional services; share of workers in trade; unemployment rate; share of high school dropouts	723 cities[a] 318 MSA, 1970, 1980, 1990, 2000	Controlling for the listed independent variables shows little effect on future city growth but does increase the impact of the education variable on the future growth rate of the MSA.

Source: Glaeser and Salt 2004; Moretti 2003; Shapiro 2006; Winters 2008.
Note: PMSA = primary metropolitan statistical area; MSA = standard metropolitan statistical area. * = results are insignificant and not reported in the results column.
a. Cities with a population of more than 30,000 in 1970.

also suggest consumption or amenity factors. Glaeser and Saiz (2004) suggest that movement in wages and house prices sheds light on the productivity and consumption story. For example, increases in nominal wages and house prices stem from production-led growth, while decreases in real wages stem from consumption-led growth. However, Shapiro (2006, 330) finds that controlling for wages and rents implies that one-third of the employment growth effect stems from "rapid improvement in the quality of life." The quality-of-life explanation operates through consumer amenities, such as bars and restaurants, rather than from improvements in crime, schools, or pollution (Shapiro 2006). The focus on quality of life and consumption-led growth has led to research into the concept of the creative city, discussed below. In fact, the creative city is a refinement of the knowledge city.

The Creative City

The concept of the creative city is a late twentieth-century construct. It gives a spatial context to creativity—the creative pursuits of individuals and industries—and suggests economic development potential. The creative city has been viewed as a home for the creative class (Florida 2002), as an engine of structural change, as a catalyst for economic revitalization, as a facilitator of public and private partnership, and as an urban success story. The creative city typology can be applied to both large and small cities, dependent on a number of factors, which are discussed further below.

The Creative Class

Florida (2002, 18) asserts that the creative class, "a fast-growing, highly educated, and well-paid segment of the workforce on whose efforts corporate profits and economic growth increasingly depend," is critical for economic growth. Roughly 38.3 million Americans or 30 percent of the U.S. workforce occupy the creative class and hold significant economic power. The average salary of a creative class worker in 1990 was US$48,752 compared to almost US$28,000 for a working-class worker and US$22,000 for a service class worker (Florida 2002). The economic effects of creativity depend on Florida's so-called three Ts: talent, tolerance, and technology:

- *Talent*, or creative share of the workforce, based largely on demographic, educational, and occupational characteristics

- *Tolerance,* or diversity, based on indexes related to sexual orientation and bohemianism
- *Technology,* or innovation, measured by patent activity and the high-technology share of the economic base.

Florida (2002) develops a *creativity index,* which is a mix of four equally weighted factors: the creative class share of the workforce, high-tech industry (using the Milken Institute's tech pole index), innovation (using patents per capita), and diversity (using the gay index). This index forms a baseline view of an area's (city or region) position in the creative economy, which Florida asserts is suggestive of a "region's longer run economic potential" (Florida 2002, 22). Florida computes the index for large cities (a ranking of 49 metro areas reporting populations over 1 million in the 2000 census), medium-size cities (a ranking of 32 metro areas reporting populations 500,000 to 1 million in the 2000 census), and small cities (a ranking of 63 metro areas reporting populations 250,000 to 500,000 in the 2000 census). Table 4.7 shows these results for the top and bottom three cities in each size category.

Each dimension—talent, tolerance, technology—is necessary to attract the creative class of worker and generate economic growth.

The creative class is involved in wide-ranging occupations from arts and entertainment to high-technology, finance, and high-end manufacturing occupations. Among these occupational groups, Florida (2002) identifies three types of creative individuals. First is a core group, the "super-creative core" who exhibit an entrepreneurial spirit in "producing new forms or designs that are readily transferable." Markusen (2006b) also identifies core cultural workers and the high rate of self-employment among this group—45 percent compared with 8 percent of the workforce as a whole. Acs and Megyesi (2007) also identify a strong entrepreneurial element in the creative city. The second group includes the creative professionals who work in knowledge-intensive industries and possess a high level of formal education. Markusen (2006b) notes the high level of investment in human capital by artists and cultural workers. Zucker (1994) notes that artists are extraordinary citizens who have high rates of political and community participation. The third group represents workers who transcend the old distinctions between white-collar and blue-collar work. As an example, Florida (2002, 19) asserts that, as today's technicians, secretaries take on "increased responsibility to interpret their work and make decisions." The result is an increase in creativity and a swelling of the creative class.

Table 4.7   Creativity Rankings in the United States, by City Size

City rank and size	Creativity index	Creative workers(%)	Creative rank	High-tech rank	Innovation rank	Diversity rank
Top three cities						
Large cities						
San Francisco, CA	1,057	34.8	5	1	2	1
Austin, TX	1,028	36.4	4	11	3	16
San Diego, CA	1,015	32.1	15	12	7	3
Medium cities						
Albuquerque, NM	965	32.2	2	1	7	1
Albany, NY	932	33.7	1	12	2	4
Tucson, AZ	853	28.4	17	2	6	5
Small cities						
Madison, WI	925	32.8	6	16	4	9
Des Moines, IA	862	32.1	8	2	16	20
Santa Barbara, CA	856	28.3	19	8	8	7
Bottom three cities						
Large cities						
Memphis, TN	530	24.8	47	48	42	41
Norfolk, VA	555	28.4	36	35	49	47
Las Vegas, NV	561	18.5	49	42	47	5
Medium cities						
Youngstown, OH	253	23.8	32	32	24	32
Scranton, PA	400	24.7	28	23	23	31
McAllen, TX	451	27.8	18	31	32	9
Small cities						
Shreveport, LA	233	22.1	55	32	59	57
Ocala, FL	263	16.4	63	61	52	24
Visalia, CA	289	22.9	52	63	60	11

Source: Florida 2002.

Given the occupational profile of the creative class worker, it is not surprising that regions with high growth, centers of learning, and expertise attract the creative class. The creative class accounts for more than one-third of the workforce in the Washington, DC, area; the Raleigh-Durham area; Boston; and Austin. Florida (2002) identifies a similar proportion of creative class worker in the college towns of East Lansing, MI, and Madison, WI. Comunian and Faggian (2011) investigate the relationship between creative cities and creative universities in the United Kingdom.

Not all regions benefit from what Florida asserts is a "new geography of class." In fact, Florida (2002) notes that inequality may increase in a creative city, where well-paid, highly educated people push out an older population who can no longer afford to live in the areas they once inhabited.

Why do some geographic areas fail to generate a creative core? In answering this question, Florida first considers why some places become destinations for the creative class. The creative class of workers values visible diversity—different food, music, people, varied nightlife, indigenous street-level culture, and outdoor recreation—as well as authenticity of place that combines urban grit alongside renovated buildings, a comingling of young and old, of people as well as place. Examples of such places that have successfully combined high-tech industry, outdoor amenities, lifestyle amenities, creativity, and innovation (the three Ts) are the greater Boston area (Route 128 suburban complex, Harvard University, Massachusetts Institute of Technology, and several charming inner-city Boston neighborhoods); the Seattle area (suburban Bellevue and Redmond, beautiful mountains and countryside, revitalized urban neighborhoods); the San Francisco Bay area (posh inner-city neighborhoods and ultra-hip districts like SoMa—South of Market—lifestyle enclaves like Marin County, as well as the Silicon Valley); and Austin (traditional high-tech developments, lifestyle centers for cycling and outdoor activities, and a revitalizing university-downtown community centered on vibrant Sixth Street, the warehouse district, and the music scene) (Florida 2002).

Failure to adapt to the "demands of the creative age" has much to do with areas trapped by their past successes (Florida 2002, 24). Olson (1982) suggests that areas that fail to transition are experiencing an "institutional sclerosis." This translates into being trapped in the "culture and attitudes of the bygone organizational age, unable or unwilling to adapt to current trends" (Florida 2002, 24). Glaeser (2011) notes that Boston has reinvented itself at least three times since the 1970s, whereas cities like Detroit and Cleveland have failed to transition to what Florida terms the "creative age."

Reinvention and Structural Change

Acs and Megyesi (2007) argue that diverse areas have lower entry barriers, making it easier for human capital with various backgrounds to enter an area and stay there. They also associate entrepreneurship with creativity and note that it is more apt to flourish in areas rich in creativity. In the same vein, Cohendet, Grandadam, and Simon (2010) refer to the creative city as a place for ideas to flourish and take shape, ultimately resulting in economic growth and wealth. Liu-Wei and Yin-Ko (2010) link the creative city to an urban environment capable of generating creativity, innovation, and, thus, income growth. Markusen (2006b, 1) suggests that the creative city "heralded a new revitalization strategy for older industrial cities" and that urban and economic development planners of communities of all sizes have increasingly turned to arts and culture as development tools. As an example, Acs and Megyesi (2007) combine data on the core group and creative professionals for Baltimore and other industrial areas (table 4.8). The benchmarked areas show a huge increase in population over the decade 1990 to 2000.

Romein and Trip (2010) suggest that structural change arising from several forces—economic (globalization and an economy built on services), geopolitical (vanishing national borders and the rise of regions as engines of growth), technological (improved information and communication technology and transport), and sociocultural (consumption, amenities)—herald the creative city. It is not just occupations that are labeled creative; entire branches of industries are also termed cultural, such as the arts, performances, heritage-based products, and creatively designed products. Creative people are therefore the most crucial resource for the economic performance of a creative city. On the basis of questionnaires and regressions, Florida (2002, 223) asserts, "Regional economic growth is driven by the locational choices of creative people—the holders of creative capital—who prefer places that are diverse, tolerant, and open to new ideas." Florida's work has been criticized for not being new and for ignoring "the productive dimensions of the cultural industries" (Pratt 2008, 2).[12] Peck (2005) lambastes Florida's promotion of the creative class, castigating it as an elitist place-marketing ploy. While Florida highlights one critical part of the creative city and contributes

Table 4.8   Creative Class Occupations, Ranked by Percentage Change

Target statistical area	% change, 1990–2000
Chicago, IL (PMSA)	169
Cleveland, OH (PMSA)	151
Pittsburgh, PA (PMSA)	139
Baltimore, MD (MSA)	126
Philadelphia, PA–NJ (PMSA)	123
Milwaukee, WI (PMSA)	123
St. Louis, MO–IL (MSA)	117
Detroit, MI (PMSA)	108

Source: Acs and Megyesi 2007.
Note: PMSA = primary metropolitan statistical area; MSA = metropolitan statistical area.

enormously to this part, his approach does not necessarily exclude the productive base of the economy.

Romein and Trip (2010) differentiate between "innovation production milieus" and "urban consumption milieus," while noting that it is the close association of both that ensures the success of the creative city. The former focuses on innovative ideas and processes from inception to market realization across clusters of firms, not all of which are creative, but all of which benefit from the close proximity that an urban environment provides. The urban consumption milieu focuses on the qualities of place and life in a city that makes individuals want to move and stay there. In a sense, capital (investments and jobs) follows creative labor. In noting the tendency of artists to gravitate to inner-city areas, Markusen (2006a) suggests a revitalizing role for areas that may have lost population. Romein and Trip (2010) identify key elements of success for creative cities—social climate; representation; labor market and employment; buzz and atmosphere; built environment; living and residential environment; amenities; clusters and incubators; and policy, government, and governance. These elements show how difficult it is to disentangle the production and consumption bases of the creative city. Pratt (2008) suggests that policy makers would achieve more successful regeneration outcomes if they would view the cultural industries as an object that links production and consumption, manufacturing and services. This is a more useful approach in interpreting and understanding the significant role of cultural production in contemporary cities and how it relates to growth.

One of the reasons why smaller towns or cities may be more successful at fostering creativity and generating economic growth may stem from their consumption base. The focus on occupations emphasizes the human capital aspect of economic growth, an aspect that has generated huge currency among growth theorists, development planners, and policy makers. The cultural sector is of particular relevance here, given that artists as core cultural workers make considerable investments in human capital, move easily across commercial, nonprofit, and community sectors, and have exceptionally high rates of self-employment (table 4.9). Markusen (2006a) applies to the cultural sector a consumption-base theory of economic growth—the portion of local economic activity that is sold to local residents and acts as a growth catalyst. Residents are assumed to spend on local cultural products that benefit the resident creative class and the local economy. Creative class workers are then assumed to spend their incomes locally, generating a positive growth multiplier for the local economy. Glaeser and Saiz (2004) find that amenities or consumption spending is

Table 4.9   Creative Workers: Consumers and Producers

Occupational title	Total employment	Self-employed	% self-employed	Primary job	Secondary job
Writers and authors	138,900	94,377	68	80,509	13,868
Visual artists	307,254	155,159	50	129,109	26,050
Artists and related workers	148,682	80,022	54	70,731	9,291
Arts directors	50,664	27,139	54	23,988	3,151
Fine artists, painters, sculptors, illustrators	23,192	12,866	55	11,372	1,494
Multimedia artists and animators	74,826	40,017	53	35,371	4,646
Photographers	130,442	65,432	52	54,024	14,408
Camera operators, TV, video, motion picture	28,130	6,705	24	4,354	2,351
Performing artists	176,463	42,724	24	38,174	4,550
Actors	63,033	10,992	17	9754	1,238
Producers and directors	76,125	24,995	33	21,683	3,312
Dancers and choreographers	37,305	6,737	18	6,737	0
Dancers	19,992	3,854	19	3,854	0
Choreographers	17,313	2,883	17	2,883	0
Musicians, singers, composers	215,425	83,121	39	56,770	26,351
Music directors and composers	54,271	21,354	39	14,584	6,770
Musicians and singers	161,154	61,767	38	42,186	19,581
Designers	531,921	168,806	32	132,827	35,979
Commercial and industrial designers	51,823	16,088	31	12,659	3,429
Fashion designers	14,844	4,353	29	3,425	928
Floral designers	103,993	33,832	33	26,621	7,211
Graphic designers	211,871	67,422	32	53,052	14,370
Interior designers	60,050	19,325	32	15,206	4,119
Merchandise displayers, window trimmers	77,221	23,881	31	18,791	5,090
Set and exhibit designers	12,119	3,905	32	3,073	832
Architects	136,378	29,678	22	23,809	5,869
Architects, except landscape and naval	113,243	24,253	21	19,457	4,796
Landscape architects	23,135	5,425	23	4,352	1,073
Total, all artistic occupations	1,506,421	573,865	38	461,198	112,667
Total, all occupations	144,013,600	11,451,600	8	9,926,000	1,525,600

Source: Markusen 2006.

more likely to catalyze growth in cities than in metropolitan areas, which rely more on increases in productivity for their economic growth.

Harnessing the Potential of Creative Cities

The United Nations (UN 2004) outlines several ways in which the potential of the creative city might be unleashed to benefit developing and developed economies:

- *Urban regeneration through culture.* The concept of the creative city has been tested in response to the economic decline of industrial cities in Australia, Europe, and the United States over the past two decades. These experiences have shown that industries in fields such as television, cinema, multimedia, music, books, and festivals can flourish in cities that provide efficient transport, communications, and public protection infrastructure combined with coordinated public policies that encourage innovation and small businesses in the creative fields.

- *Public-private partnership as a key to effective policy.* Planners take into account the role of creativity during economic policy planning in order to integrate their tangible and intangible cultural assets into the education systems, natural environment, and geographic location. Cities across the developed world are establishing municipal services to sustain the local creative economy, facilitating cooperation between the private and public sectors as well as civil society; some have even gone so far as to develop creativity indexes based on the three Ts of technology, talent, and tolerance.

- *Creativity as an unexploited opportunity.* Discussion of creativity remains at the academic level or policy level. Planners and the general public are unaware of or underestimate the value of creativity for the community; political or artistic figures do not champion the role of culture; administrative resources, skills, and capacities to manage such projects are in short supply; or clear and usable indicators do not exist for measuring success.

- *The need for UNESCO's Creative Cities Programme.* Designed to promote the social and economic development of cities in both the developed and the developing world, the program will emphasize the role of creativity and the arts and create a platform for information exchange between cities.

- *Impact far beyond the economy.* Creative cities programs have already been tried and tested on a limited scale and have proved to be innovative in finding new ways to promote social and economic development by stimulating the creation of new enterprises and cultural diversity for both struggling as well as prosperous city communities.

The Global City

The "global city"[13] is a term that was popularized by Sassen in 1991 with her book of that title (Sassen 1991). According to Sassen (2010), the global city makes new norms. In order for this to happen, the city must be complex and diverse. These factors are often a function of size, but not all large cities or megacities are global cities. For example, Tokyo is a global city, but Mumbai or São Paulo, both megacities, are not necessarily global. Sassen attests that many of the global cities of today are old-world cities that have reinvented themselves, citing Istanbul, London, and New York as examples. In contrast, Miami is a global city, combining complexity and diversity and making new norms, but it is not a megacity. This was not the case prior to the 1990s. Since then, several factors have coalesced to make Miami a global city: the infrastructure of international trade developed by Miami's Cuban population; real estate development spurred by wealthy individuals from Latin America; the opening up of Latin America and setting up of regional headquarters in Miami by firms from all over the world; a mix of cultures in a small, concentrated space; and a burgeoning creative class (Sassen 2010).

Sassen (2009) identifies key structural trends in the economy that are contributing to the rise of global cities worldwide. These trends are predicated on a growing demand for intermediate services—for example, insurance, accounting, legal, financial, consulting, software programming, and even traditional sectors. These services tend to be located in an urbanized environment where tacit and codified knowledge are maximized.

As firms become less local in their operations, expanding into national, regional, and global markets, management operations become more complex, and the firm is likely to outsource its corporate functions that previously had been managed in-house. Advances in technology have fostered outsourcing of many routinized sectors, but control remains at the center, and, with it, centralized headquarter functions have grown, facilitated by the development and growth of the intermediate sector. Cities house the headquarters.[14]

The specialized firms that emerge to fulfill these intermediate functions are themselves subject to agglomeration economies. These arise from the "mix of firms, talents, and expertise from a broad range of specialized fields" (Sassen 2009, 56). The agglomeration economies rely on the exchange of information, and the urban environment is key in providing the face-to-face communication and exchange of knowledge opportunities. Sassen (2009, 59) notes, "Cities can generate kinds of knowledge, both formal and informal, that go beyond the sum of recognized knowledge actors (e.g. professionals and professional firms in the case of the economy)," which she terms "urban knowledge capital." It has the same features as the tacit and codified knowledge identified by Lever (2002).

A key aspect of cities is their centrality, which relies on density. Density has typically been associated with a downtown or central business district. However, while centrality remains critical in today's global economy, the geography of this has extended to include other spatial forms, such as the city-region, for example, or indeed the global city-region.[15]

The Global Cities Indicators Program (GCIP), created in 2006 by the World Bank with funding from the government of Japan, helps member cities to monitor their performance.[16] The GCIP provides a framework for the collection of city indicators that are comparable and consistent over time and place. Each member city is responsible for updating its data on the web portal.[17] This effort enables "cities to measure, report, and improve their performance and quality of life, facilitate capacity building, and share best practices" (Bhada and Hoornweg 2009, 1). The Global City Indicators Facility (GCIF) at the University of Toronto[18] took over the GCIP in 2008 and oversees the development of indicators, while also assisting cities to join the program. The GCIF is structured around themes that are organized into two broad categories covering city services and quality of life (tables 4.10 and 4.11). The indicators listed are core indicators; other supporting indicators are also used (see http://www.cityindictors.org /themes.aspz#Education).

The two categories—city services and quality of life—are organized around 20 themes, consisting of core and supporting indicators. Cities are expected to report on core indicators annually and are encouraged to report on supporting indicators. There are presently 27 core indicators and 38 supporting indicators.

The GCIF has identified a set of 10 future indexes for the various themes. These are constructed as weighted combinations of the indicators and give a more complete view of city performance or quality of life (box 4.1).

Table 4.10   Global City Indicators: City Services

Theme	Indicator
Education	Percentage of children completing primary and secondary education; student-teacher ratio
Fire and emergency response	Number of firefighters per 100,000 population; number of fire-related deaths per 100,000 population
Health	Under-five mortality per 1,000 live births; number of in-patient hospital beds per 100,000 population; number of physicians per 100,000 population; average life expectancy
Recreation	Square meters of public indoor recreation facility space per capita; square meters of public outdoor recreation facility space per capita
Safety	Number of homicides per 100,000 population; number of police officers per 100,000
Solid waste	Percentage of city population with regular solid waste collection; Percentage of city's solid waste that is recycled
Transportation	Number of kilometers of high-capacity public transit system per 100,000 population; number of kilometers of light passenger transit system per 100,000 population; number of personal automobiles per capita; annual number of public transit trips per capita
Wastewater	Percentage of city population served by wastewater collection
Water	Percentage of city population with potable water supply service; domestic water consumption per capita; Percentage of city population with sustainable access to improved water source
Energy	Percentage of city population with authorized electrical service; total residential electricity use per capita
Finance	Debt service ratio (debt service expenditures as a Percentage of a municipality's own source revenue)
Governance	Percentage of women employed in the city government workforce
Urban planning	Jobs-housing ratio

Source: http://www.cityindicators.org/themes.aspx#Education.

Table 4.11   Global City Indicators: Quality of Life

Theme	Indicator
Civic engagement	Voter participation (percentage of eligible voters)
Culture	Percentage of jobs in the cultural sector
Economy	City product per capital-city unemployment rate
Environment	PM-10 concentration greenhouse emissions measured in tons per capita
Shelter	Percentage of city population living in slums
Social equity	Percentage of city population living in poverty
Subjective well-being	Subjective well-being index
Technology and innovation	Number of Internet connections per 100,000 population

Source: http://www.cityindicators.org/themes.aspx#Education.

Box 4.1

Indexes Used in the Global City Indicators Program

- Competitiveness
- Social capital
- Creativity
- Subjective well-being
- Greenhouse gas
- Total energy use
- Governance
- Urban accessibility
- Recreation and culture
- Water quality.

Source: Bhada and Hoornweg 2009.

Each city is responsible for supplying and updating its data on the web portal. The GCIF is a host for globally standardized data, providing free web-based information and assisting cities by identifying and sharing expertise on specific areas of performance so that they may strengthen their policy and management (McCarney 2010). The information can be used to generate reports by peer groups (land area, region, climate type, gross operating budget, and population or gross domestic product [GDP] per capita) or by themes. More than 30 cities have joined the GCIF since its inception, and figures for 2010 indicate 74 member cities. The city membership by population category is shown in figure 4.1.

The GCIF is an important tool for urban planners and policy makers, providing, as it does, a series of themes that facilitate measuring city performance, capturing trends over time and place, and monitoring the global role being played by cities (table 4.12).

Green Cities/Eco Cities

"Cities represent a challenge and an opportunity for climate change policy" (Corfee-Morlot et al. 2009, 3). Responsible for most of the world's economic activity, population, innovation, output, and employment, cities arguably produce most of the global greenhouse gas emissions. Furthermore, cities, especially those located along coastal regions, are

Figure 4.1   GCIF Membership in 2010, by Population Category

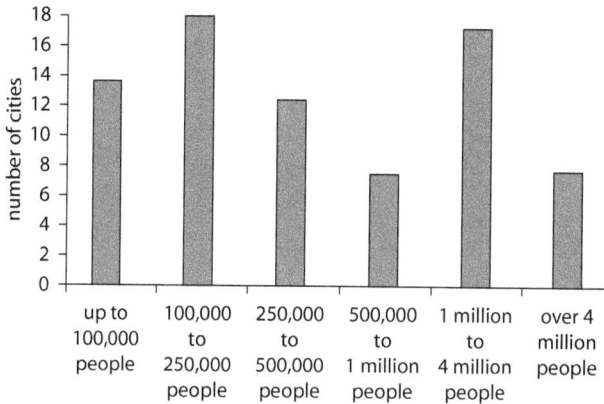

Source: McCarney 2010.

Table 4.12   Role of Standardized Indicators for Cities

Purpose	Rationale
Measuring city performance	Role of cities has expanded to include addressing climate change, partnering with private sector and civic organizations, and attracting foreign investment. Indicators are intended to determine municipal capacity for delivering services, managing growth, providing enhanced accountability, as well as determining management and financial capacity. National governments are increasingly looking at fiscal discipline at the local government level.
Capturing trends over time and across cities	There is increasing need to know the quality of life, economic and demographic trends, and environmental measures adopted in cities. Indicators enable development organizations to monitor aid effectiveness. Indicators can determine benchmarks and targets for cities based on the experience of other cities and enable cities to share best practice.
Playing a global role	In a more global world, cities are increasingly competing for investments, international events, and corporate and institutional headquarters. Cities are playing an increasingly active role in climate change negotiations. Cities are trying to "brand" themselves and become individual members of a wider urban concept.

Source: Bhada and Hoornweg 2009.

vulnerable to the effects of climate change such as urban heat island effects.

At the same time, "cities are much better for the environment" (Glaeser 2011, 201). Living in high-rises and walking to work are better for the environment than residing in leafy suburbs in large houses and driving to work (Jacobs 1961, 1969; Owen 2009). Glaeser (2011) discusses the work he carried out with Matthew Kahn on a carbon inventory of new housing throughout America (see Glaeser and Kahn 2010). Some of the results are shown in table 4.13.

Summary facts from table 4.13 and Glaeser (2011) suggest the following conclusions:

1. Big cities mean less driving: on average, when population doubles, carbon dioxide emissions per household due to driving decline by almost a ton per year.
2. City-dwellers use less gas than suburbanites.
3. Electrical appliances account for two-thirds of residential energy use; urbanites use less electricity than suburbanites.
4. The main factor explaining the difference between cities is summer heat.
5. Bigger, denser homes use less electricity. On average, a single-family detached home consumes 88 percent more electricity than the average apartment in a five-or-more-unit building.

Table 4.13   Summary of Results on Carbon Emissions per Home, 2006

Cause of carbon emissions	Highest carbon emissions per home	Lowest carbon emissions per home
Driving (A)	Southern cities; Greenville, SC; Nashville, TN; Oklahoma City, OK; Atlanta, GA	New York
Electricity (B)	Houston, TX; New Orleans, LA; Memphis, TN; Dallas, TX; Phoenix, AZ	Coastal California; Northeast; San Francisco, CA; San Juan, CA; New York, NY; Boston, MA; Las Vegas, NV
Natural gas (C)	California; Detroit, MI; Grand Rapids, MI; Buffalo, NY; Chicago, IL; Minneapolis, MN	Florida; Miami, FL
A + B + C + public transit	Houston, TX; Birmingham, AL; Nashville, TN; Memphis, TN; Oklahoma City, OK	San Diego, CA; San Francisco, CA; Los Angeles, CA; San Jose, CA; Sacramento, CA

Source: Glaeser 2011.

6. More centralized metropolitan areas use less electricity than more sprawling places.

7. Natural gas, America's primary source of warmth, is responsible for almost 20 percent of residential carbon emissions.

8. Adding household emissions (driving, electricity, natural gas) and public transit together shows that cities are greener than suburbs.

9. However, the differences between metro areas are even larger than the differences between individual cities and their suburbs.

10. Therefore, coastal California is the greenest part of the country, and the Deep South is the brownest.

Cities have not always been held in such high esteem. Ruskin, an art critic in nineteenth-century London and "an early advocate of town planning," was a proponent of the small town surrounded by a greenbelt. Greenbelts were a feature of English town planning—for example, London's greenbelt from 1947 covers 2,000 square miles—and elsewhere (Toronto, Pacific Northwest). One of the major figures in urban planning in the United States, Ebenezer Howard, championed the concept of the "garden city" that would be surrounded by a greenbelt to prevent the town from expanding beyond 32,000 inhabitants. Inhabitants of these cities would "live in nice houses and gardens at the center, walk to work in factories at the rim, and be fed by farms in an outer greenbelt" (Kunzig 2011, 132). The first garden city was Letchworth, England. A further aspect of "bringing the countryside into the city" was to build parks in cities (Glaeser 2011, 203).[19] These efforts to merge country and city—greenbelts, garden cities, and parks—were overshadowed by the development of suburbia in the late nineteenth century. Not all developers were so inclined, but the 1920s, which benefited from architects like Raymond Hood and Hugh Ferriss, turned out to be the "high-water mark for vertical America" (Glaeser 2011, 205).[20] Rising income and cheap transportation have exacerbated this trend. Furthermore, government subsidies for highways and homeownership have contributed to sprawl as well as individuals' preferences for large homes on large lots.

Urbanization continues. People are moving in droves to the cities, particularly in the developing economies; in China and India, in particular, the sheer numbers pose the biggest challenge for urban development. If, as Glaeser (2011) remarks, carbon emissions in China and India rise to U.S. levels per capita, the world's carbon consumption will increase 139 percent, even if their population stays the same. Most of the carbon emissions in China come from industry. Chinese households are thrifty energy users—the typical Beijing household emits 3.997 tons of carbon dioxide per year compared to 43 tons in the typical Washington, DC, household (Zheng et al. 2009). Both negative and positive aspects of the urbanization patterns of China and India are evident. On the positive side, both countries have cities that are extremely dense. Mumbai, with more than 50,000 people per square mile, is almost twice as dense as Bangalore, Kolkata, and New York City, each with more than 20,000 people per square mile. In China, Shenzhen has more than 15,000 people per square mile. These levels of density are compatible with public transport and are challenging for car usage. However, Shanghai and Beijing, at 20 million and 17 million inhabitants, respectively, are roughly one-tenth as dense as New York City and less than half as dense as Los Angeles. Car ownership rates in both China and India are increasing exponentially, and India's Tata Group has produced a car for US$2,500 (Glaeser 2011).

Glaeser (2011, 222) concludes, "If the future is going to be greener, then it must be more urban. Dense cities offer a means of living that involves less driving and smaller homes to heat and cool."

The manner in which cities develop offers many possibilities for the environment. Managing this change requires input from many different levels of government. The 2009 OECD report "Cities, Climate Change, and Multilevel Governance" provides an in-depth examination of this topic and advocates a multilevel governance framework to ensure that cities develop in an eco-sustainable manner (Corfee-Morlot et al. 2009). The multilevel governance framework explores the relationships between the various levels of government—local, regional, and national—in closing or narrowing any policy gaps for climate change. Policy gaps are examined along two dimensions: vertical and horizontal. The vertical dimension of multilevel governance calls for national governments to work closely with local and regional governments and vice versa. While local and regional governments may be the agents of change, change often cannot proceed without modifying the legal and institutional frameworks of the country. The horizontal dimension recognizes the chances for transmitting information and best practices between cities, regions, and nations (Corfee-Morlot et al. 2009). The report concludes with some general observations of good multilevel governance practice:

1. National policies can powerfully enable local action on climate change adaptation and mitigation.
2. There is significantly greater potential for experimentation at local scales, which in turn can be a testing ground for national governments.

3. Close collaboration between local and national authorities to build capacity to address climate change will improve the chances that local authorities will exploit potential for cost-effective mitigation and adaptation to climate change.
4. Some effective cross-sectoral regional or urban development strategies appear to be driven by the climate change imperative, where climate change mitigation and adaptation are seen to be a potential source of regional economic development (Corfee-Morlot et al. 2009).

The multilevel governance framework represents the ideal in managing climate change. The reality is far from this: "Climate policy at the city-scale remains fragmented, and the basic tools to facilitate good decision making are still lacking" (Corfee-Morlot et al. 2009, 87). The report suggests that the following tools could assist cities to be more effective in their climate change efforts:

- Harmonized inventory of greenhouse gas emissions and reporting protocols to allow cities to monitor and compare progress in mitigating emissions, to assess cost-effectiveness of additional mitigation options, and eventually to become active participants in international carbon markets.
- Regional impact science and other policy-relevant research programs to support the interface between expert information and local knowledge and promote local understanding of climate change risk and policy options—from assessment to management—for better mitigation and adaptation decision making.
- Urban climate policy networks to build on regular channels of communication among national planners and regional and local government officials as well as among local stakeholders and decision makers about targets, goals, strategies, and measures (Corfee-Morlot et al. 2009).

The report concludes by noting the progress made on a multilevel governance framework in various countries and cities.

Conclusion

The chapter has examined several constructs by which cities have been identified in recent years—the knowledge city, the creative city, the global city, and the green or eco city. These are typically developed-country constructs. This typology arises from the continuing structural change at the level of the economy, which sees more and more employment in the service sectors as routinized manufacturing moves to the edge of the cities or even farther afield. Globalization further emphasizes this trend. At the same time, urban living has become more attractive; lower crime rates in inner-city areas have attracted inhabitants, and the rise of the creative class has contributed to the economic development and sustainability of the city. Density and diversity are in vogue. Furthermore, urban living is good for the environment.

Notes

1. "Theory and empirical evidence suggest scale and knowledge externalities may interact, so that scale benefits are enhanced by knowledge accumulation—information spillovers are more beneficial the more educated the population" (Henderson 2010, 520).

2. "Moving from a city of 250,000 to one of 2.5 million is associated empirically with an 80 percent increase in commuting times and housing rental prices" (Henderson 2010, 521).

3. In addition, natural advantage is often a prime reason for the concentration of industry in a geographic location.

4. Roughly half of the 243 urban areas examined were specialized in subsectors of manufacturing, while the rest were specialized in nontraded sectors of education, banking and commerce, medical, and government services.

5. Lever (2002) cites OECD (1999) for demonstrating that investing in research and development, nationally, could be linked to competitive performance and economic growth and that this was the basis for economic development in the developed world. A similar point was made in the U.K. government white paper "Our Competitive Future: Building the Knowledge-Driven Economy" (U.K. Department of Trade and Industry 1998). At the local level, the Scottish executive advocated policy initiatives on economic sectors or clusters that are based on research, knowledge, information, and creativity (Lever 2002).

6. Four cities were excluded from the original 23 European cities owing to difficulties in measuring economic performance during the process of marketization in the 1990s, for example, Budapest, Moscow, Prague, and Warsaw.

7. "Human capital spillovers occur at the city level because skilled workers produce more product varieties and thereby increase labor demand" (Glaeser, Ponzetto, and Tobio 2011, 1).

8. Shapiro (2006), citing Glaeser, Scheinkman, and Shleiffer (1995); Glaeser and Shapiro (2003); Simon (1998, 2004); Simon and Nardinelli (2002).

9. Variables that are correlated with both education and city growth are missing from the regressions.

10. Glaeser and Saiz view dropout and unemployment rates as measures of human capital, but at the lower end of human capital distribution: "Differences in the unemployment rate across cities (less so across metropolitan areas) are generally time invariant and reflect characteristics of the labor force and the industry structure in the city" (Glaeser and Saiz 2004, 57).

11. "In other words, a local neighborhood, in contrast to a region, succeeds by avoiding large numbers of low-educated workers" (Glaeser and Saiz 2004, 58).

12. "The idea of the creative class is far from new; in fact, it is a revival of the high-tech 'boosterism' and place marketing" (Pratt 2008, 2).

13. Some writers criticize the concept of the global city as being too exclusive (McCann 2004) and too Western (Robinson 2002).

14. "The number of headquarters is what specifies a global city" (Sassen 2009, 56).

15. The global city-region was identified by Geddes (1915) and Hall (1966) and was the focus of an international conference in 1999.

16. The pilot cities were Belo Horizonte, Porto Alegre, and São Paulo in Brazil; Montreal, Toronto, and Vancouver in Canada; Bogotá and Cali in Colombia; and King County in Washington State, United States.

17. See http://www.cityindicators.org.

18. The Global City Indicators Facility offices opened in Toronto in October 2008, with support from the World Bank's Development Grant Facility, the University of Toronto, the government of Canada, and participating cities. The GCIF was officially launched in Nanjing, China, on November 3, 2008, at the United Nations World Urban Forum.

19. "In the United States, Frederick Law Olmsted specialized in bringing bucolic vistas to the heart of a city"—for example, Central Park in New York, Jackson Park in Chicago, Belle Isle in Detroit—as well as "green spaces in Buffalo, Louisville, Milwaukee, Montreal, and Washington, DC" (Glaeser 2011, 204).

20. "Between 1930 and 1933, five new buildings opened that soared above 849 feet, the height of the tallest skyscraper in Western Europe today. America would not build another tower that tall for another thirty-six years" (Glaeser 2011, 205).

References

Acs, Zoltan, and Monika I. Megyesi. 2007. "Creativity and Industrial Cities: A Case Study of Baltimore." Discussion Paper on Entrepreneurship, Growth, and Public Policy, Max Planck Institute of Economics, Jena, Germany.

Bhada, Perinaz, and Dan Hoornweg. 2009. "The Global City Indicators Program: A More Credible Voice for Cities." Directions in Urban Development, World

Bank, Washington, DC, June. http://siteresources.worldbank.org/INTURBAN DEVELOPMENT/Resources/336387-1226422021646/Directions4.pdf.

Buursink, J. 1994. "Euroservices and Euroairports: The Position of East European Cities as Eurocities." Paper presented to the conference "Cities on the Eve of the 21st Century," Institut Fédératif de Recherches sur les Economies et les Sociétés Industrielles (IFRESI), Lille, France. March.

Cohendet, Pierre, David Grandadam, and Laurent Simon. 2010. "The Anatomy of the Creative City." *Industry and Innovation* 17 (1, February): 91–111.

Comunian, Roberta, and Alessandra Faggian. 2011. "Creative Universities and Creative Cities: Exploring the Geography of Bohemian Graduates in the UK." Working Paper, School of Arts, University of Kent. An updated version appears in *Handbook of Cities and Creativity*, ed. Charlotta Mellander, Åke E. Andersson, and David Anderson. Cheltenham, U.K.: Edward Elgar, 2011.

Corfee-Morlot, Jan, Lamai Kamal-Chaoul, Michael G. Donovan, Ian Cochran, Alexis Robert, and Pierre-Jonathan Teasdale. 2009. "Cities, Climate Change, and Multilevel Governance." OECD Climate Change Working Paper 14, Organisation for Economic Co-operation and Development, Paris.

Duncan, Otis D., and Albert J. Reiss Jr. 1956. *Social Characteristics of Urban and Rural Communities, 1950*. New York: John Wiley and Sons.

Finnie, G. 1998. "Wired Cities." *Communications Week International*, May 18, 19–22.

Florida, Richard. 2002. "The Rise of the Creative Class." *Washington Monthly* 34 (May): 15–26.

Gabe, Todd, Jaison R. Abel, Adrienne Ross, and Kevin Stolarick. 2010. "Knowledge in Cities." Staff Report 470, Federal Reserve Bank of New York, September.

Geddes, Patrick. 1915. *Cities in Evolution*. London: Williams and Norgate.

Glaeser, Edward L. 2011. *Triumph of the City: How Our Greatest Invention Makes Us Richer, Smarter, Greener, Healthier, and Happier*. New York: Penguin Press.

Glaeser, Edward L., and Matthew E. Kahn. 2010. "The Greenness of Cities: Carbon Dioxide Emissions and Urban Development." *Journal of Urban Economics* 67 (3): 404–18.

Glaeser, Edward L., Giacomo A. M. Ponzetto, and Kristina Tobio. 2011. "Cities, Skills, and Regional Change." NBER Working Paper 16934, National Bureau of Economic Research, Cambridge, MA.

Glaeser, Edward L., and Albert Saiz. 2004. "The Rise of the Skilled City." *Brookings-Wharton Papers on Urban Affairs* 5: 47–106.

Glaeser, Edward L., José A. Scheinkman, and Andrei Shleiffer. 1995. "Economic Growth in a Cross Section of Cities." *Journal of Monetary Economics* 36 (1): 117–43.

Glaeser, Edward L., and J. A. Shapiro. 2003. "Urban Growth in the 1990s: Is City Living Back?" *Journal of Regional Science* 43 (1): 139–65.

Hall, Peter. 1966. *The World Cities.* New York: McGraw Hill.

Harris, Nigel. 1991. "Urbanization and Economic Development: Territorial Specialization and Policy." In *City, Class, and Trade: Social and Economic Change in the Third World,* ed. Nigel Harris, 12–64. New York: St. Martin's Press.

Henderson, J. Vernon. 1974. "The Sizes and Types of Cities." *American Economic Review* 64 (4): 640–56.

———. 2010. "Cities and Development." *Journal of Regional Science* 50 (1): 515–40.

Holko, J. 1999. "Can I Get Some Service Here? Information Technology, Service Industries, and the Future of Cities." Working Paper, Public Policy Institute of California. http://ssrn.com/abstract=985712 or doi:10.2139/ssrn.985712.

Jacobs, Jane. 1961. *The Death and Life of Great American Cities.* New York: Random House.

———. 1969. *The Economy of Cities.* New York: Random House.

Knight, Richard. 1995. "Knowledge-Based Development: Policy and Planning Implications for Cities." *Urban Studies* 32 (2): 225–60.

Kresl, Peter Karl, and Balwant Singh. 1999. "Competitiveness and the Urban Economy: Twenty-four Large U.S. Metropolitan Areas." *Urban Studies* 36 (5-6): 1017–27.

Kunzig, Robert 2011. "The City Solution to Earth's Problems." *National Geographic* (December): 124–47.

Lambooy, J. A. 2000. "Regional Growth, Knowledge, and Innovation." In *The Knowledge-Based Economy,* ed. A. Kulinski and W. M. Orlowski, 100–13. Warsaw: KBN.

Lever, W. F. 2002. "Correlating the Knowledge Base of Cities with Economic Growth." *Urban Studies* 39 (5-6): 859–70.

Liu-Wei, Li, and Pei Yin-Ko. 2010. "A Local City to a Creative City: An Examination of Taichung, Taiwan." *International Journal of Sustainable Development* 13 (1-2): 111–21.

MacKenzie, R. D. 1933. *The Metropolitan Community.* New York: McGraw Hill Book Company.

Markusen, Ann. 2006a. "A Consumption Base Theory of Development: An Application to the Rural Cultural Economy." Paper presented at the conference "Opportunities and Challenges Facing the Rural Creative Economy," Northeastern Agricultural and Resource Economics Association (NAREA),

Mystic, CT, June 13–14. http://nercrd.psu.edu/CreativeEconomy/MarkusenPaper.pdf.

———. 2006b. "Cultural Planning and the Creative City." Paper presented at the annual meetings of the American Collegiate Schools of Planning, Ft. Worth, TX, November 12.

Matthiessen, G. W., and A. W. Schwartz. 1999. "Scientific Centres in Europe." *Urban Studies* 36 (3): 453–77.

McCann, E. J. 2004. "Urban Political Economy beyond the 'Global City.'" *Urban Studies* 41 (12): 2315–33.

McCarney, P. L. 2010. "Global City Indicators Facility: City Indicators and Comparative Measurement." World Urban Forum, UN-HABITAT, Rio de Janeiro, March 24.

Moretti, Enrico. 2003. "Human Capital Externalities in Cities." NBER Working Paper 9641, National Bureau of Economic Research, Cambridge, MA.

OECD (Organisation for Economic Co-operation and Development). 1999. *Science, Technology, and Industry Scoreboard: Benchmarking Knowledge-based Economies.* Paris: OECD.

Ogburn, W. F. 1937. *Social Characteristics of Cities.* Chicago, IL: International Association of City Managers.

Olson, Mancur. 1982. *The Rise and Decline of Nations: The Political Economy of Economic Growth, Stagflation, and Social Rigidities.* New Haven, CT: Yale University Press.

Owen, David. 2009. *Green Metropolis: Why Living Smaller, Living Closer, and Driving Less Are the Keys to Sustainability.* New York: Riverhead Books.

Peck, Jamie. 2005. "Struggling with the Creative Class." *International Journal of Urban and Regional Research* 29 (4): 740–70.

Pratt, A. C. 2008. "Creative Cities: The Cultural Industries and the Creative Class." LSE Research, London.

Robinson, Jenny. 2002. "Global and World Cities: A View from off the Map." *International Journal of Urban and Regional Research* 26 (3): 531–54.

Romein, Arie, and Jan J. Trip. 2010. "Key Elements of Creative City Development: An Assessment of Local Policies in Amsterdam and Rotterdam." Delft University of Technology, OTB Research Institute for Housing, Urban, and Mobility Studies, Delft.

Rubalcaba-Bermejo, Luis, and Juan R. Cuadrado-Roura. 1995. "Urban Hierarchies and Territorial Competition in Europe: Exploring the Role of Fairs and Exhibitions." *Urban Studies* 32 (2): 379–401.

Sassen, Saskia. 1991. *The Global City: New York, London, Tokyo.* Princeton, NJ: Princeton University Press.

———. 2009. "Cities Today: A New Frontier for Major Developments." *Annals, AAPSS* 626 (November): 53–71.

———. 2010. "Swoons over Miami: Saskia Sassen Responds to FP's Global Cities Index." *Foreign Policy*, August 27. http://www.foreignpolicy.com/articles/2010 /08/27/miami_swoon?hidecomments=yes.

Shapiro, Jesse M. 2003. "Smart Cities: Explaining the Relationship between City Growth and Human Capital." Harvard University, Cambridge, MA.

———. 2006. "Smart Cities: Quality of Life, Productivity, and the Growth Effects of Human Capital." *Review of Economics and Statistics* 88 (2): 324–35.

Simon, Curtis J. 1998. "Human Capital and Metropolitan Employment Growth." *Journal of Urban Economics* 43 (March): 223–43.

———. 2004. "Industrial Reallocation across U.S. Cities, 1977–97." *Journal of Urban Economics* 56 (1): 119–43.

Simon, Curtis J., and Clark Nardinelli. 2002. "Human Capital and the Rise of American Cities, 1900–1990." *Regional Science and Urban Economics* 32 (1): 59–96.

Taylor, P. J., and D. R. F. Walker. 2001. "World Cities: A First Multivariate Analysis of Their Service Complexes." *Urban Studies* 38 (1): 23–47.

U.K. Department of Trade and Industry. 1998. "Our Competitive Future: Building the Knowledge-Driven Economy." White Paper, Department of Trade and Industry, London.

UN (United Nations). 2004. *Creative Cities: Promoting Social and Economic Development through Cultural Industries.* New York: United Nations.

Winters, J. V. 2008. "Why Are Smart Cities Growing? Who Moves and Who Stays?" Working Paper 2008-10-1, Andrew Young School of Policy Studies, Georgia State University. http://aysps.gsu.edu/usery/Papers.html.

Zheng, Siqi, Rui Wang, Edward L. Glaeser, and Matthew E. Kahn. 2009. "The Greenness of China: Household Carbon Dioxide Emissions and Urban Development." NBER Working Paper 115621, National Bureau of Economic Research, Cambridge, MA.

Zucker, Laura. 1994. "The Artist in Los Angeles County." In *The Arts: A Competitive Advantage for California*, ed. KPMG Peat Marwick, 25–34. Washington, DC: Policy Economics Group, KPMG Peat Marwick LLP.

CHAPTER 5

The Attributes and Role of "Smart Cities"

Growth in developing countries since the early 1980s has been strongly buttressed by globalization and by a wave of innovations released by new general-purpose technologies that have transformed the electronic, electrical engineering, telecommunications, and biopharmaceutical industries and created the Internet. Some countries, mainly in East Asia but also in Latin America, absorbed the new technologies and, through heavy investment in production capacity, infrastructure, and skills, emerged as successful manufacturers and exporters of industrial products.

The tempo of global change quickened in the 1990s. It slowed toward the end of that decade, because of the East Asian crisis, but recovery was swift, with world trade and capital flows expanding at record-setting rates between 2005 and 2007.[1] However, the financial crisis starting in 2008, the worldwide recession through much of 2009, the severe contraction of trade, and the urgent need for external and internal adjustments by countries with large current account imbalances have given rise to concerns over the medium-term growth prospects of the world economy and the future efficacy of the principal external drivers of growth in recent years: import demand from the leading Organisation for Economic Co-operation and Development (OECD) countries and the offshoring of tradable activities from the United States and Western Europe to economies where production costs are lower.

These concerns are motivating a reexamination in industrializing economies of development strategies reliant on processing and assembly-type industries that generate relatively little domestic value added. The viability of investment and export-led growth is being questioned, and countries with trade surpluses are looking for ways to increase the share of domestic consumption in final demand and lessen the reliance on investment as the primary driver of growth. This effort has focused increasing attention on measures to raise the contribution of total factor productivity (TFP) so as to compensate partially or wholly for a decline in investment. If TFP is to displace other sources of growth, policy makers are searching for a combination of factors that will lead to steadily increasing productivity of industry and services (Mokyr 1999).

Productivity is a function of the efficient allocation and use of resources, technological capabilities, and innovation across the full spectrum of economic activities. To maximize gains in productivity, industrializing countries will need to address four priorities:

- Products and services that will be in growing demand and subject to technological change
- A competitive business environment and a financial system that, in concert, lower the barriers to the entry and exit of firms
- Incentives for research and development (R&D) with the intention of building world-class innovation capabilities in areas with the greatest long-term commercial potential
- The quality of the scientific and technical workforce and the steady accumulation of intangible factors in business and institutions so as to raise efficiency, promote entrepreneurship, increase the returns from research, and encourage profitable innovation.

With industrial development of a modern economy almost wholly concentrated in cities, productivity gains accruing from technological progress and from innovation will be spearheaded by urban centers. The experience of advanced countries suggests that a country has only a few such centers of innovation or "smart cities." Hence, the viability of a "productivity-led" strategy in an industrializing context will rest on the effectiveness of policies—national and local—to groom one or a small number of smart cities that not only are technologically dynamic and innovative but also realize the industrial scale needed to contribute substantially to the overall growth rate of the national economy.

This chapter profiles smart cities and discusses policies that can contribute to their flowering and growth. Smart cities are not called into existence by the wave of a policy maker's wand. In recent times, they have morphed from cities that have a strong base of industries with large research content. Therefore, the chapter first underscores the significance of productivity as a source of growth and identifies those industries and products with robust growth prospects, which are the focus of rapid technological change and could provide the underpinnings of a smart city. It draws on the experience of China, which, among the middle-income countries, is most aggressively pursuing the objective of developing smart cities. The chapter then examines the attributes of smart cities that are responsible for their success. It concludes with policy suggestions for how aspiring countries could develop the potential of a few nascent smart cities.

Growth and Technology-Intensive Subsectors

The centrality of capital for growth in the world as a whole since 1980 is highlighted by Jorgenson and Vu Khuong (2009), who show that capital was the source of 54 percent of growth in 1989–95 and 41 percent during 2000–06, exceeding the contribution of other factors. However, the compelling development is the increasing importance of TFP, which accounted for 36 percent of growth in the most recent period compared with less than a fifth in the first. If this trend persists, TFP will become the principal driver of growth, as it already is in the advanced countries (Comin and Hobijn 2010),[2] and its persistence will depend less on the intersectoral transfer of resources and more on technology advances, the diffusion of technology, and the narrowing of technological gaps among production units within a subsector. Innovation, or the successful exploitation of new ideas and technology, is the cornerstone of this process.[3]

A striking example of the salience of total factor productivity is apparent from the partitioning of the sources of growth in China, the second largest and fastest-growing economy in the world (Bosworth and Collins 2007). Capital and TFP contributed 3.2 and 3.8 percent, respectively, to China's gross domestic product (GDP) growth between 1978 and 2004.[4] During the period 1993 to 2004, their shares were 4.2 and 4.0 percent, respectively (table 5.1). Capital and TFP contributed 2.2 and 4.4 percent of industrial growth during 1978–2004 compared with 3.2 and 6.2 percent during 1993–2004 (table 5.2). Cross-country empirical evidence from other countries suggests that TFP has risen much faster in the technology-intensive electrical and nonelectrical machinery subsectors (Jorgenson, Ho, and Stiroh 2007). This has enlarged the output share of those industries and raised the average TFP for manufacturing as a whole.

Table 5.1   Sources of GDP Growth in China, 1978–2004
annual % rate of change

Source	1978–2004	1993–2004
Output	9.3	9.7
Employment	2.0	1.2
Output per worker	7.3	8.5
Physical capital	3.2	4.2
Land	0.0	0.0
Education	0.2	0.2
Factor productivity	3.8	4.0

Source: Bosworth and Collins 2007.

Table 5.2   Sources of GDP Growth in the Industrial and Services Sectors in China, 1978–2004
annual % rate of change

Source of growth	Industry		Services	
	1978–2004	1993–2004	1978–2004	1993–2004
Output	10.0	11.0	10.7	9.8
Employment	3.1	1.2	5.8	4.7
Output per worker	7.0	9.8	4.9	5.1
Physical capital	2.2	3.2	2.7	3.9
Education	0.2	0.2	0.2	0.2
Factor productivity	4.4	6.2	1.9	0.9

Source: Bosworth and Collins 2007.

Over the same two periods, capital contributed 2.2 and 3.2 percent to industrial growth in China, respectively, and TFP contributed 4.4 and 6.2 percent. In 1978–2004, services derived 2.7 percent of growth from capital and 1.9 percent from TFP. The contribution of TFP to services (a sector where technological advances have been slower) fell to just 0.9 percent a year between 1993 and 2004.

With China investing more than 46 percent of GDP in 2009–10 and capital spending subject to decreasing returns, as is evident from rising incremental capital output ratios (Yu 2009), the scope for squeezing out additional growth through even larger injections of capital has been largely exhausted. Investment as a share of GDP must decline, and if growth rates in the 7–8 percent range are to be maintained, the share of TFP would need to rise even higher. This also applies to other middle-income countries, where the investment rates are trending downward and threaten to depress growth rates that are already well below the peaks reached in the 1990s. Undoubtedly, reducing intersectoral and intrasectoral gaps in productivity will boost TFP in all the industrializing economies, but raising and maintaining the contribution of TFP to levels in excess of the 1.5 percent average in most countries will require accelerating technological change and innovation, which in turn will be paced by the evolving composition of industry.

This raises an important question regarding subsectors that are growing most strongly, are likely to undergo rapid technological change, and are likely to register the largest productivity gains. Answers must necessarily be hedged because an examination of past trends casts a narrow beam of light into the near future only. International and Chinese experience suggests that manufacturing is the leading source of technological innovation. It has more links to other activities, including services, and the highest direct and indirect job multipliers (see Yusuf and Nabeshima 2010). This is borne out by recent trends in production, trade, patenting activity, and exports. These are not a sufficient basis for targeting industry, but they do indicate the nature of industrial opportunities for countries seeking to restore their growth rates through the midwifery of smart cities.

Export Composition and Growth

From the data on the fastest-growing global exports during 1997–2007 and the most rapidly expanding exports for the Asia region (tables 5.3 and 5.4), three manufactured products stand out: optical devices, telecommunications and transport equipment, and white goods. In 1985, more than 60 percent of China's exports were resource- and agro-based products and primary products. Electronics and other high-technology products accounted for a little more than 5 percent of the total. Five years later, the share of the former group had been cut almost by half, and by

Table 5.3   Fastest-Growing Manufactured Exports Worldwide, 1997–2007

Type of product	Average growth rate (%)
Optical instruments and apparatus	77.0
Platinum and other metals	74.0
Glycosides; glands or other organs	50.7
Other nitrogen-function compounds	49.0
Other articles of precious metal	48.4
Nickel and nickel alloys, unwrought	46.4
Nickel and nickel alloys, worked	40.3
Cyclic hydrocarbons	40.0
Orthopedic appliances	39.2
Medicaments (including veterinary)	39.2

Source: UN Comtrade data.

Table 5.4   Fastest-Growing Manufactured Exports from Asia, 1997–2007

Type of product	Average growth rate (%)
Dish washing machines, household	1,703.0
Other articles of precious metals	198.7
Radiotelegraphic and radiotelephonic	147.8
Cellulose acetates	135.5
Silver, unwrought, unworked or semimanufactured	135.1
Aircraft	126.1
Optical instruments and apparatus	122.1
Reaction engines	111.4
Nickel and nickel alloys, unwrought	109.5
Drawn or blown glass, unworked	104.6

Source: UN Comtrade data.

2006, it was down to 12 percent. The big gainers were exports of electronic and telecommunications products and office equipment, the shares of which grew from 5.4 percent in 1985 to more than one-third in 2006. A very similar transformation can be seen in the export mix of other Southeast Asian countries.

Further information on China's exports can be gleaned from tables 5.5 and 5.6. Transport equipment, electrical equipment, chemicals, and machinery emerge as the leading industries that are also contributing the most exports.

Pattern of Imports

Imports of manufactures by industrializing countries, many of which are from technologically more advanced countries, provide further clues by highlighting the demand for products and services that cannot be met competitively from local sources and pointing to opportunities for upgrading and diversification. Again, China can illuminate the situation because it is a large importer of intermediate and capital goods that support its assembly industries. China's imports for 2002–08 are presented in table 5.7. The data are highly aggregated, but they indicate that growth rates for electronics, computers, telecommunications, and optoelectronics are slowing and their shares in total imports are falling (table 5.8). The demand for life sciences and biotechnology products remains robust, and their share of total imports, although still small, is on the rise. Scale favors electronic components and telecommunications, while growth is in the life sciences.

R&D and Patenting

The R&D intensity of individual industries and trends in patenting during 2005–09, by identifying the most technologically dynamic subsectors,

Table 5.5   Fastest-Growing Manufacturing Industries in China, 1996–2003

Industry	Average growth rate (%)
Transport equipment	505.3
Iron and steel	496.4
Industrial chemicals	476.8
Machinery, except electrical	474.0
Food products	464.8
Machinery, electric	352.8
Professional and scientific equipment	17.6
Petroleum refineries	16.0
Furniture, except metal	14.4
Nonferrous metals	14.1

Source: UN Comtrade data.

Table 5.6   Top 10 Exports from China, 2006

Description	Trade value (US$ millions)
Complete digital data-processing machines	43,384
Peripheral units, including control and adapting units	37,594
Television, radio broadcasting, transmitters, other	35,776
Parts, nes of and accessories for machines of headings 7512 and 752	32,786
Parts, nes of and accessories for apparatus falling in heading 76	31,474
Electronic microcircuits	21,306
Other sound recording and reproducer, nes; video recorders	21,266
Footwear	21,015
Children's toys, indoor games, and so on	18,011
Outerwear, knitted or crocheted, not elastic or rubberized; other, clothing accessories, nonelastic, knitted or crocheted	14,892

Source: UN Comtrade data.
Note: nes = not elsewhere specified.

offer additional guidance on industrial prospects. For this purpose, patents registered with the U.S. Patent and Trademark Office (USPTO) and the World Intellectual Property Organization (WIPO) can provide a global perspective and also reveal the trends in patenting by Chinese residents. Because it is costly to register with the USPTO and the WIPO and the evaluation process is both standardized and exacting, the patents approved by these bodies tend to be, on average, of higher quality than patents registered elsewhere.

Table 5.7   Imports to China, 2002, 2005, 2008
US$ (100 millions)

Indicator	2002	2005	2008
Total merchandise	2,951.7	6,599.5	11,325.6
Total industrial products	2,459.0	5,122.4	7,701.7
Machinery and electronics	1,555.9	3,503.8	5,386.6
Percentage of merchandise	52.7	53.1	47.6
Percentage of industrial products	63.3	68.4	69.9
High-tech products	828.4	1,977.1	3,418.2
Percentage of merchandise	28.1	30.0	30.2
Percentage of industrial products	33.7	38.6	44.4

Source: Ministry of Science and Technology (http://www.sts.org.cn/sjkl/gjscy/index.htm); State Statistics Bureau; General Administration of Customs.

Table 5.8   Imports of High-Tech Products as a Percentage of Total Imports in China, 2002, 2005, 2008

Imports	2002	2005	2008
Computers and telecommunications	9.50	9.10	7.03
Life science technologies	1.00	0.70	0.70
Electronics	11.50	15.30	14.20
Computer-integrated manufacturing	3.10	2.50	2.20
Aerospace	1.60	1.30	1.20
Optoelectronics	0.50	0.50	4.30
Biotechnology	0.04	0.02	0.03
Materials	0.70	0.40	0.50
Other technologies	0.20	0.03	0.04

Source: Ministry of Science and Technology (http://www.sts.org.cn/sjkl/gjscy/index.htm); State Statistics Bureau; General Administration of Customs.

As presented in table 5.9, the top five categories approved by the USPTO are drug, bio-affecting and body treating compositions (3.1 percent), semiconductor device manufacturing process (2.9 percent), active solid-state devices (2.7 percent), multiplex communications (2.4 percent), and telecommunications (2.0 percent). Residents of China who registered with the USPTO received the largest number of patents for electronic and electrical devices, followed by communications devices, software, pharmaceutical compounds, and optical devices.

The two leading categories of patents approved by the WIPO are electronic and electrical devices and chemical compounds, including pharmaceutical and biotech products (table 5.10). These are followed by mechanical engineering patents and patents for instruments, including optical devices. Electronic and electrical industries dominated patenting

Table 5.9   Top USPTO Patents Worldwide, 2005–09

Class	Class title	% of total patents
424	Drug, bio-affecting and body-treating compositions (includes class 514)	3.1
438	Semiconductor device manufacturing: process	2.9
257	Active solid-state devices (for example, transistors, solid-state diodes)	2.7
370	Multiplex communications	2.4
455	Telecommunications	2.0
435	Chemistry: molecular biology and microbiology	1.7
532	Organic compounds (includes classes 532–70)	1.6
375	Pulse or digital communications	1.3
359	Optical: systems and elements	1.3
385	Optical waveguides	1.1
123	Internal-combustion engines	1.0
356	Optics: measuring and testing	0.9
280	Land vehicles	0.7
530	Chemistry: natural resins or derivatives; peptides or proteins; lignins or reaction products thereof	0.5
296	Land vehicles: bodies and tops	0.5
180	Motor vehicles	0.4
426	Food or edible material: processes, compositions, and products	0.2
99	Foods and beverages: apparatus	0.1
452	Butchering	0.1

Source: USPTO.

in the United States from 1960 to 2005 and also contributed the most to gains in productivity (tables 5.11 and 5.12).

The R&D data and patent statistics provide a window on the distribution of technological activity and point to those industries that are likely to be a focus of innovations as patented knowledge is commercialized. When the data on patents are combined with the data on trade, electronic and optical devices are in the lead with respect to global demand and technological prospects. Chemical products and transport and engineering products fall into second and third places. This is the crude ranking of industrial activities that emerges from trends in a few select indicators. This ranking is in line with casual empiricism and the information presented in the business literature: over the next five or more years, electronic, communication, and optical industries will remain the leading subsectors in the world. Chemical and biological products, drawing on the vast amount of research in the life sciences, will also be of significance.

Table 5.10   Share of WIPO Patents, by Sector, 2007–09

Sector and field of technology		% of all patents issued	% of China's patents	China's patents as % of all patents
	Total	100.00	100.00	3.15
I	*Electrical engineering*	29.48	53.14	5.67
1	Electrical machinery, apparatus, energy	5.20	5.38	3.25
2	Audio-visual technology	3.16	2.46	2.45
3	Telecommunications	4.61	11.33	7.73
4	Digital communication	4.69	25.76	17.28
5	Basic communication processes	0.87	0.78	2.84
6	Computer technology	6.37	5.11	2.53
7	IT methods for management	1.27	0.70	1.72
8	Semiconductors	3.31	1.62	1.54
II	*Instruments*	16.23	7.86	1.52
9	Optics	2.96	1.59	1.69
13	Medical technology	5.90	2.72	1.45
III	*Chemistry*	29.61	18.49	1.97
15	Biotechnology	3.61	1.98	1.73
16	Pharmaceuticals	37.67	4.55	2.34
18	Food chemistry	1.11	0.72	2.04
19	Basic materials chemistry	3.42	1.68	1.54
20	Materials, metallurgy	2.00	1.37	2.16
21	Surface technology, coating	2.04	1.08	1.67
22	Microstructural and nanotechnology	0.25	0.04	0.45
23	Chemical engineering	2.76	2.08	2.38
24	Environmental technology	1.51	1.20	2.49
IV	*Mechanical engineering*	18.31	12.93	2.22
32	Transport	3.46	2.21	2.01

Source: China State Intellectual Property Office.

Note: Under the WIPO approach, one application may have several classes of intellectual property and may belong to different fields of technology. In this case, every technology field is counted. As a result, the sum of the total number of all technology fields could be larger than the total number of applications in the year.

Table 5.11   Top Five Patenting Industries in the United States, 2006

Rank	Industry
1	Electronic components and accessories and communications equipment
2	Office computing and accounting machines
3	Professional and scientific instruments
4	Electrical transmission and distribution equipment
5	Industrial organic chemistry

Source: World Intellectual Property Organization.

Table 5.12   Top Five Industries Contributing to TFP Growth in the United States, 1960–2005

Rank	Industry
1	Computers and office equipment
2	Electronic components
3	Telephone and telegraph
4	Food
5	Rubber and miscellaneous plastics

Source: World Intellectual Property Organization.

This suggests that the aspiring smart city in an industrializing country should be building on an emerging or established comparative advantage in such manufacturing activities. This is not to say that other industries and tradable services should be excluded from consideration, only that virtually all of the dynamic smart cities in the world have achieved their standing because of the electronic, information technology (IT), telecommunications, transport, and biotech industries. For some, these are now providing the stepping-stones to the development of "green" industries, new materials, and advances in nanotechnology. Having established a strong presence in several of the most dynamic industries, Chinese firms, for example, are eager to move up the value chain from the assembly and testing of standardized products to the design and manufacture of differentiated parts and components and innovative products that generate higher profit margins.[5]

What Makes Cities Smart

From the perspective of tomorrow's smart cities, IT, electronics, biotech, chemical, and yet undiscovered general-purpose technologies[6] will serve as the springboards for tackling a new generation of problems with novel solutions and laying the groundwork for new industries. As W. Brian Arthur (2009, 164, 169) observes, "Innovation arises when people are faced with ... well-specified problems.... Novel technologies arise from a combination of existing technologies." He rightly notes that a general-purpose technology "does not just offer a set of limited functions, it provides a vocabulary of elements that can be put together—programmed—in endlessly novel ways for endlessly novel purposes" (Arthur 2009, 88). Thus, the makings of the next technological revolution are already in place and primed for a new round of innovation. What is needed is the orientation of research efforts toward key longer-term problems backed by the credible commitment

of resources to the deepening of scientific knowledge and to the nurturing of technologies that weave together findings from relevant
fields. National policy can provide the incentive framework for technology development and urbanization, but, because of trade and competition, the forces of comparative advantage are exacerbating the
differences among the regions of a country. For this reason, municipal
policies and local innovation systems will determine the emergence of
smart cities (Acs 2000).

When East Asian and Latin American economies were attempting to
accelerate industrialization and exports, it was important to build production capacity in processing industries as widely as possible, and in those
circumstances, breadth and scale mattered most. By investing in productive assets and borrowing technology from abroad, manufacturing industries could be quickly built up using tried incentives. This explains the rise
of industrial cities in Asia, Eastern Europe, and Latin America. A few
could become smart cities.

In the Right Place

Cities with long-term technology or innovation potential are likely at a
minimum to be distinguished by (a) a strategic location in a prosperous
and growing urban region, (b) a robust recent history of urban development and industrialization, and (c) adequate land area to accommodate
future growth. Climate, environmental conditions, accessibility, and
potential amenities have traditionally favored coastal cities, which tend to
have first-mover advantages and rich hinterlands and are the focus of
migration. For these reasons, China's "open cities" of the 1980s were all
coastal cities. But some smart cities in Europe and the United States are
located in the interior, and some are emerging in China as well—cities
such as Changsha, Wuhan, Xian, and Zhengzhou. Virtually all of the
European and North American cities owe their standing to a strategic
location, an industry with one or several leading firms, or the presence of
established major teaching and research institutions.

Harnessing Intelligence

Before industrial cities can become smart cities, enhancing the depth and
quality of human capital is critical. Smart cities require institutional
mechanisms and research infrastructure for generating ideas and ways of
debating, testing, and perfecting these ideas. Smart cities can achieve
rapid and sustainable growth of industry by bringing together and fully
harnessing four forms of intelligence: the human intelligence inherent in

local knowledge networks, the collective intelligence of institutions that support innovation through a variety of channels, the production intelligence of the industrial base, and the artificial intelligence that can be derived from the effective use of digital networks and online services (Komninos 2008). Smart cities are open to ideas and thrive on the heterogeneity of knowledge workers drawn from all over the country—and the world. Moreover, such cities are closely integrated with other global centers of research and technology development, and their teaching and research institutions must compete with the best for talent and validation of their own ideas. Last but not least, because smart cities are at the leading edge of the knowledge economy, their design, physical assets, attributes, and governance need to reflect their edge over others. Industrial cities can become smart cities, and a strong manufacturing base is an important asset, as in Munich, Seattle, Seoul, Stuttgart, Tokyo, and Toulouse. But industry is not a necessary condition: Cambridge (United Kingdom), Helsinki, Kyoto, and San Francisco are not industrial cities; they are smart cities that have acquired significant high-tech or IT production capabilities.

Being Big or in an Urban Region

Research on agglomeration economies has pointed to the productivity gains that accrue to large cities from scale, diversity, and density of activities and from the apparent superlinearity (albeit modest) of innovations in relation to the size of the city (Carlino, Chatterjee and Hunt 2007; Carlino and Hunt 2009; Gill and Goh 2010; Glaeser and Gottlieb 2009; Rosenthal and Strange 2004; World Bank 2009).[7] Diversified urban economies recover more quickly from shocks. Moreover, evidence suggests that, because of their greater innovativeness, large cities can serve as nurseries for high-tech, new start-ups (Carlino, Chatterjee, and Hunt 2007; Duranton and Puga 2001). However, it is desirable not to overstate the advantages of size, especially for smart cities. A meta-study of the empirical research on agglomeration economies finds that the productivity gains are in the 3 percent range (Melo, Graham, and Noland 2009). Furthermore, many cities noted for innovation are medium-size cities such as Austin, Boston, Raleigh, San Francisco, and Seattle in the United States and Cambridge (United Kingdom), Eindhoven, Helsinki, Munich, Stockholm, and Toulouse in Europe.[8] Even the entire population of Silicon Valley does not exceed 2.6 million. Productivity gains from localization economies can be realized by mid-size cities that specialize in manufacturing activities (Henderson 2010). If they are located in an urban region, they can realize economies of agglomeration, specialization, and scale (a polycentric urban region).[9]

A typical urban region in an industrializing country is likely to be composed of a large core city ringed by smaller satellite or edge cities. The core city with a broad economic base and clusters of business services serves as the hub of the region and the major source of knowledge generation and spillovers. The more specialized neighboring cities, with lower land and housing costs, host clusters of industrial firms and other activities. The urban core can provide the technological leadership and many of the supporting business services, but innovation is frequently a region-wide activity, and smart cities can be the smaller ones, with specialized clusters and other attributes, which are examined below.

Human Capital and High Technology

Almost by definition, export-oriented and sustainable cities are (and will be) ones that produce and attract large numbers of skilled and technical workers, raise the quality of human capital,[10] and nurture a local innovation system.[11] The quality of human and knowledge assets is what makes a city smart and entrepreneurial. International research suggests that the presence of "star scientists" can initiate virtuous spirals in the fields where innovation is keyed to scientific advances. The biotech cluster in San Diego arose because several star scientists chose to locate there because the city was enticing and the university offered singular opportunities.

First, smart cities have a high ratio of science and technology (S&T) workers in the labor force. Table 5.13 provides a classification of S&T workers for whom data are available in the United States. A similar classification is available for China and other countries. Second, smart cities host several universities, and tertiary-level enrollment is high. Third, the industrial composition of the city favors industries that employ large numbers of S&T workers and have high rates of patenting (see table 5.14). Fourth, smart cities usually attract one or a few major firms with a focus on dynamic industries that invest heavily in R&D and rely on innovation to maintain competitiveness. Table 5.15 lists U.S. cities ranked by the percentage of high-tech jobs in the total workforce. Table 5.16 does the same for IT jobs.

Smart cities use information and communication technology (ICT) to support industry, the education and research infrastructure, and governance. In the future, ICT will be critical to sustainability because it will enable urban centers to contain energy consumption (for example, in Singapore), provide better services, and build more resilient infrastructure.

Table 5.13   Science and Technology Occupations in the United States

Occupation employment statistics code	Occupational title
13017	Engineering, math, natural sciences managers
22102	Aeronautical and astronautical engineers
22105	Metallurgists or metallurgical, ceramic, and materials engineers
22108	Mining engineers
22111	Petroleum engineers
22114	Chemical engineers
22117	Nuclear engineers
22121	Civil engineers
22123	Agricultural engineers
22126	Electrical and electronic engineers
22127	Computer engineers
22128	Industrial engineers, except safety
22132	Safety engineers, except mining
22135	Mechanical engineers
22138	Marine engineers
24102	Physicists and astronomers
24105	Chemists, except biochemists
24108	Atmospheric and space scientists
24111	Geologists, geophysicists, and oceanographers
24199	All other physical scientists
24302	Foresters and conservation scientists
24305	Agricultural and food scientists
24308	Biological scientists
24311	Medical scientists
25102	Systems analysts
25103	Database administrators
25105	Computer programmers
25111	Programmers, numerical tool, and process control
25310	Mathematical scientists
25312	Statisticians

Source: Markusen et al. 2004.

Smart cities have also taken the lead in providing affordable housing and space for industry and tradable services, thereby ensuring that new industries and talented people remain and contribute to local development. By retaining industry and not segregating the population by income, the city avoids sharp cleavages in income distribution.

A city that is top ranked with respect to high-tech and IT scores is Seattle, the home of Boeing and Microsoft. Table 5.17 shows the composition of employment in Seattle by subsector, underscoring the importance of activities notable for their technology intensity, such as aircraft

Table 5.14   S&T Jobs in Selected High-Tech Industries in the United States, 1997

Standard industrial classification	Description	1997 U.S. employment	S&T occupations as % of industry total
376	Guided missiles and space vehicles and parts	76,808	42.7
737	Computer programming, data processing	1,425,663	40.7
381	Search, detection, navigation, guidance equipment	185,888	34.1
871	Engineering, architectural, and surveying services	938,469	30.5
357	Computer and office equipment	277,495	30.1
873	Research, development, and testing services	491,699	26.7
366	Communications equipment	294,531	20.8
372	Aircraft and parts	415,022	17.0
482	Telegraph and other message communications	815,427	16.4
131	Crude petroleum and natural gas	100,308	15.9

Source: Markusen et al. 2004.
Note: S & T = science and technology.

Table 5.15 High-Tech Jobs in Selected Cities in the United States, 1997

Metropolitan statistical area	Share of workforce (%)	Number of jobs (thousands)
San Jose, CA	41.3	289.1
Seattle, WA	21.1	174.9
Boston, MA	20.9	281.5
Washington, DC	20.3	321.6
Austin, TX	19.7	75.7
Orange County, CA	18.4	152.4
Raleigh-Durham, NC	16.8	69.0
San Diego, CA	16.4	112.7
Dallas, TX	16.4	197.9
Salt Lake City, UT	16.2	60.6

Source: Markusen et al. 2004.

and measuring instruments, and for IT intensity, such as insurance, computer programming, and architectural services.

Industrialized and Export Oriented

From the experience of the OECD countries and the evidence cited earlier in this chapter, it appears that an export-oriented manufacturing base

Table 5.16   IT Jobs in Selected Cities in the United States, 1997

Metropolitan statistical area	Share of workforce (%)	Number of jobs (thousands)
San Jose, CA	21.2	148.7
Washington, DC	17.5	277.1
Boston, MA	16.2	218.5
Orange County, CA	13.9	114.9
Denver, CO	13.5	88.0
Raleigh-Durham, NC	13.5	55.2
Minneapolis–St. Paul, MN	12.5	133.5
Dallas, TX	12.5	150.8
Austin, TX	11.5	44.0
San Diego, CA	11.2	77.1

Source: Markusen et al. 2004.

Table 5.17   Key High-Tech Sectors in Seattle

Standard industrial classification	Description	Employment
367	Electronic components and accessories	4,787
372	Aircraft and parts	74,500
381	Search, detection, navigation, guidance equipment	15,593
382	Laboratory apparatus and analytical, optical instruments	5,166
384	Surgical, medical, and dental instruments	5,606
631	Life insurance	4,235
737	Computer programming and data-processing services	23,174
871	Engineering, architectural, and surveying services	14,906
874	Management and public relations services	7,406
	Total high-tech industry employment	174,902
	High-tech specialization index	2.23

Source: Markusen et al. 2004.

is a precondition for the rise of a smart city. As noted, some kinds of manufacturing industries are among the leading innovators and have registered the highest gains in productivity. Even in the U.S. economy, with its heavy emphasis on services, manufactures account for 62 percent of exports (in 2008), with the 10 leading metropolitan areas responsible for a large

share of the total. Istrate, Rothwell, and Katz (2010, 7) note, "The introduction of innovative products often precedes exports ... and metro areas
are the home to most inventors of patents and a disproportionate share
of R&D, science, and even venture capital investments .... There is evidence [also] that export-oriented industries produce more patents if they
are located near other firms in the same industry." Industries that nurture
a dense network of suppliers facilitate innovation by reducing the cost of
bringing ideas to fruition.[12] Manufacturing industries are also more likely
to attract foreign direct investment (FDI) and to benefit from spillovers.[13]
The significance of manufacturing as the basis for technology-intensive
and innovative activities is even more apparent in the industrializing
countries, such as Brazil, China, Malaysia, Poland, and Thailand. Smart
cities in these countries will arise from the ranks of the leading centers of
industry, such as Bangkok, Penang, Shanghai, and Shenzhen.

Walkable

Cities that are livable, energy efficient, and well furnished with social
capital are designed to be *walkable*. This means, in practice, that they are
compact, zoned for mixed use, safe, pedestrian friendly (with green
spaces, sidewalks, shaded lanes, street lights, and underpasses integrated
into the walking experience), and have readily accessible public transport.
Designing a city to be walkable also minimizes the likelihood of urban
sprawl, which results in a healthier population and reduces energy and
infrastructure costs (Frumkin, Frank, and Jackson 2004). Compactness
and density facilitate face-to-face encounters, which, as Venables (2010, 2)
observes, "allow high-frequency exchange of ideas and complex dis-
course ... the building of trust .... [Moreover,] larger and thicker labor
markets can improve the quality of the match between firms with particular skill needs and workers with particular skill attributes, can increase
competition in the matching process, and can increase the frequency of
meetings." Wuhan, for example, has the topography and the potential to
morph into a city as attractive for the Chinese (and, eventually, international) creative class as Austin or San Diego or Singapore, but the potential of its many watercourses has yet to be exploited, and little attention
has been paid to redesigning the city to reverse its drabness and sprawl.
Penang equally has the makings of an innovative city, but it lacks a comprehensive action plan (see Yusuf 2008).

Sustainable

Sustainability has taken on much greater significance in the face of
impending climate change, but not only because global temperatures

are rising.[14] For a city to thrive and to grow, the availability of adequate supplies of water and energy is a must, as is the effectiveness of infrastructure for disposing sewage and waste and of regulations for managing environmental pollution. Sustainable cities are notable for the quality of governance, and they maintain sound finances with the help of fiscal planning, local tax instruments, intergovernmental transfers, budgetary rules, and accounting procedures. Sustainability in the context of an urban region demands systematic coordination among municipalities to ensure the effective planning of infrastructure and also coordination of taxation and zoning.[15] In the future, sustainable cities will need to be much more energy frugal and "green" and to strengthen their ability to sustain shocks—financial and weather or climate related. A sustainable urban center in the average lower-middle-income country will need to plan on accommodating a large increase in the population and adopting measures to avoid the spread of urban poverty and of slums (see Linn 2010). In middle-income countries, cities will also have to prepare for the aging of populations. Even the most dynamic Chinese and Indian cities do not meet most of the criteria of sustainability.[16] Existing metropolitan regions will need to be significantly reshaped, and emerging cities will need to be much better designed. Because China, India, and other developing countries in Asia and Africa are only partly urbanized, there is scope for improvement, but past mistakes will be costly to undo.

Connected

Urban connectedness is important at two levels. Successful metropolitan cities are open, trade oriented, and innovative. In a globalized environment, this depends on the quality of the transport and the ICT infrastructure that links the city to the rest of the country and the world and facilitates the flow of goods, services, and capital as well as the circulation of people and ideas. Connectedness at the local level using ICT can deliver efficient solutions for the development of energy, transportation, housing, and buildings. It can promote commercial, social, and academic networking and the creation of social and research capital (it induces face-to-face encounters), which is good for productivity and for livability. Villa and Mitchell (2009, 11) observe, "Knowledge workers are opting for more collaborative and flexible forms of work that allow them to contribute when they want, from virtually anywhere, and with almost anyone. At the same time, the speed demands and complexity of knowledge work have increased significantly, driving the need to collaborate and engage a broader workgroup to obtain needed results."

Catalyzing Innovation

Cities become innovative because existing industries or institutions help to nucleate new activities and start a chain reaction. The process can be initiated by any number of catalysts: the transformation of a local university, the creation of a new institution, the arrival of a major firm, a small cluster of dynamic start-ups, or some other catalytic event that energizes a combination of intellectual and productive activities. There are virtually no instances in the past two decades of innovative cities being successfully made to order anywhere in the world. The attempts to engineer science cities such as Tsukuba in Japan and Daejeon in the Republic of Korea as well as other technopoles in Europe have rarely lived up to expectations. Most often, existing urban centers became innovative places because a critical mass of human capital, productive assets, and infrastructure and service providers was catalyzed by a firm, a leader, a university chancellor, or some other event. China is currently taking a top-down approach to creating smart cities. Only time will tell whether the outcomes will match expectations.

Toward an Urban Innovation Strategy

For smart cities, openness and connectivity are more important than scale. They contribute to the productivity of research and the generation as well as the testing of ideas. However, a minimum level of urbanization economies arising from industrial diversity can confer important benefits by providing a mix of technologies and production expertise out of which innovations can arise and which provide the soil for new entrants to take root. Connectivity via state-of-the art telecommunications and transport infrastructure is a source of virtual agglomeration for an intelligent city that confers the advantages of a large urban center without the attendant disadvantages of congestion and pollution. In this respect, the smaller smart cities of Europe and the United States enjoy the advantages of livability without sacrificing the productivity gains accruing from agglomeration.

The inland cities of China, such as Changsha, Wuhan, Xi'an, Zhengzhou, and others, have a broad and diverse industrial base; all have the scale to become smart cities, but they do not fit the description of "open" cities connected to other nodes of innovation in China and the rest of the world. These cities remain inward looking and protective of local industry. Wuhan is a production center for optoelectronics, but it is not comparable, for example, with Warsaw (Indiana) in the United States, a small city that has become the global leader of the medical equipment and devices industry and the home of leading companies such as Biomet, Medtronic, Symmetry, and Zimmer. Neither can Wuhan's leading universities, which are among the best in China, compare with the expertise accumulated by Purdue University (in Indiana) and Indiana University in medical technologies. Likewise, Penang in Malaysia hosts a large cluster of electronics firms and is a major source of Malaysia's exports, but in spite of the efforts of the national and local authorities, Penang is far from becoming a smart city.

To exploit the innovation potential inherent in virtual agglomeration, smart cities need to network actively with other centers throughout the region and the world and build areas of expertise, as Wuhan can in optoelectronics. This calls for embracing a culture of openness and activism on the part of major local firms and universities to translate such a culture into commercial and scientific linkages that span the globe. Wuhan will be recognized as an innovation hotspot for optoelectronics when a few local firms enter the ranks of the world's leading companies in this field and local universities are viewed as doing path-breaking research in optoelectronics.

The remarkable feature of China's leading inland cities is that each one has moved aggressively to build tertiary institutions and research facilities, trains thousands of engineers and scientists, and is home to one or two universities, which are among the top ranked in China. Chengdu, Xi'an, Zhengzhou, and the others have managed to groom a few firms that could become industrial anchors for local clusters, much like ARM and Cambridge Consultants served as the anchors for the electronics cluster in Cambridge (United Kingdom).[17] Several inland cities such as Chengdu, Chongqing, Dalian, and Shenyang have also been successful in persuading multinational corporations to set up production facilities, which augment manufacturing capabilities and create the preconditions for a concentration of the value chain.[18] Moreover, the leading inland cities are investing in the transport infrastructure to improve connectivity, and all have established industrial parks to provide space and services for industry to grow. These, plus a full suite of incentives, satisfy most of the preconditions for the emergence of innovative industrial clusters. What might be missing is focus. The inland cities want to develop several of the industries designated as high tech. For example, electronics, automobiles, biotech, renewable energy, and advanced materials are on the shopping list of all cities vying to become the smart cities of tomorrow. All of these cities are attempting to upgrade local industries so as to move "up the value chain" and to link this with a localization of the innovation value chain. All are aiming to increase local value added so as to maximize well-paid jobs and expand the urban revenue base. Although this sets the stage for intense competition, it also could lead to a waste of resources, as cities bid for a limited pool of talent, offer generous incentives to attract domestic and international companies, and protect local producers in an effort to deepen technological capabilities.

The end result could be a suboptimal dispersion of scientific talent and of research and production facilities. Instead of a few world-class centers with substantial innovation capabilities and a focus on one or a few technologies, there is the risk that the inland cities would fail to acquire the critical mass of expertise in any area and fail to build innovative clusters. The competition among cities can lead to a massive expenditure on R&D infrastructure and on production capacity, most of it redundant, as each city attempts to raise local value added and reel in more of the innovation value chain. This may have worked when Chinese cities were beginning to produce manufactures for an expanding global market and investing in production capacity was a safe bet. Developing innovative capacity in various smart cities requires a different approach, and capacity building is only one part of the strategy.

The innovativeness of cities is related directly to the quality of human talent. China's coastal cities have been quicker off the mark because they have been more successful in nurturing quality, retaining the most talented knowledge workers, and attracting the cream of the knowledge workers from other parts of the country. The coastal cities are also more open and accessible to outsiders and have integrated with global knowledge networks. For smaller inland cities to become innovative smart cities, they will need to specialize and pull in some of the best brains in their fields of specialization from across the country. Any serious attempt to become an innovative city built on the quality of talent, which after all is the life blood of innovation, will have to combine urban design and renewal with a focus on developing a few core areas of world-class expertise.

It may be misleading to think that the only industries appropriate for smart cities are the so-called high-tech ones with the largest number of patents in recent years. These deservedly attract the most attention and resources; however, many traditional industries can generate handsome returns through innovations that leverage findings in the life sciences and ICT. The dairy industries in Denmark and New Zealand, two of the leading exporters, have enhanced competitiveness and profitability with the help of innovations that improve herd management, optimize the feed of animals, and monitor the condition of individual head of cattle. Efforts to reduce water consumption by the meat-packing and beverage industries and to control pollution are prompting a host of innovations that contribute to the bottom line of firms. The textile industry is improving the variety of its offerings and the attributes of materials as a result of advances in nanotechnology. The huge construction materials industry is primed for technological change, as the efforts to minimize greenhouse gases gather momentum. Likewise, manufacturers of machinery and equipment, at the heart of the industrial economy, are also faced with the challenge of designing machines and techniques so as to use different kinds of materials, reduce waste, and lessen energy consumption. The point is that successful smart cities in industrializing countries do not all have to join the rush toward the electronics, biotech, transport, and renewable energy sectors. There are plenty of other low-hanging fruit, and there are numerous innovations to be made in seemingly mundane industries, some of which will require an adroit combination of technologies— the food-processing industry being one. This industry, which is a natural for cities in northeastern China, such as Changchun, is ripe for innovations to cut back sharply on waste, pollution, and energy and water use and to introduce foods that are more nutritious and safeguard health.

Aspiring smart cities hosting medium-tech industries can consider whether the future focus of innovative activities could be on some of these industries rather than the fashionable high-tech ones. Their comparative advantage in innovation might lie in food processing and not in the auto industry. And food processing may call for the development of research in the life sciences in a few specific areas, such as packaging. In other words, a realistic assessment of innovation potential must start from a clear understanding of existing competitive advantage and promising future niches for which competition will not be too fierce. In electronics and auto parts, competition will be deadly, and inland cities might well consider whether they want to invest scarce human resources and capital in becoming, at best, the second-ranked innovative cities in a high-tech industry as opposed to the leading innovative city in a medium-tech or even a formerly low-tech industry, which they are able to revolutionize through innovation. Such innovation is more likely to be inclusive than innovation in advanced materials, for example.

Although human talent is the main contributor to the intelligence of cities, the firms that conduct most of the downstream research have a large role to play. The innovativeness of the business sector is a function of many factors, some of which, such as management and the investment climate, are listed above. With respect to cities in several industrializing countries, two points need to be emphasized. First, state-owned and state-controlled enterprises continue to account for a significant share of production in key industries. Second, although the innovation systems created by the cities are encouraging new entrants, it is not apparent from the low rate of exit that truly innovative firms are being groomed or that struggling firms are being allowed to fail in sufficient numbers. State-owned enterprises tend to be among the least innovative firms and low on the scale of productivity. The larger their share of gross value of industrial output (GVIO) and R&D spending, the more protective municipal governments will be of local industry and the less easy it will be for inland cities to enhance innovation capabilities. Furthermore, attempting to build high-tech industries by supporting the entry of firms producing standardized products using well-established technologies is not a promising strategy.

Policy Measures That Facilitate Technological Upgrading and Innovation

Some policy options with regard to the two-track strategy are outlined below. More efficient business and technical services and government procurement can facilitate the success of the two-track approach.

Building "Smart Cities"

The central government can promote urban innovation capabilities through several measures.

First, the government can enhance the incentives to innovate countrywide by taking steps to increase the integration of the national economy and discourage local protectionism. This would intensify the degree of competition among domestic firms and the competitive pressures from imports, increasing both entry and exit of firms and encouraging firms to compete on the basis of technology. Pricing energy and other nonrenewable resources appropriately, setting national standards (including environmental standards and standards encouraging energy efficiency) for products, and enforcing these standards would also generate pressures to upgrade technologies, which some Western countries have done to good effect. The ability of smaller firms to meet these standards would be facilitated by strengthening the industrial extension system and providing smaller firms with access to laboratory, testing, and certification facilities.

The German Fraunhofer Institutes and the Industrial Development Corporation of Norway are good models for industrializing countries to adapt. In Japan, the TAMA (Technology Advanced Metropolitan Area) Association provides its member firms, most of which are of small and medium sizes, with laboratory facilities and testing equipment plus other services.

Second, the central government can take the initiative in building countrywide research networks that enhance the sharing, absorption, and development of technology. Research consortia in Japan, Korea, and the United States have assisted in disseminating the latest technologies and pushing the technology frontier in selected areas. Recognizing the cost and complexity of research in frontier fields, even the largest firms are finding it desirable to specialize and to form partnerships with other firms or with universities when developing sophisticated new products or technologies. In addition to consortia, the technological and innovative capabilities of nascent smart cities would benefit if both domestic and foreign firms could be persuaded to locate some of their R&D centers, not just their production facilities, in the cities.

Third, international experience suggests that smart cities house leading research universities that compete with each other and with other universities throughout the country. Smart cities are home to at least two to three of a country's top-ranked schools, and these institutions can mobilize the funding to sustain cross-disciplinary postgraduate and postdoctoral programs and set up specialized, well-staffed research institutes so as to achieve a level of performance comparable to that of institutions in more advanced countries.

Many high-tech multinational corporations are investing in R&D facilities outside of their home countries. Smart cities can derive spillovers from facilitating such investment in R&D infrastructure and in the creation of intangible assets. Cities also gain from significant spillover effects arising from the knowledge and experience imparted to the local workforce, the reputational gains for cities that will come to be seen as science hubs, and the contribution that such research can make to industrial upgrading locally.

Fourth, the most important contribution universities can make to innovation is by generating ideas and serving as a breeding ground for entrepreneurs who are the vehicles for transforming ideas into commercial products and services. Central and municipal governments are in a position to enlarge the share of basic research and to ensure the continuity of funding, both of which could build innovation capacity in the smart cities. The National Institutes of Health in the United States played a central role in the boom in the life sciences because it was and is a source of large and stable funding, much of it for basic research done in universities. This funding financed countless research programs, trained thousands of PhDs, supported postdocs, and created the depth of expertise that enabled the United States to become the leader in the field of biotech. To maximize the spillovers from the government-sponsored research and contests to develop particular types of technologies, one possibility is to make the findings of this research widely available. In the 1950s and 1960s, the research on electronics financed by the U.S. government was shared generously, and this enabled many companies to come up to speed and become innovators themselves. Good research is inseparable from a stringent and disciplined process of refereeing and evaluation of research findings. The research community needs to take the initiative in this area, but the government could provide the parameters. The universities can also take the lead in thickening the scientific culture of their cities by promoting public lectures and exhibitions and contributing to the teaching of science in local schools.

Fifth, there is the perennial issue of risk capital for innovative firms. Although some public risk capital is available in the industrializing countries, private venture capital for smaller private firms that are trying to scale up is still scarce. One partial solution is to increase lending by banks to high-tech private firms—and not mainly to government-linked companies. Such lending by local banks to local firms and the creation of bank-led relational networks are a mode of financing that seems to work in the United Kingdom and the United States and complements the resources of entrepreneurs, "angel" investors, and venture capitalists. Too little bank financing goes to private firms, especially the riskier high-tech ones.

Sixth, high-tech industry depends on a vast range of technical skills to staff factories, render IT support, repair complex equipment, and provide myriad other services. Smaller firms and start-ups frequently have difficulty finding such skills and can rarely afford to provide much training in-house. Hence public-private initiatives to secure and replenish the base of technical skills essential for a smart city can circumvent market failures and promote desirable forms of industrial activity, aside from minimizing both frictional and structural unemployment. Labor market institutions can be strengthened and made nondiscriminatory by setting up multilevel professional advisory agencies and increasing the provision of vocational training for which there would be a demand from expanding and new enterprises.

Industrial cities have attracted a range of business service providers such as engineering research centers and productivity centers, but many of them lack market orientation and suffer from funding and skills shortages. It is important to make them more functional and more responsive to private sector needs through a public-private partnership approach. However, there are some good examples in China that could be replicated. Figure 5.1 illustrates the example of Shanghai's R&D public service platform, which offers a wide range of business and extension services. These services cover the innovation development process, including the sharing of scientific information, technology testing and transfer services, and support for entrepreneurship and management.

Seventh, although universities across the industrializing world churn out huge numbers of graduates each year, the quality of the training provided is frequently weak. In the meantime, employers experience a serious

Figure 5.1   Shanghai R&D Public Service Platform

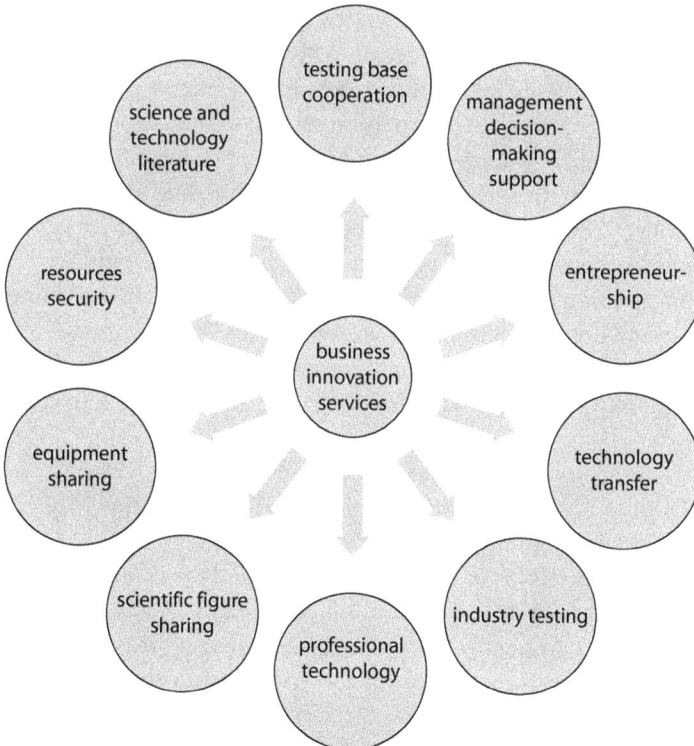

Source: Shanghai Municipality Science and Technology Commission 2006.

shortage of highly skilled technicians, engineers, and executives. This combination of low-skill glut and high-skill shortage poses a difficulty for the skill transfer that companies need to improve the quality of their output or move to a more value added link in the chain. Transfer of managerial experience is one of the key ways in which FDI contributes to the Chinese economy. In effect, the education system in China does not sufficiently encourage creativity and initiative, meaning that new graduates often lack the skills most needed as the economy strives for technological maturity.

To move forward, both the private sector itself and the government need to invest more in improving human resources management in private small and medium enterprises (SMEs). The following measures can be considered through a public-private partnership approach (for more details, see Zhang et al. 2009):

- Using the legal instruments of confidentiality agreements and competition restrictions to protect technical secrets from being taken by R&D personnel when they leave the firm
- Improving labor market conditions by using relevant services. For example, local governments could create skill development centers to (a) provide SMEs with management and technical training, especially related to innovation; (b) provide information on the demand for and supply of various skills and the premium on various job categories through close relationships with schools, training institutions, and the labor market; (c) collect and disseminate success stories about the management of skilled employees and the promotion of an innovation culture
- Strengthening policies supporting training and vocational education by reviewing the ceiling on tax-deductible training expenditures (2.5 percent of wage bill) of enterprises and redefining the role of the government in vocational education.

In addition to human resources management, improvements can also be made in facilitating the collaboration of SMEs with knowledge institutions and enhancing innovation services.

Eighth, scope exists for making better use of demand-side instruments such as government procurement and standard setting. Combined with adequate efforts to guard against the potential risks of rent seeking and protectionism, this would go a long way to encourage the demand for innovation services. However, the procurement policy can be a double-edge sword. The key to success lies in open competition. Some potential risks in this area need to be carefully addressed: (a) the risk of turning the government procurement instrument into one that protects national and local products from international and national competition, (b) the challenge of following the procedures laid out to identify the "indigenous innovation products" for the government catalogue, and (c) the risk of making government merely a passive taker of what domestic suppliers offer, rather than a demanding buyer of technologically sophisticated products (Zhang et al. 2009).

The demand for innovation could be increased through government standard setting. Standard setting allows governments and other entities to generate demand for advances in, for example, the performance, safety, energy efficiency, and environmental impact of products. To generate more demand for innovation, certain measures could be taken: (a) focusing exclusively on product improvement and resisting the temptation to use standard setting to protect or help domestic or local industry; (b) taking European Union or U.S. standards as a technical starting point, while looking for ways to improve product performance; (c) involving industry leaders more in standard setting (this needs to be done in a productive way); and (d) changing the role of government from sole standard setter to time-sensitive driver of industrial consensus (Zhang et al. 2009).

Identifying and Promoting Smart Cities

Industrializing countries need to embark on a new urban development strategy to realize their growth expectations. Such a strategy will have to be centered on transforming the leading urban centers into smart cities that are not only industrially dynamic but also fruitful sources of innovation.

Various cities would benefit from such policies; however, because each city differs with respect to resource base and comparative advantages, additional polices differentiated according to the circumstances would be needed to accelerate the transition to a smart city and create the foundations for sustainable innovation. Such differentiated policies that factor in the capabilities of a city, actual and potential, can be constructed using longitudinal data on trade, investment, industrial composition, and the labor market, combined with the gathering of qualitative information from the principal players in a local innovation system (see the annex to this chapter). Picking tomorrow's smart cities is both easy and difficult. The easy part is identifying cities that are already demonstrating their innovativeness and need to smarten up their act. The hard part is identifying the future performers from a long list.

Annex: Technology Capability and Innovation Criteria

Cities: Profile and technological capacity

- Population of city
- Population growth
- GDP per capita
- Overall GDP growth rate since 2000 and growth by sectors (in comparison with main competitors in China)
- Number of high-tech companies
- Percent of workers in high-tech fields
- Percent of workforce with advanced degrees
- Number and skill composition of in-migrants (since 2000); where do they go?
- Number and skill composition of out-migrants
- FDI

Science and technology input-output indicators

- Number of firms filing research joint ventures
- Number of research institutes
- Number of full-time R&D personnel
- Total public funds invested in R&D (and distribution of spending)
- R&D funds per capita of R&D personnel
- Patents registered by residents at their national offices
- Receipts of royalty and license fees
- Number of scientists and engineers in workforce
- Number of scientific publications (in major journals, past five years)

University sector

- Number of tertiary institutions and enrollment or number of graduates; percentage in science and engineering disciplines
- Percentage of high-achieving graduates who stay in municipality (top 5 percent of class); where do those who leave go?
- Enrollment in doctoral programs
- Enrollment in postdoctoral programs
- Spending on research as a fraction of university budgets; as a fraction of total spending on R&D in municipality
- Number of spinoffs
- Number of contracts with enterprises; what kinds of contracts?

- Number of patent applications; number of patents granted?
- Strongest university departments (by what criteria? national ranking)
- Leading research institutes (by what criteria? national ranking)

Manufacturing sector

- Largest three manufacturing sectors (percent of GVIO)
- Fastest-growing three manufacturing sectors (and share of GVIO)
- Top five exports to rest of the country and the world in 2000 and latest year; top five fastest-growing exports
- Largest five firms by turnover
- Top three firms in the three fastest-growing manufacturing subsectors (how does the largest firm in this set compare in size with the leading firm in this subsector?)
- Number of new entrants in these three subsectors in the past five years
- Number of exits from these subsectors in the past five years
- Number of high-impact firms in these subsectors; that is, firms that doubled their output value in five years
- R&D spending by subsectors as a percentage of turnover
- Expenditure on technology licensing in the past five years
- Number of patents applied for; number granted
- FDI in these subsectors over the past five years; national investment in these subsectors; national firms with subsidiaries in city
- Labor force composition of fastest-growing subsectors; increase in employment in three fastest-growing subsectors
- Number of industrial and technology parks and incubators; numbers of firms in parks, change in number since 2005

Firms in selected subsectors (based on firm surveys)

- Proportion of enterprises that conduct R&D activities to total number of enterprises
- Proportion of R&D expense to total sales income
- Proportion of R&D personnel to total staff
- Proportion of enterprises that apply for patents
- Proportion of enterprises that possess patents
- Proportion of enterprises creating new products in the past three years
- Percentage of sales derived from new products

- Proportion of enterprises making any technique improvement in the past three years
- Proportion of enterprises having cooperation with high-level education and research institutes
- Proportion of product export-oriented enterprises
- Enterprises whose proportion of sales of new products or products using new techniques is more than 25 percent of total sales
- Proportion of employees with tertiary- or graduate-level qualifications
- Proportion of staff who received training abroad
- Firm size
- Plant vintage
- Foreign ownership or part of multinational group
- Existence of formal R&D department

Policies and incentives

- Principal industrial policy objectives
- Key policy incentives for achieving these objectives employed since 2000–01
- Results of policy incentives; which were most effective?
- Main problem areas and policy challenges

Notes

1. The stability of the renminbi during this difficult period assisted the recovery of East Asian economies. World merchandise trade rose by almost 7 percent a year, and annual inflows of foreign direct investment increased from US$959 billion in 2005 to US$1.8 trillion in 2007 (UNCTAD 2008; WTO 2008).

2. Helpman (2004, 33) observes, "More than 60 percent of the variation in income per worker is explained by differences in TFP. The role of TFP is even greater in explaining the cross-country differences in the growth rate of income per worker rather than the differences in the level of income per worker. In the former case, differences in TFP account for 90 percent of the variation."

3. The literature on the use of knowledge for economic growth originated with the writings of Fritz Machlup in the early 1960s (Machlup 1973). Machlup's *The Production and Distribution of Knowledge in the United States* launched the idea of the information revolution and the knowledge society. See Lin (2007) for a detailed account of the genesis and elaboration of the knowledge economy concept.

4. The sources of growth in China are estimated, among others, by Badunenko, Henderson, and Zelenyuk (2008); Urel and Zebregs (2009), and Wang and Yao (2003); all of whom find that capital played the leading role. Time-series analysis arrives at similar results. A more recent estimate by Kuijs (2010) pegs the contribution of TFP during 1995–2009 at 2.7 percent and the contribution of capital at 5.5 percent.

5. Although China's exports of manufactures overlap with those of the United States, there are wide differences in quality and technological sophistication (Edwards and Lawrence 2010).

6. With general-purpose technologies, countries can expect growth through innovations to accelerate quickly after a period of gestation. See Helpman (2004).

7. In the United States, 10 large metro regions are responsible for a third of all patents.

8. Two-thirds of the patents in the United States are not assigned to parties from a large metropolitan area.

9. A background empirical study based on micro-level data in 2007 shows that industrial agglomeration has played a significant role in determining the productivity of industrial enterprises in China. The productivity effects of industrial agglomeration, however, differ across regions, scales, and sectors. The coastal region has especially benefited from agglomeration, and there is scope for interior regions to replicate the coastal region's experiences (He and Wang 2010).

10. This involves improving the quality of education and of health services.

11. Universities can play a large part in drawing students from other parts of the country and overseas to a city. After they graduate, some stay, adding to the talent pool and helping to create a critical mass of entrepreneurship and skills. See Berry and Glaeser (2005).

12. Helsley and Strange (2002) make the point that the concentration of an industry facilitates not just the generation of ideas but also their realization.

13. A large literature links industrial productivity to exports and to FDI (with qualifications). A recent study by Istrate, Rothwell, and Katz (2010) points to the contribution of large metropolitan areas to U.S. exports, in particular, exports of manufactures.

14. Kahn (2010) discusses how climate change is likely to drive adjustment, innovation, and a redistribution of the population among cities through the price mechanism.

15. The absence of coordination can lead to the decline of cities and the out-migration of industry. See, for instance, Pugh O'Mara (2002) on the plight of Philadelphia, where the lack of coordination among the 238 local municipalities

in the Greater Philadelphia area has contributed to the industrial decline of the city.

16. Sanyal, Nagrath, and Singla (2010) describe and discuss the limited progress to date by Indian cities.

17. ARM (Advanced RISC Machines) was established in 1990 as a joint venture between Acorn Computers, Apple, and VLSI Technologies. It is the leading producer of microprocessors for mobile telecommunications.

18. However, most of the more than 600 R&D centers established by multinational corporations are in the coastal cities, chiefly Beijing and Shanghai.

References

Acs, Zoltan. 2000. *Regional Innovation, Knowledge, and Global Change.* London: Pinter

Arthur, W. Brian. 2009. *The Nature of Technology: What It Is and How It Evolves.* New York: Free Press.

Badunenko, Oleg, Daniel J. Henderson, and Valentin Zelenyuk. 2008. "Technological Change and Transition: Relative Contributions to Worldwide Growth during the 1990s." *Oxford Bulletin of Economics and Statistics* 70 (4): 461–92.

Berry, Christopher R., and Edward L. Glaeser. 2005. "The Divergence of Human Capital Levels across Cities." Discussion Paper 2091, Harvard Institute of Economic Research, Cambridge, MA, September. http://ssrn.com/abstract= 794551 or doi:10.2139/ssrn.794551.

Bosworth, Barry, and Susan M. Collins. 2007. "Accounting for Growth: Comparing China and India." NBER Working Paper 12943, National Bureau of Economic Research, Cambridge, MA.

Carlino, Gerald A., Satyajit Chatterjee, and Robert M. Hunt. 2007. "Urban Density and the Rate of Invention." *Journal of Urban Economics* 61 (3): 389–419.

Carlino, Gerald A., and Robert M. Hunt. 2009. "What Explains the Quantity and Quality of Local Inventive Activity?" Working Paper 09-12, Federal Reserve Bank of Philadelphia, Philadelphia, PA.

Comin, Diego A., and Bart Hobijn. 2010. "Technology Diffusion and Postwar Growth." NBER Working Paper 16378, National Bureau of Economic Research, Cambridge, MA, September.

Duranton, Gilles, and Diego Puga. 2001. "Nursery Cities: Urban Diversity, Process Innovation, and the Life-Cycle of Products." *American Economic Review* 9 (5): 1454–77.

Edwards, Lawrence, and Robert Z. Lawrence. 2010. "Do Developed and Developing Countries Compete Head to Head in High Tech?" NBER Working Paper 16105, National Bureau of Economic Research, Cambridge, MA.

Frumkin, Howard, Lawrence D. Frank, and Richard Jackson. 2004. *Urban Sprawl and Public Health: Designing, Planning, and Building for Healthy Communities.* Washington, DC: Island Press.

Gill, Indermit S., and Chor-Ching Goh. 2010. "Scale Economies and Cities." *World Bank Research Observer* 25 (2): 235–62.

Glaeser, Edward L., and Joshua D. Gottlieb. 2009. "The Wealth of Cities: Agglomeration Economies and Spatial Equilibrium in the United States." *Journal of Economic Literature* 47 (4): 983–1028.

He, Canfei, and Junsong Wang. 2010. "Spatial Restructuring of Chinese Manufacturing and Productivity Effects of Industrial Agglomeration." World Bank, Washington, DC.

Helpman, Elhanan. 2004. *The Mystery of Economic Growth.* Cambridge, MA: Belknap Press of Harvard University Press.

Helsley, Robert W., and William C. Strange. 2002. "Innovation and Input Sharing." *Journal of Urban Economics* 51 (1): 25–45.

Henderson, J. Vernon. 2010. "Cities and Development." *Journal of Regional Science* 50 (1): 515–40.

Istrate, Emilia, Jonathan Rothwell, and Bruce Katz. 2010. "Export Nation: How U.S. Metros Lead National Export Growth and Boost Competitiveness." Metropolitan Policy Program, Brookings Institution, Washington, DC, July. http://www.brookings.edu/~/media/Files/rc/reports/2010/0726 _exports/0726_exports_istrate_rothwell_katz.pdf.

Jorgenson, Dale W., Mun S. Ho, and Kevin J. Stiroh. 2007. "The Sources of Growth of U.S. Industries." In *Productivity in Asia: Economic Growth and Competitiveness*, ed. Dale W. Jorgenson, Masahiro Kuroda, and Kazuyuki Motohashi, Northampton, MA: Edward Elgar.

Jorgenson, Dale W., and M. Vu Khuong. 2009. "Growth Accounting within the International Comparison Program." *ICP Bulletin* 6 (1): 3–28.

Kahn, Matthew. 2010. *Climatopolis: How Our Cities Will Thrive in the Hotter Future.* New York: Basic Books.

Komninos, Nicos. 2008. *Smart Cities and Globalization of Innovation Networks.* New York: Routledge.

Kuijs, Louis. 2010. "China through 2020: A Macroeconomic Scenario." Working Paper 9, World Bank, Beijing.

Lin, B. C. 2007. "A New Vision of the Knowledge Economy." *Journal of Economic Surveys* 21 (3): 553–84.

Linn, J. F. 2010. "Urban Poverty in Developing Countries: A Scoping Study for Future Research." Wolfensohn Center for Development Working Paper 19, Brookings Institution, Washington, DC.

Machlup, Fritz. 1973. *The Production and Distribution of Knowledge in the United States.* Princeton, NJ: Princeton University Press.

Markusen, Ann, Karen Chapple, Daisaku Yamamoto, Gregory Schorock, and Pingkang Yu. 2004. "Gauging Metropolitan 'High-Tech' and 'I-Tech' Activity." *Economic Development Quarterly* 18 (1): 10–24.

Melo, Patricia C., Daniel J. Graham, and Robert B. Noland. 2009. "A Meta-Analysis of Estimates of Urban Agglomeration Economies." *Regional Science and Urban Economics* 39 (3): 332–42.

Mokyr, Joel. 1999. "Editor's Introduction: The New Economic and the Industrial Revolution." In *The British Industrial Revolution: An Economic Perspective*, 2d ed., ed. Joel Mokyr, 1–127. Oxford: Westview Press.

Pugh O'Mara, Margaret. 2002. "Learning from History: How State and Local Policy Choices Have Shaped Philadelphia's Growth." *Greater Philadelphia Regional Review* (March).

Rosenthal, Stuart S., and William C. Strange. 2004. "Evidence on the Nature and Sources of Agglomeration Economies." In *Handbook of Urban and Regional Economics*, Vol. 4, ed. J. Vernon Henderson and J. F. Thisse, 2119–71. Amsterdam: Elsevier.

Sanyal, Sanjeev, Sumati Nagrath, and Gorika Singla. 2010. "The Alternative Urban Futures Report: Urbanisation and Sustainability in India; An Interdependent Agenda." Report prepared by Mirabilis Advisory, Gurgaon, India, for the World Wildlife Foundation India.

Shanghai Municipality Science and Technology Commission. 2006. "The Innovation System of Shanghai." Presentation made to an Organisation for Economic Co-operation and Development delegation, Shanghai, October 9.

UN Comtrade (United Nations Commodity Trade). Statistics Database. http://comtrade.un.org/db/.

UNCTAD (United Nations Conference on Trade and Development). 2008. "Foreign Direct Investment May Have Peaked in 2007, Annual Report Reveals." Press Release, UNCTAD, Geneva.

Urel, Bulent, and Harm Zebregs. 2009. "The Dynamics of Provincial Growth in China: A Nonparametric Approach." *IMF Staff Papers* 56 (2): 239–62.

Venables, Anthony J. 2010. "Productivity in Cities: Self-Selection and Sorting." Discussion Paper Series 507, Department of Economics, University of Oxford, October.

Villa, Nicola, and Shane Mitchell. 2009. "Connecting Cities: Achieving Sustainability through Innovation." Paper presented at the Fifth Urban Research Symposium 2009, "Connected Urban Development," Cisco Systems, Internet Business Solutions Group.

Wang, Yan, and Yudong Yao. 2003. "Sources of China's Economic Growth, 1952–99: Incorporating Human Capital Accumulation." *China Economic Review* 14 (1): 32–52.

World Bank. 2009. *World Development Report 2009: Reshaping Economic Geography.* Washington, DC: World Bank.

WTO (World Trade Organization). 2008. "Developing, Transition Economies Cushion Trade Slowdown." Press Release, WTO, Geneva.

Yu, Yongding. 2009. "China's Policy Response to the Global Financial Crisis." Richard Snape Lecture, Productivity Commission, Melbourne.

Yusuf, Shahid. 2008. "Can Clusters Be Made to Order?" In *Growing Industrial Clusters in Asia: Serendipity and Science,* ed. Shahid Yusuf, Kaoru Nabeshima, and Shoichi Yamashita. Washington, DC: World Bank.

Yusuf, Shahid, and Kaoru Nabeshima. 2010. *Two Dragon Heads: Contrasting Development Paths for Beijing and Shanghai.* Washington, DC: World Bank.

Zhang, Chunlin, Douglas Zhihua Zeng, William Peter Mako, and James Seward. 2009. *Promoting Enterprise-Led Innovation in China.* Directions in Development. Washington, DC: World Bank.

CHAPTER 6

Globalization, Urban Regions, and Cluster Development

Globalization has resulted in not just a closer integration of economies but also a tightening of the links among major cities. Advances in information and communication technology (ICT) and transport technologies, together with the modernization of urban infrastructure, have further facilitated interaction among cities at many different levels and contributed to the emergence of global urban regions. Cities, like Bangkok, Seoul, and Shanghai, lie at the core of urban regions and benefit from agglomeration economies that arise from specialization and scale of production and from industrial diversity that promotes spillovers and the emergence of new activities. Research suggests that each doubling of city size can raise productivity by between 3 and 14 percent. Urban regions are characterized by a concentration of services, high-tech and creative activities, and nascent industries in the core city, with large-scale manufacturing coalescing in nearby medium-size cities and more specialized cities. This arrangement optimizes the gains from urbanization economies in the core city and localization economies in the hierarchy of medium and small-size cities in the urban region.

A Holistic Approach to Development

Globalization has created new channels for comparing experiences and sharing lessons. At the same time, it has sharpened the competition for final goods and mobile human capital. This competition is multidimensional, and it is forcing cities within urban regions to take a holistic approach to development and to compete on many different fronts—the business climate and the urban infrastructure being just two areas, with others, such as livability and urban amenities, acquiring more significance.

To attract resources and sustain the momentum of development, cities need to demonstrate their ability to enhance growth potential by cultivating several vibrant and preferably interlaced leading subsectors. Growth potential depends also on the age structure of the population, whether it is expanding or not, and the quality of the workforce. Quality, more than volume, of human capital appears to be the most significant determinant of growth. Recent research also suggests that, in view of the importance of entrepreneurship, innovation, adaptation, and invention for technological convergence among countries, the absolute quality of talent and skills might have a strong bearing on economic performance.

Growth potential also depends on how close firms are to technological frontiers. Proximity to the frontier increases returns to research and development (R&D) and the scope for raising productivity through enhanced technological capabilities. In this context, cities signal their potential by their reputation for technological dynamism and openness to ideas.

The Role of Clusters

The growth imparted by leading sectors can be magnified by the formation of specialized clusters of networked firms that compete, cooperate, and deepen markets for labor, give rise to intangible capital, generate technological spillovers, and promote start-up activity.

A symbiotic relationship between manufacturing firms and service providers, as is emerging in the Bangkok, Thailand; Hong Kong SAR/Shenzhen/Guangzhou/Dongguan, China; and Seoul, Republic of Korea urban regions, for example, can lead to an unbundling of activities and greater specialization, to the advantage of both parties. A significant share—close to 37 percent—of the employment generated by the export of manufactures by U.S. companies is in upstream and downstream services. In fact, manufacturing gives rise to employment multipliers of up to five and six that are far larger than the multipliers associated with services.

Clusters generally form around nuclei. Urban centers with a strong development orientation and leadership, such as Beijing and Shenzhen, are attractors, and those with a preexisting industrial base can be a source of skills and intangible assets. These assets, which include scientific and non-scientific R&D, software, worker training, brand equity, product design, and organizational capability, have accounted for 27 percent of the growth in the United States since 1995. Major research-oriented firms or multinational corporations can provide a nucleus as well, and there are plenty of examples from Cambridge (United Kingdom), Medicon Valley, San Diego, Silicon Valley, and elsewhere of firms such as CCL and Acorn, Hewlett Packard, Hybritech, and Novo Nordisk spawning scores of daughter enterprises and helping to scale up the activities of a cluster. Multinational corporations and local firms are also giving rise to spinoffs and new start-up firms in Beijing, Seoul, Shenzhen-Guangzhou, and Taipei-Hsinchu.

To thrive and grow, clusters require anchors. The size and affluence of the urban market (as in Seoul, Shanghai, and Tokyo) is one of the most important, but there are other anchors of consequence as well. Research universities have an increasing role if they can supply high-quality skills, contribute to network formation—local and global—and enrich the local knowledge economy by way of tacit knowledge, workshops, patenting, publications, trouble shooting, and the dialogue on technology. Vocational training institutions, physical and social infrastructure, affordable housing, and recreational facilities are among some of the other anchors. How a city goes about developing these anchors determines its overall competitiveness in the global economy.

Competitive clusters must be capable of upgrading, diversifying, and incubating new industries. Silicon Valley, for example, has served as a breeding ground for several kinds of clusters, and both Beijing and Shanghai are attempting to develop multiple high-tech activities. A dynamic cluster has several attributes. It has an entrepreneurial culture that leverages the resources of universities and firms; it benefits from the local presence of "angel" investors and venture capitalists who support and mentor local activities; it combines the advantages of specialization in key fields with an openness to new ideas; it has the capacity to learn from mistakes and to unlearn; and it has a "buzz" in national and global circles.

History shows that many clusters formed accidentally because of a decision to locate an important facility (such as the National Aeronautics and Space Administration center in Houston, Texas), a university, or a firm that emerged as a major player in the industry (for example, Dell in Austin, Texas, and, perhaps, Huawei in Shenzhen). History further shows that these chance events might have foundered were it not for supporting initiatives taken by urban leaders and national governments.

Policies to Support Clusters

The supporting policies can take many forms. Strategic foresight exercises can assist governments in mapping out a long-term cluster development strategy and providing the stable long-term financing for R&D that research-intensive activities frequently require (for example, the backing by the National Institutes of Health has been critical to the success of biopharmaceutical research in the United States and the training of a legion of researchers). Complementing these are policies to ensure the supply of quality skills.

For cities, policies that attract industry—domestic and foreign—need to be supplemented by policies that secure the city finances and ensure that services and housing meet the expectations of industries that are aware of and compare opportunities in other cities throughout the world. But providing services and infrastructure is not enough: cities must also market themselves aggressively by organizing events and seeking out business nationally and internationally. Such marketing is the most reliable way of infusing capital and ideas into existing clusters and sowing the seeds of new clusters.

Governments seek to stimulate the geographic dimension of innovation and industrial clustering by promoting technopoles, high-tech parks, bio-parks, and industry parks and by encouraging venture capital and financial services to be located in the vicinity of such parks. This is in line with the knowledge spillovers that Marshall ([1890] 1920) first envisaged.[1] Firms and areas in close proximity to vibrant areas will benefit and learn from each other, leading to increasing returns and further agglomeration. Knowledge is transferred through interpersonal contacts and interfirm mobility of workers. Knowledge and innovation tend to spill over locally first and to diffuse geographically over time. The pace and extent of this reaction-diffusion varies geographically and depends on the stage of industry life cycle and the importance of tacit knowledge. Closer proximity of firms, which helps to lower transaction and transport costs, also contributes to this process of diffusion.

Sustaining Clusters

Learning and knowledge transfer occur through networking—social and economic—such as user-producer relationships, user associations, mobility of workers, spinoffs of new firms from larger, old firms, local libraries and information centers in the area, and so on. The ability of local firms to tap into such tacit knowledge depends on the existence of social links and open lines of communication in the area. In general, it is the creative atmosphere in the locality that contributes the most. New clusters are formed when a pool of skilled labor and university-trained human capital is available. In this context, there is an important role of diaspora, where returning human capital comes back, bringing some savings for risk taking and investment in new firms.

For well-established clusters to continue to thrive, it is necessary to have an external link or source of knowledge and learning. Therefore, links to regional innovation systems or some new source of knowledge are necessary for the local area to upgrade itself. Localization and globalization coexist in high-tech clusters. Over longer distances, collaboration between the Silicon Valley and Chinese provincial governments and universities would benefit China. The Indian Institutes of Technologies benefited from their cooperation with U.S. firms and clusters. For newly formed clusters, the local areas need more intense places of interaction in the local area, and external links are less important for a while. How do multinational corporations that locate within a local cluster respond to such localization? Multinationals are no longer the key vehicle for ICT development and diffusion. Instead, managers and skilled human capital are the main actors in this process. Therefore, free mobility of these carriers of tacit knowledge is needed to sustain a cluster.

Starting a cluster is entirely different from sustaining a cluster. Starting a cluster requires managerial skills, technical specialists, and access to technology and market opportunities. Empirical evidence indicates that governments should help to support specific new firms (say, specific tech firms) through industrial policy rather than invest large amounts in starting an industrial cluster.

As entrepreneurs in emerging markets take the lead in research and innovation, there is increased recognition of their impact on global business structures. Previously, companies set up manufacturing units in Asia mainly for their cheap labor, while keeping the managerial functions in the West. However, in keeping with rising incomes and consumption in the emerging markets, the supply chains are now being altered. To understand these changes, there is a need to understand the reasons why some regions and countries are becoming the new innovation hubs, while other regions and countries are being left out. Initial research in developing countries indicates that the following factors are important for innovation clusters:

- *Urbanization.* The rapid concentration of population in metropolitan cities reveals an increasing scope of opportunities that are attracting the young and educated to these hubs.
- *Educational improvement.* A more educated working population attracts jobs requiring higher skills, including research and development skills. Thus, better education at the higher secondary and university levels will have a great influence on the level of innovation.
- *Business growth.* A growing business sector indicates greater market interactions and, therefore, greater potential for innovation.
- *Macroeconomic factors.* A stable and growing economy is necessary for innovative practices. Thus, indicators like gross domestic product and value added by a sector are important yardsticks for measuring the health of the economy in general.
- *Infrastructure improvement.* A lack of infrastructural support would be an impediment to any business, including an entrepreneurial undertaking. Therefore, basic facilities like electricity, roads, transportation, and Internet access are necessary factors for innovative businesses, especially start-ups.

A review of 24 cities for which data are available indicates a positive correlation between agglomeration economies, population, and other indicators. For example, the percentage of urban population is positively correlated with the other indicators (figure 6.1).

Conclusion

Innovation clusters are important for economic development, locally, nationally, and internationally. Yet, too few exist. Mills, Reynolds, and Reamer (2008, 6) lament the "thin and uneven (presence of clusters) in levels of geographic and industry coverage, level and consistency of effort, and organizational capacity." Furthermore, traditional clusters—for example, the automobile cluster in the Midwest—are under tremendous economic stress,[2] which includes the individual worker, the supply chain, and the host community.

Two key elements for successful innovation clusters are place and access to finance. Feldman (2009) notes that competitive advantage may be inherent to a certain locale. Seed and early-stage financing

Figure 6.1   Ranking of Metropolitan Cities

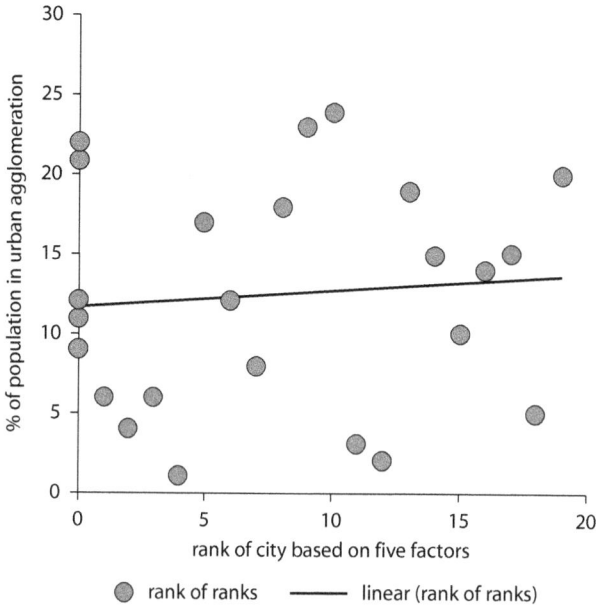

Source: Authors based on data from the World Bank and Brookings Institution.

capital is critical in order for innovative firms to be able to realize their ideas from inception through to market and commercialization. Policy makers can help.

For example, the Obama administration has put forth an initiative describing a national innovation policy for the United States. Sallet, Paisley, and Masterman (2009) examine the innovation environment in the United States in which this national policy would operate.

1. In regions around the country, clusters of universities and high-tech companies partner with local and regional governments to boost tech-based economic growth and create jobs. The two best examples are Silicon Valley for computer technology and the Boston corridor for biotech development.

2. Job creation and business creation, the main economic benefits coming from innovative clusters, mostly spring from so-called "high-impact" companies (high-tech start-ups and established companies alike) that sell goods and services outside their clusters to both national and international markets, drawing revenue back into the cluster (Acs, Parsons,

and Tracy 2008). These "traded" services boost regional economic growth and national economic competitiveness. As measured by patent rates, productivity rates, and other innovation metrics, an innovation cluster creates new companies and new jobs in a helter-skelter but overall positive direction.

3. The federal government provides large sums of funding for basic scientific research and boasts a variety of programs to help companies and state and local governments to prepare executives and workers for employment at young, innovative companies seeking to commercialize this research.

4. The national innovation policy under consideration by the federal government would link clusters with R&D firms and academic institutions, companies, and local and regional policy makers. The United States devotes 1 percent of the nation's basic R&D budget to programs that support regional clusters, while Europe and China invest more.

Notes

1. "Marshall ([1890] 1920) suggests that locations thick with similar activity generate valuable agglomeration economies for firms—namely, better access to skill labor (labor market pooling), specialized suppliers (shared inputs), and knowledge spillovers from competing firms" (Alcácer and Chung 2010, 1).

2. Automobile parts manufacturers told the Treasury Department early in 2009 that 130,000 jobs had been lost in 18 months (*Economist* 2009).

References

Acs, Zoltan J., William Parsons, and Spencer Tracy. 2008. "High-Impact Firms: Gazelles Revisited." Study for the Office of Advocacy, U.S. Small Business Administration. http://www.sba.gov/advo/research/rs328tot.pdf.

Alcácer, Juan, and Wilbur Chung. 2010. "Location Strategies for Agglomeration Economies." Harvard Business School Working Paper 10-071, Harvard University, Cambridge, MA.

Economist. 2009. "The American Car Industry." *The Economist*, February 19. http://www.economist.com/business/displaystory.cfm?story_id=13145718.

Feldman, Maryann. 2009. "Place Matters: Innovation Springs from Many Seeds, But Soil Is Equally Important." Science Progress, Center for American Progress, Washington, DC, January.

Marshall, Alfred. [1890] 1920. *Principles of Economics: An Introductory Volume*, 8th ed. London: Macmillan.

Mills, Karen G., Elisabeth Reynolds, and Andrew Reamer. 2008. "Clusters and Competitiveness: A New Federal Role for Stimulating Regional Economies." Policy Brief, Brookings Institution, Washington, DC. http://www.brookings .edu/reports/2008/04_competitiveness_mills.aspx.

Sallet, Jonathan, Ed Paisley, and Justin R. Masterman. 2009. "Geography of Innovation: The Federal Government and the Growth of Regional Innovation Clusters." Science Progress, Washington, DC, September 1.

CHAPTER 7

Urban Development and Growth

The world's population crossed the 7 billion people mark in 2011, more than half of whom now make their home in a city.[1] Each week, the ranks of urban residents are growing by 1 million, and on every single day some 20,000 new dwellings and 160 miles of road are added to the existing stock. China alone constructs 2 billion square miles of floor space each year, which is approximately half of the global total. By the middle of the century, demographers project a population of close to 9 billion, barring unexpected changes in fertility trends and unforeseen calamities;[2] an estimated 70 percent of this vast number will rub shoulders in cities. More people and more cities are an inescapable part of the future, and if urban densities continue declining at about 2 percent a year, as they have through much of the twentieth century, the built-up area will expand at a far faster rate than the urban population. By one estimate, the urban population in developing countries could double by 2030, whereas the built-up area encompassed by cities would triple. Clearly, we and future generations are in for exciting times.

The authors are greatly indebted to Lopamudra Chakraborti for assistance with the research for this chapter.

The importance of cities predates the industrial revolution. Ancient civilizations arose in urban settings, starting with the earliest cities germinating in the marshy areas beyond Baghdad.[3] Greek civilization would be a desert if it were emptied of Athens, Corinth, Sparta, Thebes, and other cities. The Roman Empire was a "world of cities," with Rome and later Constantinople as its political, administrative, and cultural axes.[4] Islamic civilization, the Renaissance, the glory of China under the Sung and Ming dynasties, the remarkable architectural achievements of the Mughals, and the later rise of capitalism are all inextricably linked to cities.[5] Abstract from the urban context, drain out the technological, intellectual, political, economic, and artistic achievements that flowered in cities, and most of the richness of history simply melts away. The industrial revolution gave cities added prominence by enormously enlarging their economic significance. Agriculture and rural industry, long the economic heartland of nations, was displaced in a matter of decades by the concentration of economic power in cities, which were quick to exploit the potential of steam and the technologies that transformed the textile, metallurgic, machine building, chemical, and other industries starting in the mid-nineteenth century. European countries that embraced industrialization experienced rapid urbanization and the transfer of the economic center from the rural to the urban sector. Henceforth, national wealth was increasingly derived from manufacturing industry powered by fossil fuels. In nations where modern industry was slow to gain traction or did not take root at all, urban development was much feebler. With the widening use of steam power, cities became even more attractive because the factory-based manufacturing industry needed pools of labor (especially female workers),[6] markets to absorb increased output (local, national, and international), and supporting infrastructure and services. Cities could provide all of these relatively efficiently and cheaply, and they simplified the logistics of input supplies, reduced the cost of intermediate goods, and facilitated the distribution of products to other markets.

Until well into the 1960s, the growth and dynamism of cities in Western countries and Japan were paced by manufacturing activities.[7] Thereafter, the role of industry as the leading sector was displaced by services, and the character of urbanization began inexorably to change. From the late 1950s onward, many more countries, many of which had recently gained independence, began pursuing development along Western lines by emphasizing industrialization. Assisted by tariff protection and other government-provided incentives,[8] manufacturing industries, frequently state owned, were established in the primary cities, with the capital city, the seat of administrative authority, being the preferred location. This led to the emergence of new business and professional classes that quickly allied themselves with administrative and military elites controlling the state and responsible for making policy and distributing rents. Thus began the concentration of wealth and power[9] in the primary urban centers of developing nations, mimicking to some degree similar trends in the industrial countries, with an important difference: urbanization took off in the developing world without industry providing the main impetus in many cities. The research since the 1960s shows that urbanization is closely correlated with industrialization, but industry does not cause urbanization (Henderson 2010), as it arguably did between 1850 and 1960 in Western countries. What then explains the surge since 1950 that has carried the urbanization rate from less than 30 percent to more than half of the global population in 2010?

Urbanization: From Canter to Gallop

Five factors account for accelerating urbanization, and its structural characteristics and their persistence determine its dynamics, challenges, and policy implications, which will be discussed in the balance of this chapter.

First, the demographic transition—a sharp decline in infant mortality and increasing life expectancy, followed by a much more gradual reduction in fertility—has resulted in a ballooning of populations in developing nations. The natural increase has caused cities to grow and led to in situ urbanization—small towns and villages have mushroomed into cities in Brazil, China (Zhu et al. 2009), and Pakistan, for example. Brazil, in particular, achieved European rates of urbanization by 2000.[10] Greater rural population densities have pushed people to migrate, and the "urban advantage" (a point emphasized by UN-HABITAT 2010) and income gradients have exerted a parallel pull.[11] With population pressures rising, cities are seen as beacons of opportunity that are disappearing in rural areas. And urbanization has been correlated with rising living standards, although inevitably the transfer of populations has led to rising rates of poverty (Ravallion, Chen, and Sangraula 2007). Those living on less than US$1 a day in urban areas rose from 19 to 24 percent between 1993 and 2002; over the same period, the urban share of the population as a whole rose from 38 to 42 percent. The urbanization of poverty was most rapid in Latin America, with the proportion of the poor living in urban areas rising from 50 to 60 percent between 1993 and 2002. By contrast, less than 10 percent of East Asia's poor live in urban areas, largely because absolute poverty in China is overwhelmingly rural.

Second, agricultural production is becoming less labor intensive, with machinery, chemicals, and energy serving as substitutes.[12] Fewer hands are needed on farms, and if the highly productive agricultural systems in advanced economies are a mirror of what developing economies can expect, the share of the agricultural labor force in low- and middle-income countries will drop below 10 percent of the national total from the average of about 25 percent in 2007. Furthermore, dispersed small-scale rural industry, inefficient and polluting as it is,[13] fights a losing battle against urban producers, which enjoy manifold advantages compounded by declining costs of surface transport and increasing efficiencies in distribution and marketing technologies.

Third, technological advances and the evolving income elasticity of demand are responsible for structural changes that have enlarged the role of services. A stream of innovations has raised the productivity of manufacturing,[14] contributing to growth, but also to a decline in relative prices of manufactures and employment in industry (table 7.1 shows the fall in the share of manufacturing between 1980 and 2008). Thus, the share of manufacturing in gross domestic product (GDP) is a shrinking proportion of the output in larger cities, although it remains high in smaller cities with industrial specializations. Meanwhile, rising demand for urban services and much slower gains in productivity have increased the share of urban services in GDP and employment. With the exception of China, services now dominate GDP everywhere,[15] and in most cities in advanced countries, services provide the majority of jobs and generate more than half of the income. In fact, with industry pushed to the margins of some urban economies, services are the economy. A fraction of services are tradable, but most urban services in developing countries are nontradable, and services constitute a small share of the exports of low- and middle-income countries, tourism being the largest.[16] This has

Table 7.1 Contribution of Manufacturing and Services to GDP, 1980–2008

	Manufacturing value added (% of GDP)		Services value added (% of GDP)	
	1980	2008	1980	2008
World	25	17	56	70
Middle income	26	21	41	54
Low income	12	13	42	49

Source: World Bank 2011a.

long-term implications for the number and type of jobs that the urban economy is likely to create, for growth, and for exports to balance the city's trade accounts. To be viable over the longer term, cities—much like countries—must have something to sell, with any shortfall being offset through capital transfers. Until a few decades ago, all growing cities were industrial cities with export potential. This has ceased to be the rule with the rise of formal and informal services,[17] which suspends the question over the future of urban centers that depend on transfers for their survival.

Fourth, cities enable firms to specialize and realize scale advantages. These so-called localization economies are an important asset for mid-size industrial cities and a source of productivity gains from labor markets, technological spillovers, and the benefits of clustering (proximity to other producers and suppliers of services). For larger urban centers, urbanization economies are more prominent. These are the economies arising from the multiplicity of industry and services that open the door to diversification and induce the entry of new firms. Together, these lead to significant productivity gains and higher average incomes (see figure 7.1 on the relationship between city size, industrial composition, city clustering, and incomes in China). Currid (2007, 460) notes, "Agglomeration may be even more important to maintaining the social mechanisms by which the cultural economy sustains itself [through nonmarket transactions]." A vast literature, mostly on cities in developed countries, has attempted to estimate the gains from agglomeration, whether from localization or urbanization or scale economies.[18] Researchers differ on which gains matter more, but all agree that agglomeration pays, although how much productivity can be traced to size and diversity varies from 3 to 12 percent.[19] A meta-analysis of elasticities drawn from 34 studies cautions that the gains from largeness should not be exaggerated (see Melo, Graham, and Noland 2009), but there is little or no evidence indicating that growth is disadvantageous for cities. Nevertheless, casual empiricism suggests that, as cities grow larger and become more complex, management and services provision become increasingly more challenging, and congestion, pollution, and crime diminish the quality of life, as, for instance, in Bangalore and many booming cities in China's Pearl River Delta. Whether these collectively erode the productivity-enhancing advantages of size has been difficult to establish, and the debate on the merits of largeness continues.[20] This point is examined further below.

The fifth and final factor contributing to the vigor of urbanization is the role of cities in sparking ideas, stimulating social change by inculcating

Figure 7.1 Strong Correlates of Urban Productivity (City GDP per Capita) in China, 2007

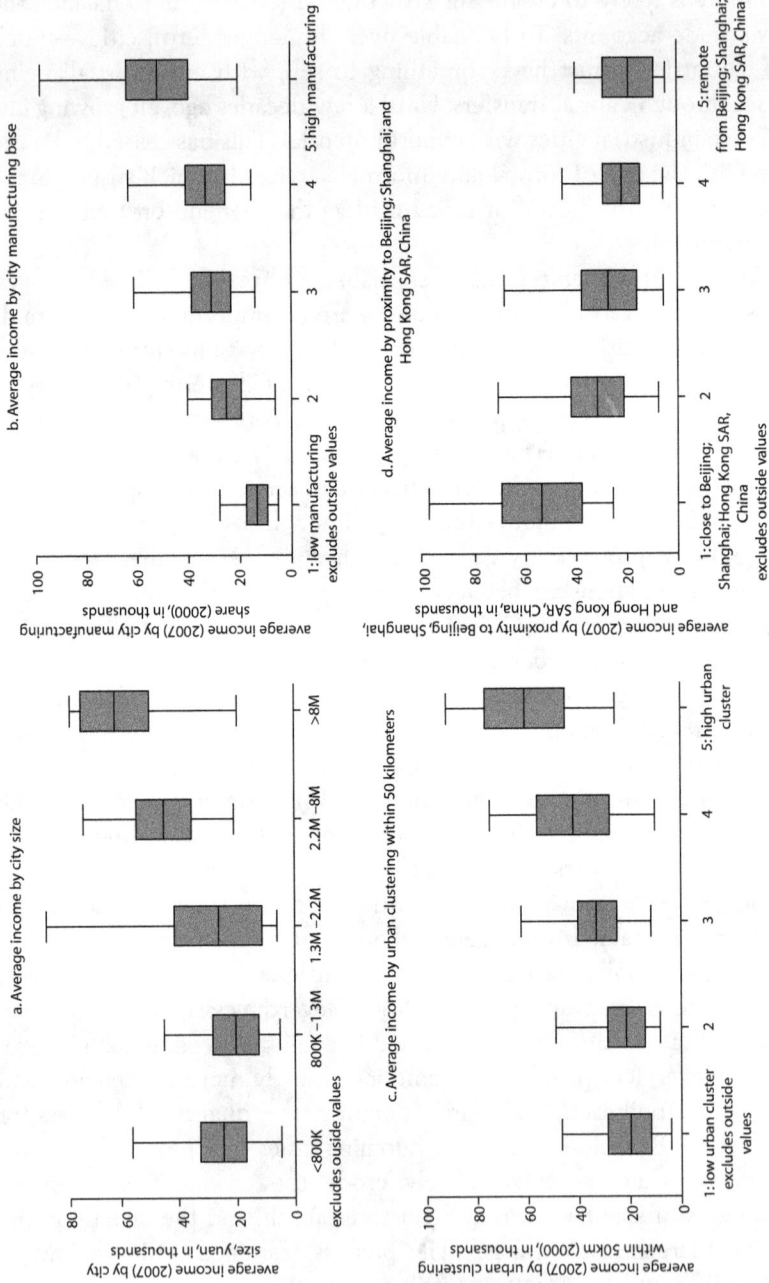

a. Average income by city size

b. Average income by city manufacturing base

c. Average income by urban clustering within 50 kilometers

d. Average income by proximity to Beijing; Shanghai; and Hong Kong SAR, China

Source: Lall and Wang 2011.

Note: Average city income is measured by GDP per capita.

142

new values, and encouraging innovation in every sphere of life. Steven Johnson (2010, 16, 162) compares cities in all their variegated complexity to coral reefs "powerfully suited to the creation, diffusion, and adoption of good ideas. ... They cultivate specialized skills and interests, and they create a liquid network where information can leak out of those subcultures and influence their neighbors in surprising ways. This is one reason for superlinear scaling in urban creativity."[21] Such innovation has buoyed productivity; equally, it has enhanced human capabilities and raised the quality of life. As cities in developing countries attempt to come to grips with increasing size, complexity, and the pressures arising from climate change, the innovative potential of cities will become ever more important and the basis not just of survival but also of prosperity.

While continued urbanization appears to be a given, urban development is likely to evolve in different directions, with implications for growth and the quality of life. From the perspective of this book, the interesting issues pertain to the potential of the metropolitan model of urban development and how creatively metropolitan centers address the challenges coming from many directions.

The Metropolitan Powerhouse

Megacities with populations of 10 million and more have increased in number from 9 in 1985 to 23 in 2010 and account for almost half of the world's wealth.[22] Moreover, some of the megacities in East Asia account for a third or more of national GDP. A striking characteristic of the urbanizing tendencies in East Asia, Latin America, and the United States is the emergence of metropolitan regions composed of a cluster of cities that may or may not include a megacity. Bangkok, Jakarta, and Seoul are examples of metropolitan economies in which the core primary city has brought (or created) dormitory, secondary, and edge cities into its orbit. Guangzhou and Hong Kong SAR, China, encompass another vast metropolitan region that arose with great rapidity once China adopted the Open Door Policy in 1979, and industry began transferring from Hong Kong SAR, China, to the Pearl River Delta.[23] The Washington, DC, metro region and others in the United States and in Europe are examples of networked city flotillas. For many reasons, urbanization might take the form of the metro region in the future, with isolated cities becoming endangered species.[24]

It is a commonplace that urban development flourishes in certain geographic locations. In the United States, more than half of the population live within 50 kilometers of a coastline, and mild climates attract people.[25]

A prosperous hinterland, space for a city to expand, and adequate supplies of water are other geographic considerations.[26] Some of the world's
largest cities have been established at strategic points on riverine plains
and close to river deltas, locations that facilitate the transport of goods.
Most of the choice spots are taken, and because the availability of fresh-
water and climatic considerations may bulk larger, urbanization will most
likely concentrate around the most promising existing centers, although
rising sea levels will imperil several low-lying coastal regions and cities
and some of the 360 million people who currently live in these areas
(figures 7.2 and 7.3 show the countries in East Asia with the most vulnerable populations; China is in the forefront, followed by Indonesia). The
need to economize on energy use and on the cost of providing urban
infrastructure makes the metropolitan model, with its compact design, a
more viable proposition than a relatively isolated city (Glaeser 2011).
The metropolis can also internalize urbanization and localization economies by combining a portfolio of cities in a single urban domain. The core
city with diverse services and the advanced emerging industries that

Figure 7.2   Exposure of People to Cyclones and Earthquakes, 2000 and by 2050

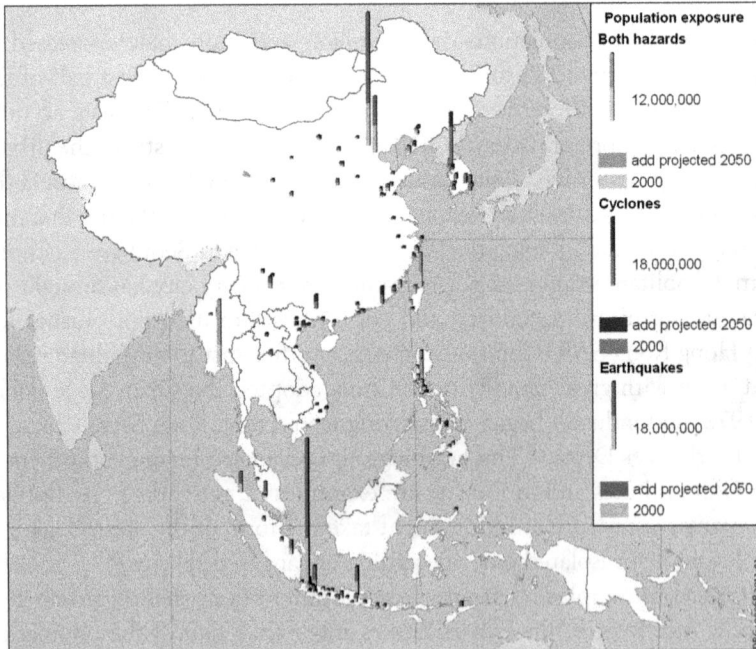

Source: Jha and Brecht 2011 (adapted from *National Disaster, UnNatural Disasters: The Economics of Effective Prevention,* World Bank and United Nations, 2010).

Figure 7.3   Coastal Population of Selected Countries That Are Highly Vulnerable to Sea Level Rise

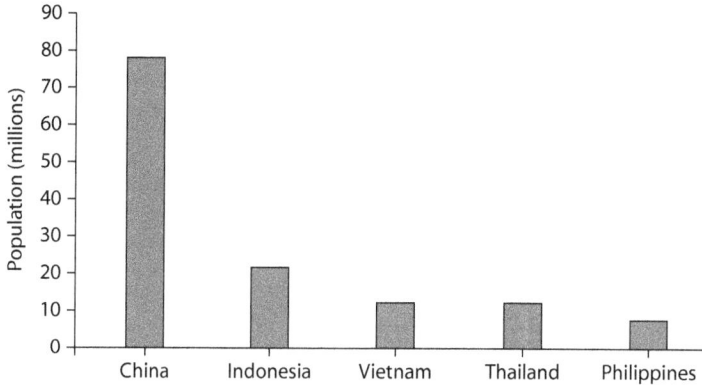

Source: Jha and Brecht 2011, adapted from Prasad et al. 2009.

draw oxygen from proximity to centers of research can be the primary source of urbanization or Jacobs economies, while smaller peripheral specialized cities can serve as sites for industrial activities requiring cheaper land for factories and cheaper accommodations for workers. By yoking these different kinds of cities together with an efficient multi-modal transport system, the metropolitan region can maximize the gains from agglomeration and market size economies. By expanding in the vertical plane, it can also squeeze a lot more people into a place with proven locational advantages and capitalize on an existing foundational infrastructure and possibly a brand name.

A broad economic base and a large urban market make it easier for a metropolitan region to meet its financing needs and minimize fluctuations in revenue streams, while keeping tax rates at moderate and competitive levels. Revenue adequacy underwrites industrial capabilities and provides the means for a city to adapt to changing circumstances, calling for the displacement of older industries by newer ones and the renewal of infrastructure and buildings so as to incorporate the latest technologies (such as information and communication technologies and green technologies enabling buildings to use less water and energy) and accommodate changing lifestyles.[27]

"Green technologies" is a loose term currently embracing a range of technologies aimed at conserving nonrenewable resources, controlling and minimizing waste, and squeezing greater productivity out of available resources through new technological fixes. Green technologies come in many flavors, such as materials that reduce the weight and facilitate the recycling of auto bodies and parts; technologies that substitute nontoxic for toxic materials and cut down waste; sensor technologies that help to smooth traffic flows, provide early warning of impending infrastructure breakdowns or disasters, improve land productivity by monitoring soil moisture content, and detect toxic pollutants; software that helps to manage smart grids and energy use throughout the economic system and software that simplifies equipment and cuts capital costs, for example, of diagnostic and measuring devices; and design innovations that lessen energy and water consumption in cities and buildings or allow for efficient disposal, salvage, recycling, and longevity of products (Tomlinson 2010). The list goes on and includes manufacturing technologies that are energy frugal and reduce waste, technologies for the construction and food-processing industries—both vast consumers of resources—and new technologies for the information technology industry itself, a major user of energy (for production and use of products) and rare metals and a generator of toxic waste (see Fiksel 2009). Several of these technologies—in particular, those associated with transport, energy generation, food production and processing, and construction and maintenance of infrastructure—give rise to dense links with manufacturing and services activities. Replacing the global stock of automobiles and internal combustion engines with hybrid and electric vehicles with smaller direct carbon signatures has enormous implications for industry. So does the building of equipment for urban public transport. The three biggest sources of greenhouse gases (excluding humans, rice cultivation, and cattle) are power plants, transport equipment, and buildings. If the vast majority needs to be replaced to minimize climate change and "green" becomes the order of the day, manufacturing industry will have to take on a challenge. And once green is "it," every other activity will be affected, requiring redesign, software retooling, and change in the structure of industry.

No metropolitan region ever optimizes on all of these fronts, and when there are many adjacent municipal jurisdictions, coordinating infrastructure development, embarking on revenue-raising arrangements, and sharing financial burdens can be severely challenging. By failing to arrive at coherent and mutually advantageous outcomes through negotiated give-and-take, multijurisdictional metropolitan entities are squandering the economic and financial benefits of agglomeration.

Metropolitan Challenges

Too many cities in advanced and developing countries are failing to exploit the urban advantage and are struggling to cope with the growth of populations and the associated crowding, pollution, traffic, shortages of housing and services, increasing poverty and inequality, spread of slums, and environmental degradation.[28] Very few cities in developing countries are able to generate enough jobs for the growing workforce, and unemployment is endemic. Where economic performance falls short of potential or where revenue effort is weak, urban services suffer, which affects business activity and quality of life, especially of the poor. Most cities have barely begun to come to grips with the physical and institutional changes required to contain greenhouse gas (GHG) emissions[29] and to engineer the resilience demanded by the threat of climatic extremes.[30] If a doubling of urban populations and an increase in average temperatures by 2° or more are inevitable by mid-century, then delay is becoming increasingly costly.[31]

For cities in most developing countries, certain inescapable facts demand an adequate response—if not immediately, then definitely in the not too distant future—if cities are to reap the urban advantages and sustain their long-term viability. Demographic trends and a youth bulge, most notably in the Middle East and South Asia, will necessitate employment-augmenting policies to maintain adequate growth in incomes and social stability.[32] For an expanding global economy, energy and resource scarcities will be mounting concerns requiring a change in urban design, in modes of transport, and in soft and hard infrastructure. And climate change will expose cities to pressures and shocks rarely experienced before. Few cities will be spared, and many coastal and semiarid locations may only remain habitable through major injections of capital.[33]

It is possible for metropolitan centers to thrive and for even the most vulnerable to avoid being plunged into vicious spirals leading to steadily worsening conditions. Inevitably, there is no infallible recipe, no sufficient conditions to assure success. However, the collective experience of scores of urban centers, many of which have embarked on innovative policies and introduced new technologies, provides reliable guidelines on how to create a dynamic metropolitan region that would provide most inhabitants with jobs and a decent life.

Wealth of Cities and National Policies

If cities are truly the drivers of economic growth, how closely is that performance keyed to the national policy and overall national economic conditions? In other words, can cities forge ahead by dint of good urban policies more or less independently of what is happening at the national level? Singapore surely fits this description, being a city-state, but other cities, even the largest and most prosperous such as Bangkok, São Paulo, Seoul, Shanghai, Tokyo, and the complex of Guangzhou and Hong Kong SAR, China, depend on the enabling matrix of national trade, investment (domestic and foreign),[34] fiscal, education, and other policies to provide the springboard for their own development. Even though decentralization and localization have transferred more administrative and fiscal discretion and policy initiative to subnational governments, and even though cities are at the leading edge of development, fundamental national policies define policy parameters, incentives, and the degrees of freedom available to city managers and determine the fiscal and financial resources they can mobilize. The industrialization of Seoul and Shanghai was enabled by planning, day-to-day decision making conducted by city authorities, and a host of local regulations, rules, standards, and licensing requirements, but the opportunities for the cities were delineated and circumscribed by exchange rate, trade, industrial, labor, education, and technology policies of the central government. Both cities successfully groomed highly competitive export industries that generated economic momentum and employment and catalyzed the development of other sectors of the urban economy. Seoul took a lead in establishing a world-class infrastructure to harness the potential of information and communication technologies (ICTs), with Shanghai now close behind. These measures initiated the process of modernization and integration with the global economy, and the end result as of now are two metropolitan economies that rank among the world's most vibrant. However, in both instances—and these examples can be multiplied—urban outcomes were prompted and shaped by national policies. The government of the Republic of Korea, once it had embraced export-oriented industrialization, viewed Seoul as the engine room of the economy,[35] and urban development complemented other policies—more recently, policies to develop an ICT-supported knowledge economy. The industrialization of the Seoul metro region propelled the Korean economy during the high-growth era starting in the mid-1960s and continues to do so as Korea enters a postindustrial stage. Seoul not only has served as the seat of government and the nation's cultural hub, but also is home to several of Korea's leading export industries, including textiles, machinery, electronics, and now the creative industries.[36] Once China set its sights on reform and catching up with the leading East Asian economies and designated Shanghai as one of the principal Dragonheads,[37] the city authorities had the green light to pursue an ambitious urban industrial

strategy that was amply supported by resources from the central government and supplemented by foreign direct investment (FDI) induced
through central policies reinforced by municipal incentives. Shanghai's
development since the early 1990s is the stuff of legend, and it owes
much to the vision and energy of a succession of local officials,[38] but it
was the central government that loosened the corsets binding Shanghai,
encouraged the local authorities to raise their sights, and created the
policy environment that allowed the city to harness its vast latent capabilities and bid for resources from elsewhere in China and from abroad.

It is the central government that sets the stage and to a greater or lesser
extent choreographs, through policies and other interventions, urban
development in positive as well as negative directions. Where central
governments are missing in action, passive, obstructive, or predatory,
urbanization may continue, as it has in Sub-Saharan Africa and in South
Asia, but the urban development that results in growth, exports, and jobs
may be slow to materialize, if it surfaces at all. Some cities in Africa, such
as Dar es Salaam and Kinshasa, have become more populous over the
past decade, but not because of development. Urbanization in Zimbabwe
and the Democratic Republic of Congo is the direct outcome of conflict
and worsening conditions in rural areas. Development has gone into
reverse because the states have faltered or are failing (see World Bank
2011b). Thus, the policy making and administrative capabilities of the
state and its urban strategy broadly define the opportunities for urban
development. Some cities, especially capitals, are favored over others, and
they have a head start; however, it is up to the municipal authorities and
other stakeholders to derive maximum benefits from the urban assets at
their disposal, to enhance competitive advantage in profitable directions,
to augment the local resource base, and to encourage investment that can
maximize long-run growth.

Notes

1. Annual births average 140 million, and deaths average 57 million, leading to
   a net population gain of 83 million each year.
2. The most recent projections point to 9.3 billion people by 2050 (UN 2011).
   According to John Bongaarts (2011), the margin of error for 2050 estimates
   could be plus or minus 1 billion.
3. An aerial remote-sensing investigation conducted by Jennifer Pournelle, a
   student of Robert McCormick Adams, suggests that settlements were constructed on small ridges in marshy areas called "turtlebacks" (Pournelle 2007,

35), and these eventually grew into cities such as Eridu and Uruk—the birth-place of writing; Vanderbilt (2011a); McCormick Adams (1966).

4. The speeches of Greek and Roman orators are laced with praise for their cities, and such praise was often modeled on praise of individuals. The rec-ognition accorded to the fallen hoplites in Pericles's "Funeral Oration" is "subsumed into an account of the moral and political virtues of the city of Athens" (Grafton, Most, and Settis 2010, 202). Price and Thoneman (2010) observe that there were more than 300 cities in the Asian part of the Roman Empire alone and that the empire in its entirety contained several thousand cities.

5. Bosker, Buringh, and van Zanden (2008) attribute the cultural and commer-cial retreat of Arab cities from the heights they had scaled through the twelfth century and their lagging performance thereafter relative to European cities to the autonomy and "producer" orientation of the European urban centers in northern Italy, for example, and the grip of predatory states on the Arab and Islamic cities, which became oriented toward "consumption."

6. Kim (2005). Immigration to the United States contributed to the growth of the cities and supplied the workforce for industrialization.

7. The share of manufacturing production in the United States peaked in 1979. However, cities such as New York and Philadelphia had entered the spiral of deindustrialization in the 1950s. New York's garment industry, which invented ready-to-wear clothing, gave birth to the Singer sewing machine and accounted for 70 percent of all women's clothing and 40 percent of mens-wear in the United States in 1910, was battered by the rise of low-cost pro-ducers in East Asia and by the revolution in telecommunications and in transport. The fact that it survives at all is because some products governed by tight schedules require close face-to-face coordination among suppliers, service providers, designers, and those who actually sew the various parts of a garment (Vanderbilt 2011b).

8. Most countries adopted the strategy of import-substituting industrialization.

9. In some countries, land reform accelerated the transfer of power by disman-tling feudal systems of privilege, wealth, and political control, for example, in the Republic of Korea. In others, such as Pakistan, the political sway and social influence of the landowning class has eroded much more slowly.

10. Brazil's urban population rose from 36 percent in 1950 to 77 percent in 1990.

11. This is the so-called Harris-Todaro effect of higher urban incomes. See Fields (2007).

12. See Smil (2008, 2011) on the energy (and nitrogen fertilizer) intensity of modern agriculture.

13. Township and village enterprises blossomed in China with the spread of agricultural reforms in the early 1980s. By 1996, they accounted for 26 percent of China's GDP and employed 30 percent of the rural workforce. But growth slowed thereafter, as urbanization began pulling industry away from rural locations.

14. Most striking is the decline of employment in high-tech manufacturing in the United States between 1990 and 2008.

15. Between 1977 and 2007, the share of services in global GDP rose from 55 to 70 percent, and it rose to 75 percent in the Organisation for Economic Co-operation and Development countries (Francois and Hoekman 2010).

16. See Eichengreen and Gupta (2009, 2011) on the role of services with reference to India; Ghani (2010) on how growth in India could continue to be propelled by services; and Spence and Hlatshwayo (2011) on the contribution of nontradable services to the bulk of the employment created in the United States since 1990.

17. In 2007, the global value of cross-border trade in services amounted to US$3.3 trillion or about a fifth of total trade. However, the share is closer to 50 percent when measured by direct and indirect value added (Francois and Hoekman 2010). Its growth is impeded by regulatory restrictions and by the greater protection accorded to services.

18. Gill and Goh (2010); Glaeser and Gottlieb (2009); Rosenthal and Strange (2004); World Bank (2008). Geoffrey West (2010) compares large cities to big animals whose size is a source of scale economies. When a city doubles in size, the resources required to sustain it grow 85 percent. See Lehrer (2010).

19. Rosenthal and Strange (2007) note that a doubling of city size can lead to an increase in productivity of between 3 and 8 percent.

20. Cohen (2004) presents data underlining the inexorable increase in average city size over the past two centuries. In 1800, the largest 100 cities in the world had an average population of 200,000. By 1990, the population of the top 100 had risen to 5 million. Beijing was the only city with 1 million inhabitants at the beginning of the nineteenth century, and 100 years later only 16 cities had attained this size. By 1950, their number had swelled to 86.

21. Superlinear scaling refers to a faster than exponential rate of increase. Thus, as cities grow, according to Geoffrey West and his coworkers at the Santa Fe Institute, such superlinearity is evident in telecommunications traffic, patenting, and pedestrian speed. See SENSEable City Lab MIT (2009).

22. UN-HABITAT (2010) points to the emergence of the mega region—an endless city. However, the bulk of the urban population resides in mid-size and small cities.

23. See McGee et al. (2007) on the rise of the region comprising Guanghzhou and Hong Kong SAR, China; Berger and Lester (1997) on the transfer of industry from Hong Kong SAR, China, to emerging cities on the mainland of China.

24. Eventually some of these will end up as ghost towns, as younger people migrate, revenues decline, services atrophy, and infrastructure deteriorates.

25. The concentration of people in coastal areas is described by Rapaport and Sachs (2003). The migration of the U.S. population toward the south and away from colder areas is described by Glaeser (2011).

26. The contribution of geography to city formation in Europe is analyzed in depth by Bosker and Buringh (2010).

27. Smaller household size, increasing numbers of older people, and the explosion in relational networking are among the factors influencing lifestyles and demands on urban infrastructure and services. Per capita consumption of energy is greater in smaller households. http://www.statcan.gc.ca/pub/11 -526- s/2010001/part-partie1-eng.htm.

28. Inequality is greatest in African cities (Gini coefficients of 0.58), but it is rising most rapidly in Asia (UN-HABITAT 2010). Although the percentage of those living in urban slums is estimated to have declined—from 39 to 32 percent between 2000 and 2010—the absolute numbers have risen. If current trends continue, almost 900 million people will be living in slums by 2020 (UN-HABITAT 2010).

29. Cities account for 80 percent of all GHG emissions, with the top 50 cities releasing 2.6 trillion tons of GHGs per year (Oxford Analytica 2011).

30. The topic of urban resilience has brought forth a considerable literature. See Newman, Beatley, and Boyer (2009); World Bank (2008); see the ICLEI, Local Governments for Sustainability website: http://resilient-cities.iclei.org /bonn2011/about/.

31. Heat island effects will only exacerbate the problem for cities, a foretaste of which was experienced by Chicago in 1995 and by Europe in 2003.

32. Recent unrest in the Middle East, sparked by unemployment and growing inequality of incomes and opportunities, has demonstrated the seriousness of the challenge.

33. In some instances, this will include expenditures on infrastructure for augmenting the water supply with the help of transfers from other parts of the country, as in China, and desalination of seawater.

34. FDI is an important source of capital and technology transfer for industrializing countries and is likely to remain a vital conduit. Singapore was the leading urban recipient of FDI projects in 2009, followed by Shanghai, London, and Dubai. In Latin America, Bogotá, Mexico City, and São Paulo led the field. See FDI Intelligence (2011).

35. Even though the Korean government was painfully aware of Seoul's vulnerability to an attack from the Democratic People's Republic of Korea given that it was just 30 miles from the demilitarized zone, it acknowledged and exploited the city's strategic location and long-standing role in the national economy.

36. These include online video games, multimedia, and publishing. See World Bank (2008); Yusuf, Nabeshima, and Yamashita (2008).

37. Its past history made Shanghai a logical choice. See Yusuf and Nabeshima (2006, 2010); Yusuf and Wu (1997).

38. Some of the mayors who contributed to Shanghai's resurgence were Wang Daohan (mayor, 1981–85); his protégé and successor, Jiang Zemin (mayor, 1985–89, and later Party chief of Shanghai); and Zhu Rongji (mayor, 1989–91).

References

Berger, Suzanne, and Richard Lester. 1997. *Made by Hong Kong.* New York: Oxford University Press.

Bongaarts, John. 2011. "One Minute with..." *NewScientist*, April 2, p. 40.

Bosker, Maarten, and Eltjo Buringh. 2010. "City Seeds: Geography and the Origins of the European City System." CEPR Discussion Paper 8066, Centre for Economic Policy Research, London.

Bosker, Maarten, Eltjo Buringh, and Jan Luiten van Zanden. 2008. "From Baghdad to London: The Dynamics of Urban Growth in Europe and the Arab World, 800–1800." CEPR Discussion Paper 6833, Centre for Economic Policy Research, London.

Cohen, Barney. 2004. "Urban Growth in Developing Countries: A Review of Current Trends and a Caution Regarding Existing Forecasts." *World Development* 32 (1): 23–51.

Currid, Elizabeth. 2007. "How Art and Culture Happen in New York." *Journal of the American Planning Association* 73 (4): 454–67.

Eichengreen, Barry, and Poonam Gupta. 2009. "The Two Waves of Service Sector Growth." NBER Working Paper 14968, National Bureau of Economic Research, Cambridge, MA.

———. 2011. "The Service Sector as India's Road to Economic Growth." NBER Working Paper 16757, National Bureau of Economic Research. Cambridge, MA.

FDI Intelligence. 2011. "Manufacturing Makes a Comeback: FDI Global Outlook Report 2011." FDI Special Report, *Financial Times*, London, April–May.

Fields, Gary S. 2007. "The Harris-Todaro Model." Working Paper 21, Cornell University, Ithaca, NY. http://digitalcommons.ilr.cornell.edu/working papers/21.

Fiksel, Joseph. 2009. *Design for Environment: A Guide to Sustainable Product Development*. New York: McGraw Hill.

Francois, Joseph, and Bernard Hoekman. 2010. "Services Trade and Policy." *Journal of Economic Literature* 48 (3): 642–92.

Ghani, Ejaz, ed. 2010. *The Service Revolution in South Asia*. New York: Oxford University Press.

Gill, Indermit S., and Chor-Chung Goh. 2010. "Scale Economies and Cities." *World Bank Research Observer* 25 (2): 235–62.

Glaeser, Edward L. 2011. *Triumph of the City: How Our Greatest Invention Makes Us Richer, Smarter, Greener, Healthier, and Happier*. New York: Penguin Press.

Glaeser, Edward L., and Joshua D. Gottlieb. 2009. The Wealth of Cities: Agglomeration Economies and Spatial Equilibrium in the United States." *Journal of Economic Literature* 47 (4): 983–1028.

Grafton, Anthony, Glenn W. Most, and Salvatore Settis. 2010. *The Classical Tradition*. Cambridge, MA: Harvard University Press.

Henderson, J. Vernon. 2010. "Cities and Development." *Journal of Regional Science* 50 (1): 515–40.

Jha, Abhas, and Henrike Brecht. 2011. "Building Urban Resilience in East Asia." *Eye on East Asia and Pacific* 8, Washington, DC, World Bank. http://siteresources .worldbank.org/INTEASTASIAPACIFIC/Resources/226262-1291126731435/EOEA_Abhas_Jha_April2011.pdf.

Johnson, Steven. 2010. *Where Good Ideas Come From: The Natural History of Innovation*. New York: Penguin Group.

Kim, Sukkoo. 2005. "Industrialization and Urbanization: Did the Steam Engine Contribute to the Growth of Cities in the United States?" *Explorations in Economic History* 42 (4): 586–98.

Lall, Somik, and Hyoung Gun Wang. 2011. "China Urbanization Review: Balancing Urban Transformation and Spatial Inclusion." *Eye on East Asia and Pacific* 6, World Bank, Washington, DC.

Lehrer, Jonah. 2010. "A Physicist Solves the City." *New York Times*, December 19. http://www.nytimes.com/2010/12/19/magazine/19Urban_West-t.html.

McCormick Adams, Robert. 1966. *The Evolution of Urban Society: Early Mesopotamia and Prehispanic Mexico*. Chicago: Aldine Publishing.

McGee, Terry, George C. S. Lin, Mark Wang, and Andrew Marton. 2007. *China's Urban Space: Development under Market Socialism*. Routledge Studies on China in Transition. London: Routledge.

Melo, Patricia C., Daniel J. Graham, and Robert B. Noland. 2009. "A Meta-Analysis of Estimates of Urban Agglomeration Economies." *Regional Science and Urban Economics* 39 (3): 332–42.

Newman, Peter, Tim Beatley, and Heather Boyer. 2009. *Resilient Cities: Responding to Peak Oil and Climate Change*. Washington, DC: Island Press.

Oxford Analytica. 2011. "International: Cities Spearhead Climate Initiatives." Oxford Analytica, Oxford, March 24. http://www.oxan.com/display.aspx?Item ID=ES167025.

Pournelle, Jennifer. 2007. "KLM to CORONA: A Bird's Eye View of Cultural Ecology and Early Mesopotamian Urbanization." In *Settlement and Society: Essays Dedicated to Robert McCormick Adams*, ed. E. C. Stone, 29–62. Cotsen Institute of Archaeology, University of California, Los Angeles; Oriental Institute of the University of Chicago, Chicago, IL.

Prasad, Neeraj, Federica Ranghieri, Fatima Shah, Zoe Trohanis, Earl Kessler, and Ravi Sinha. 2009. *Climate Resilient Cities: A Primer on Reducing Vulnerabilities to Disasters*. Washington, DC: World Bank.

Price, Simon, and Peter Thoneman. 2010. *The Birth of Classical Europe: A History from Troy to Augustine*. London: Penguin.

Rapaport, Jordan, and Jeffrey D. Sachs. 2003. "The United States as a Coastal Nation." *Journal of Economic Growth* 8 (1): 5–46.

Ravallion, M., S. Chen, and P. Sangraula. 2007. "New Evidence on the Urbanization of Global Poverty." *Population and Development Review* 33(4): 667–701.

Rosenthal, Stuart S., and William C. Strange. 2004. "Evidence on the Nature and Sources of Agglomeration Economies." In *Handbook of Urban and Regional Economics*, Vol. 4, ed. J. Vernon Henderson and J. F. Thisse, 2119–71. Amsterdam: Elsevier.

———. 2007. "The Micro-Empirics of Agglomeration Economies." In *A Companion to Urban Economics*, ed. R. J. Arnott and D. P. McMillen. Oxford: Blackwell Publishing.

SENSEable City Lab MIT (Massachusetts Institute of Technology). 2009. "City Gravity: Visualizing Communications Traffic across the US Reveals Surprising Patterns of Innovation and Urban Growth." *Seed* (February): 24–26. http://www.carloratti.com/publications/on_us/20090101SeedMagazine.pdf.

Smil, Vaclav. 2008. *Energy in Nature and Society: General Energetics of Complex Systems*. Cambridge, MA: MIT Press.

———. 2011. "Nitrogen Cycle and World Food Production." *World Agriculture* 2: 9–13.

Spence, Michael, and Sandile Hlatshwayo. 2011. "Evolving Structure of the American Economy and the Employment Challenge." Working Paper, Council on Foreign Relations, New York.

Tomlinson, Bill. 2010. *Greening through IT: Information Technology for Environmental Sustainability*. Cambridge, MA: MIT Press.

UN (United Nations). 2011. "World Population to Reach 10 Billion by 2100 if Fertility in All Countries Converges to Replacement Level." Press Release, United Nations, New York, May 3. http://esa.un.org/unpd/wpp/other-information/Press_Release_WPP2010.pdf.

UN (United Nations)-HABITAT. 2010. *State of the World's Cities 2010/2011: Cities for All; Bridging the Urban Divide.* Nairobi: UN-HABITAT.

Vanderbilt, Tom. 2011a. "Did the First Cities Grow from Marshes?" *Science* 331 (6014): 141.

———. 2011b. "Long Live the Industrial City." *Wilson Quarterly* (Spring): n.p.

West, Geoffrey. 2010. "A Physicist Solves the City." *New York Times,* December 17. http://www.nytimes.com/2010/12/19/magazine/19Urban_West-t.html?pagewanted=all.

World Bank. 2008. *Climate Resistant Cities: A Primer on Reducing Vulnerabilities to Climate Change Impacts and Strengthening Disaster Risk Management.* Washington, DC: World Bank, Global Facility for Disaster Reduction and Recovery (GFDRR), United Nations International Strategy for Disaster Reduction (ISDR), June. http://siteresources.worldbank.org/EASTASIAPAC IFICEXT/Resources/climatecities_fullreport.pdf.

———. 2011a. *World Development Indicators, 2011.* Washington, DC: World Bank.

———. 2011b. *World Development Report: Conflict, Security, and Development.* Washington, DC: World Bank.

Yusuf, Shahid, and Kaoru Nabeshima. 2006. *Postindustrial East Asian Cities: Innovation for Growth.* Washington, DC: World Bank.

———. 2010. *Two Dragon Heads: Contrasting Development Paths for Beijing and Shanghai.* Washington, DC: World Bank.

Yusuf, Shahid, Kaoru Nabeshima, and Shoichi Yamashita. 2008. *Growing Industrial Clusters in Asia: Serendipity and Science.* Washington, DC: World Bank.

Yusuf, Shahid, and Weiping Wu. 1997. *The Dynamics of Urban Growth in Three Chinese Cities.* New York: Oxford University Press for the World Bank.

Zhu, Yu, Xinhua Qi, Huaiyou Shao, and Kaijing He. 2009. "The Evolution of China's in Situ Urbanization and Its Planning and Environmental Implications: Case Studies from Quanzhou Municipality." In *Urban Population-Environment Dynamics in the Developing World: Case Studies and Lessons Learned,* ed. Alex de Sherbinin, Atiqur Rahman, Alisson Barbieri, Jean-Christophe Fotso, and Yu Zhu. Paris: Committee for International Cooperation in National Research in Demography (CICRED). http://www.ciesin.columbia.edu/repository/pern/papers/urban_pde_zhu_etal.pdf.

CHAPTER 8

Elements for Future Success of Metropolitan Regions

Size and agglomeration economies can influence urban fortunes through productivity, but there are too many examples of metropolitan regions that are punching far below their weight. There are megacities where the development of industry and tradable services is creeping along or in retreat, where growth is stagnating, and where the supply of housing and public services is struggling to keep up with the demand because the productive economic base and revenue effort are both weak. Cairo, Johannesburg, Karachi, Manila, and São Paulo belong to this category of cities that are deriving few advantages from size and suffer instead from the diseconomies of unbridled agglomeration. What differentiates these cities from metropolitan regions that are economically dynamic and registering high growth rates? For low- and middle-income countries that are experiencing lagging urban development in the face of rising urbanization, the missing ingredient is exploding business activity represented by the entry and growth of firms producing tradables (whether manufactured products or services), creating good jobs,[1] generating exports, and serving as a channel for new technologies absorbed from overseas and supplemented by own adaptation and innovation. Bangalore, Bangkok, and Shenzhen owe their dynamism to the continual value-adding and growth-enhancing churning of the business scene, with new—domestic and foreign—firms serving as a conveyor belt for investment and technology and competitive pressures sharpened by exposure to global markets continually weeding out the laggards.

The entry of new firms and the growth of the most entrepreneurial firms are the lifeblood of the metropolitan region.[2] The dynamic cities not only benefit from high rates of entry, but also, as in Beijing or in Dongguan, encourage the formation of clusters, which give rise to technological spillovers, stimulate productivity, and create conditions conducive to the formation of new firms.[3] Entry, cluster formation, and growth of the more productive firms can promote exports, which, in turn, further stimulate economic expansion.[4] In fact, urban industrialization in the current context and for all but the largest countries is inseparable from participation in the international market.[5] This broadens market opportunities for venturesome firms, which are a minority everywhere—but an important one—and spurs productivity growth. Firms with the greatest managerial, organizational, and technical capabilities grow, and in both East Asia and Latin America, participation in international value chains has provided firms with technology and growth ladders. The experience of Taiwan, China, in particular, highlights this process of urban industrialization through a proliferation of small and medium enterprises, their entry into trade, their proactive absorption of technology, and their emergence as globally competitive entities that drive the economies of cities in Taiwan, China, and the nation.

Once urban development takes off, the large metropolitan region has several advantages. The medium-size peripheral cities are likely to grow quickly—a worldwide trend—to have a large youthful population that can provide entrepreneurial dividends, and to have lower-priced land to encourage new starts, especially in manufacturing. The core city, with a concentration of services and unskilled workers, offers a different range of opportunities, with many more niches for new start-ups and easier access to financing for existing firms or clusters of firms and for small and medium enterprises (SMEs).[6] The core city is better supplied with business development services, which can be valuable for start-ups. The core city is also the focus of academic and cultural activities. Together, the concentration of universities, research and consulting services, and recreational facilities provides the opportunities for knowledge workers with diverse skills to exchange and breed new ideas, some of which are enriched by being at the intersection of two or several disciplines.

The metropolitan region that combines the advantages of medium-size and large cities has strong economic credentials, but its full developmental potential is only realized when certain other criteria are met in whole or in part. These are as follows: (a) industrial composition and clustering, (b) connectedness, (c) compactness, (d) urban smarts, (e) governance, and (f) sustainability and resilience.

These criteria or attributes were not uppermost in the minds of city planners, managers, and developers; when metropolitan cities were taking shape in the twentieth century, fuel was cheap, abundant land was available for development, pollution and population pressures were less obtrusive, and sprawling low-rise cities appeared appropriate for the foreseeable modes of economic activity and lifestyles. Few if any city authorities seriously considered adopting a holistic approach, which seems warranted from the vantage point of current knowledge. But in the future, to succeed in attracting resources and talent and to maintain adequate growth rates, cities will need to monitor progress with reference to the above, moving farther along some axes than others, depending on circumstances, without neglecting any one.

The Industrial Matrix

It is appropriate to start with industrial composition because this is of immediate relevance for growth, employment, and exports, and the current mix foreshadows future options for a metropolis. The type and competitiveness of productive activities dominating the city's economy are the principal indicators of growth prospects through sales in domestic and foreign markets. They indicate the gains to be derived from productivity, from innovation, or from technological catch-up. Figure 8.1, on total factor productivity (TFP) by industrial sector in the United States between 1960 and 2007, demonstrates the edge that certain high-tech industries, but also services benefiting from information technology (IT), have over other activities. Figure 8.2 points to the research and development (R&D) intensity of key subsectors among 10 Organisation for Economic Co-operation and Development (OECD) countries, which is a reliable indicator of innovation and productivity growth. And the industrial composition points to employment elasticities and the types of skills likely to be in demand. When firms cluster in ways that promote spillovers, the productivity bonus can be larger.

The IT-enabled services sector in Bangalore[7] and in Gurgaon, the second largest city in Haryana and located about 30 kilometers south of New Delhi, are clusters of proven competitiveness and export success, employing highly skilled workers and diversifying into more complex services

Figure 8.1   Industry Contributions to Productivity Growth in the United States, 1960–2007

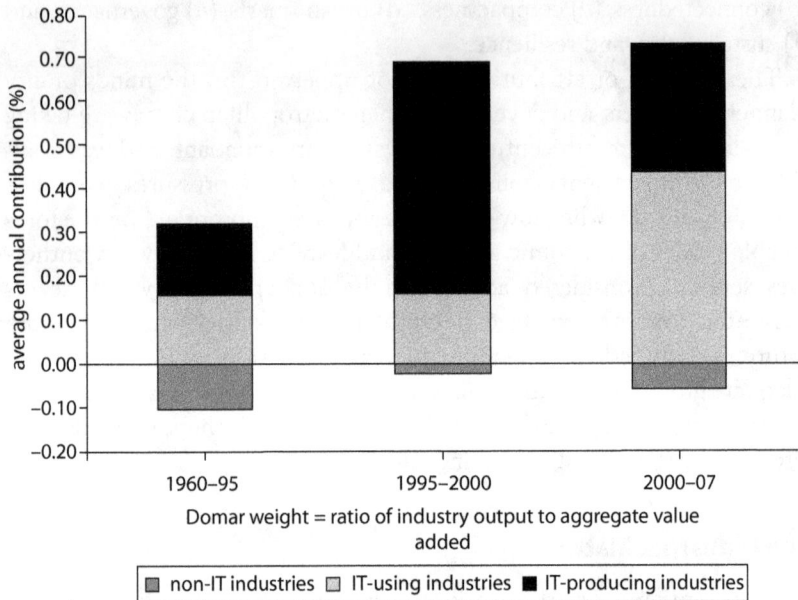

Source: Jorgenson, Ho, and Samuels 2010.

offering larger rewards. This kind of industry, with good long-term potential and significant local linkages, is an asset for the metropolis, not the least because it is an industry with low entry barriers, which encourages the proliferation of businesses in societies where demonstration effects can uncork pent-up entrepreneurial energies.

Dongguan, one of the fastest-growing metro cities in China, is the center of manufacturing covering a spectrum ranging from textiles to electronics.[8] These industries provide jobs for skilled and unskilled workers, and the diversity is fertile soil for new businesses. Manufacturing activities in Dongguan target foreign markets, and major multinationals such as Foxconn and Nike have located their main manufacturing assets in the city. This further enriches the industrial ecology of the city because large factories owned by multinational corporations (MNCs) exploit scale economies and buy inputs from or subcontract with thousands of specialized suppliers.[9] The MNCs nourish the ecosystem with capital and production technologies and boost the development of local research and testing facilities.[10] No less important from the productivity angle are the

Figure 8.2   R&D Intensity, by Industry Average across 10 OECD Countries

(average across 10 countries in %)

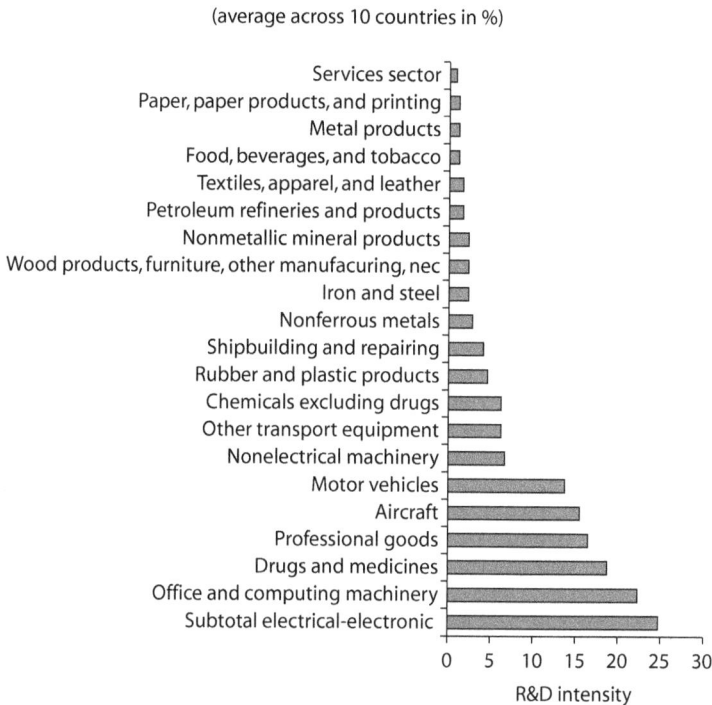

R&D intensity

Source: van Pottelsberghe 2008.
Note: nec = not elsewhere classified.

managerial, design, and marketing techniques and the habit of many-faceted, incremental innovations that the MNCs introduce. That manufacturing productivity is increasing by 10 percent or more in cities such as Dongguan testifies to the speed at which technologies are being disseminated, and this helps to absorb rising wages, while maintaining healthy profit margins.[11]

Bangkok is yet another example of a dynamic industrial metropolis. The core city is richly supplied with services, and around it has sprung a necklace of secondary cities crowded with manufacturing firms that rely on the providers of IT, finance, management, marketing, logistics, and human resource management services located in Bangkok.[12] The metropolitan economies and the advantages accruing from the presence of the central government are such that efforts to disperse economic activities to other cities in Thailand have largely failed. Other cities, such as Cairo,

Johannesburg, or Rio de Janeiro, with a modest suite of tradable activities pay a price. Cairo's manufacturing sector is smaller, mainly low-tech, and low also on the scale of competitiveness. Services cater mostly to domestic demand. This constrains productivity gains, technological change, diversification, and growth. Rio de Janeiro is in a similar predicament, having deindustrialized and failed to substitute departing industries with tradable services other than those serving tourists.[13] Rio de Janeiro, for all its natural beauty, is a city without the leading export and research-intensive sectors that can deliver high rates of growth and employment and lessen the city's dependence on budgetary transfers from the center.[14]

In spite of its strong mining and engineering sectors, Johannesburg also has to cope with slow growth, largely because of the decline in mining and manufacturing activities,[15] which tend to be skill intensive and offer few jobs for South Africa's legions of unemployed, youthful, unskilled workers. Growth prospects of the Johannesburg-Gauteng region, while adequate for the near term, look increasingly dim over a longer horizon unless industrial trends are reversed.

What we learn from Chinese and some Southeast Asian metropolitan centers is that, for low- and middle-income countries, a broad manufacturing base—complemented, as in Bangkok, Shanghai, and Taipei, by the densification of services industries—promises growth and the scope for diversification. Analysis using the Hausmann-Rodrik-Hidalgo product space mapping technique indicates that production systems lying on the periphery of the product space without many links to other product categories, as in the case of Johannesburg and Rio de Janeiro, face difficulty in acquiring the richly networked core activities that contribute to a deepening of industrial capabilities with better longer-term growth prospects.[16]

Figures 8.3 and 8.4 present the sectors with the highest rates of productivity increase in the United States over a 47-year period. These industries also rank high in the trade statistics, and the manufacturing industries on the list are among the most research intensive, underscoring the likely longer-term growth potential.

The list of activities is illustrative: these are some of the subsectors that performed well in the recent past and boosted city economies. However, productive highfliers can be stingy sources of jobs. Whether it is finance and insurance or electronics and biotechnology, leading innovative activities are more productive and more intensive in their use of capital and skills. If recent trends persist, and there is reason to think that they will

Figure 8.3 Contributions to Productivity Growth in the United States, by Industry, 1960–2007

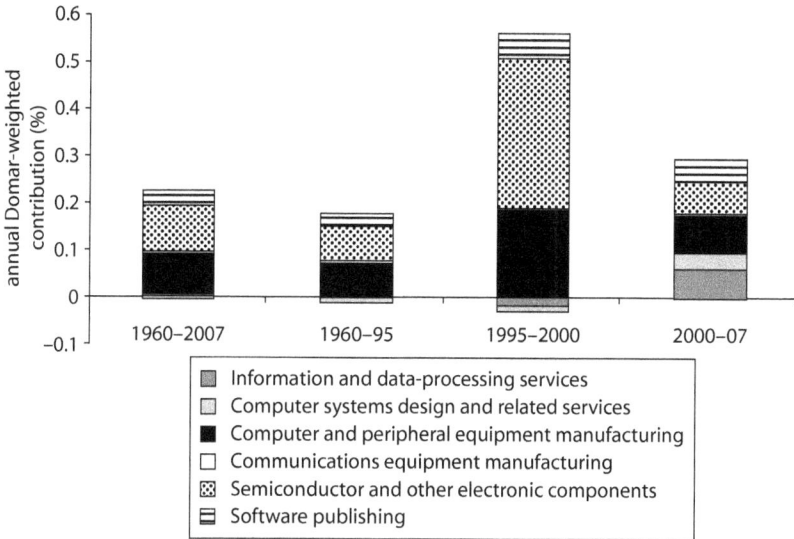

Source: Jorgenson, Ho, and Samuels, 2010.

for at least a decade, metropolitan centers with a large share of the tradables in the most productive categories could grow faster than other centers, but if they wish to produce an abundance of jobs, they will need to nurture many nontradables, mainly services.

Connectivity

A highly connected metropolitan region enhances productivity and maximizes the benefits from increased trade and capital flows, the circulation of talented people, and the collaborative efforts of researchers in different countries. Connectedness has several facets, but the two that deserve the most attention are the quality of the information and communication technology (ICT) and transport infrastructure and the links they help to create.

A wealth of research has pieced together evidence mainly from developed countries showing that the cross-sectoral absorption of ICT in myriad activities has raised productivity and induced innovation. Erik Brynjolfsson believes that IT is changing the innovation process itself. He claims, "IT is setting off a revolution on four dimensions simultaneously: measurement, experimentation, sharing, and replication that reinforce

Figure 8.4   Industry Contributions to Productivity in the United States, 1960–2007

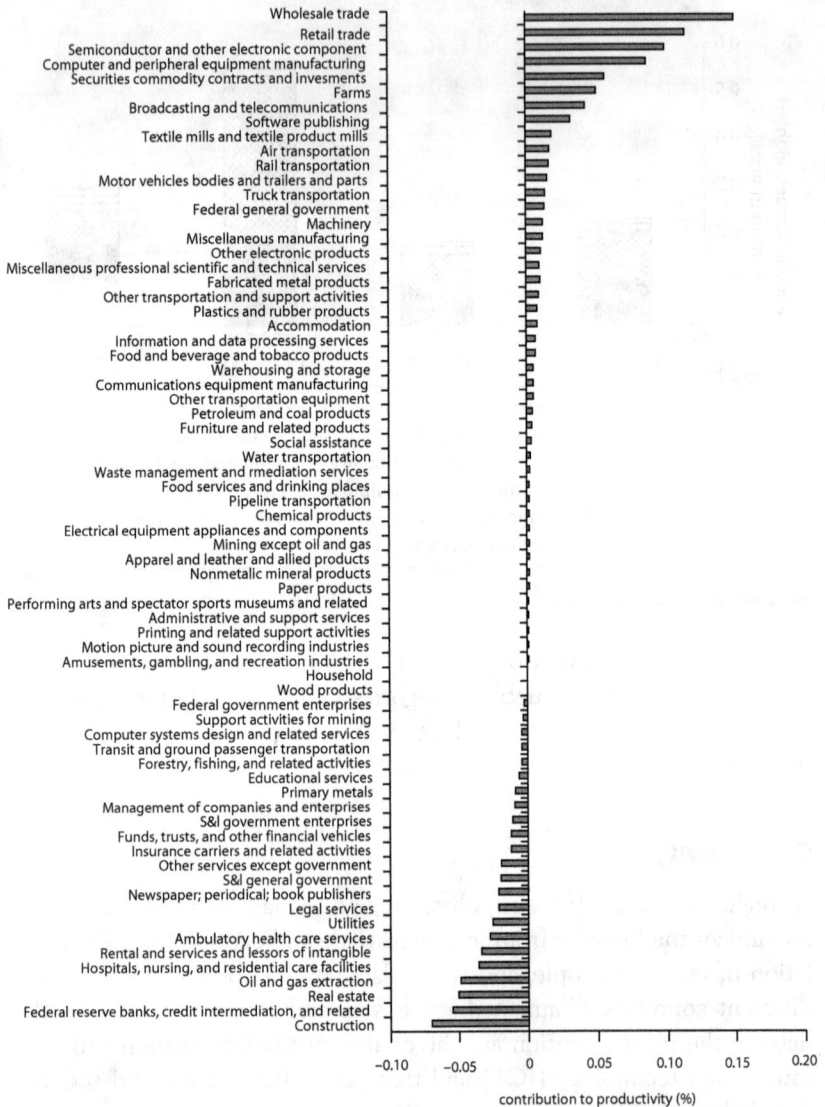

contribution to productivity (%)

Source: Jorgenson, Ho, and Samuels, 2010.

and magnify each other" and permit the rapid scaling up of innovations (quoted in Hopkins 2010, 52). The United States has been the leader in this regard, although European countries have also benefited, and some developing countries are catching up.

The centrality of capital for growth in the world as a whole since 1980 has been highlighted by Jorgenson and Vu Khuong (2009), who show that capital was the source of 54 percent of growth in 1989–95 and that its share was still as high as 41 percent during 2000–06, exceeding the contribution of other factors. The compelling development since the mid-1990s is the increasing importance of total factor productivity, which accounted for 36 percent of growth in 2000–06, compared with less than a fifth in 1989–95. If this trend were to persist—and Jorgenson, Ho, and Samuels (2010) acknowledge that productivity will be vital for maintaining U.S. living standards over the longer term—then TFP could draw abreast or even pull ahead of capital as a driver of growth. However, as Jorgenson and his coauthors observe, "With only replication [of established technologies] and without innovation, output will increase in proportion to capital and labor inputs. By contrast, the successful introduction of new products and new or altered processes, organization structures, and business models generates growth of output that exceeds the growth of capital and labor inputs. This results in growth of multifactor productivity or output per unit of input" (Jorgenson, Ho, and Samuels 2010, 13–14). Innovation, or the successful exploitation of new ideas and technology, is becoming the cornerstone of growth, and ICT is the leading driver of such growth.[17] As Jorgenson, Ho, and Samuels (2009) show,[18] the contribution to growth of IT-producing and IT-using industries in the United States has increased steadily, and IT capital now makes a substantial contribution to gains in productivity. Additional evidence on the salience of ICT is provided by Brynjolfsson and Saunders (2010) and the research conducted by the Information Technology and Innovation Foundation on urban activities deriving productivity gains from IT.[19]

The point to be noted is that the use of ICT for industrial, commercial, or social purposes is to a great extent an urban phenomena and, because frequent exchanges via electronic media also increase face-to-face encounters (Leamer and Storper 2001), a metro region well furnished with ICT infrastructure and recreational amenities is the ideal setting for the circulation of information, the testing of ideas, and the fruiting of innovation.

Seoul is a classic example of a city with state-of-the-art ICT infrastructure providing locals with unparalleled access to the Internet and the latest advances in mobile telecommunications. Seoul's edge over most other cities derives from the government's ambitious plans, launched in 1995, to wire the nation in enlightened anticipation of a tectonic shift in communications and the use of media[20] and subsequent initiatives to develop IT-based activities. Such activities include the Digital Media City to support the growth of the digital content industry, a major source of high-value-adding jobs in the metro area.

Productivity gains aside, the large strides made in weaving ICT into the fabric of urban life in the Republic of Korea have spurred innovation, as evidenced by increasing patent output and, more important, the rise in international collaboration between Korean and foreign researchers. Domestic connectivity strengthened urban civil society and energized social and intellectual activities. International connectivity is tightening the links that Korea needs to sustain its competitiveness.

Singapore is another city that has leveraged ICT to maximize the gains from globalization and made its business environment the envy of other countries in the region and beyond. Singapore is a leader in technologies to expedite the operations of its busy container port and its world-class airport.[21] It also uses electronic pricing to smooth traffic flows and to minimize congestion. Singapore's e-government platform is the benchmark for other cities, and the government is continuously searching for ways to prune transaction costs further. Through these investments in ICT as well as others in education and health care, Singapore has strengthened connectivity and raised total factor productivity. Other cities taking note of the benefits accruing to Seoul and Singapore have begun investing in infrastructure and training, but they frequently neglect to adopt a comprehensive approach, which is the key to mutually reinforcing gains from several interlocking activities.

A major metropolis seeking greater connectivity must also look to its airport and port facilities (if it is a coastal city). An urban economy reliant on trade—and the foremost metropolitan regions depend on trade to boost domestic sources of demand by a few percentage points—must enlarge and grease the channels through which trade flows.[22] The economic significance of ports has long been recognized. A busy port has a large footprint, employing tens of thousands and consuming a wide assortment of services produced locally.[23] The contribution of a major international airport equals and may exceed that of a port. By value, close to one-third of global trade is now shipped by air.[24] This includes high-value electronic products and pharmaceuticals, cut flowers, meat, and other farm products requiring a cold chain—and the percentages are rising as the cost of air transport declines in relative terms with the introduction of larger fuel-efficient aircraft. In addition, airports serve as the gateways for the export of tourism and business travel services, which cities such as Bangkok, Cairo, Cape Town, and Rio de Janeiro depend on for the large slice of their earnings from trade. As air transport has increased its share of trade, major airports with space around them are becoming the foci of industrial and services clusters. A classic example is Dulles airport serving the Washington, DC, area, which is the axis of IT, telecommunications, and defense industry clusters and the driver of growth for the metropolitan region.[25] Other cities are also discovering that airports can stimulate clustered industrial activities through connectivity and induced employment. Songdo City,[26] which is sprouting IT activities adjacent to Seoul-Incheon airport, is one example; Bangkok's new Suvarnabhumi airport is another. Both cities see these airports as hubs for new activities with a high trade component.

The Smarter Metropolis

The globally connected metropolis, which is a "smart city" like Seoul or Singapore or San Francisco or San Jose, is doubly advantaged because it has the capabilities to exploit the opportunities arising from globalization. There is no precise definition of the smart city. Being smart is associated with several attributes, including a large percentage of the population with a college degree, state-of-the-art ICT infrastructure,[27] and the early adoption of environmentally friendly and green technologies. However, for our purposes, urban "smarts" or intelligence derives from a concentration of skills and the quality of governance. In other words, being smart has to do with the brainpower a city can marshal to manage and accelerate its development with the help of innovation at many different levels. Alongside depth and quality of human capital, these cities require institutional mechanisms and basic research for generating ideas and ways of debating, testing, and perfecting these ideas.

The smart city can achieve rapid and sustainable growth of industry by bringing together and fully mobilizing four forms of intelligence: the human intelligence inherent in local knowledge networks enriched by the inmigration of people with diverse talents;[28] the collective intelligence of institutions that support innovation through a variety of channels and serve to urbanize technologies, shaping them to suit the environment and making them easily available to users; the production intelligence of its industrial base; and the collective intelligence that can be derived from the effective use of digital networks and online services—a kind of involuntary crowd sourcing that contributes to problem solving and a progressive upgrading of the urban environment (Komninos 2008). Cities positioning themselves to become innovative hotspots are open to ideas and thrive on the heterogeneity of knowledge workers drawn from all over the country and the world. Moreover, such cities are closely integrated with other global centers of research and technology development—they are a part of the global innovation system—and their teaching and research institutions must compete with the best for talent and validation of their own ideas. Last, but not least, because smart cities are at the leading edge of the knowledge economy, their design, physical assets, attributes, and governance need to reflect their edge over others. Industrial cities can become innovative cities, and a strong manufacturing base can be an asset, as it is for Munich, Seattle, Seoul, Stuttgart, Tokyo, and Toulouse. But industry is not a necessary condition: Cambridge (United Kingdom), Helsinki, Kyoto, and San Francisco are not industrial cities; they are innovative cities that have acquired significant high-tech or IT production capabilities. As long as a city is part of a metro region or adjacent to one, size can be a secondary consideration and overridden by the advantages of livability. Medium-size industrial cities, by exploiting localization economies, can promote the formation of vibrant industrial clusters. And because they tend to be less congested, medium-size cities can appeal to younger age groups, who are concerned about cost of living and environmental quality,[29] as well as to members of the creative class, who place a high premium on quality of life (see tables 8A.1–8A.5 at the end of this chapter, which rank cities with respect to quality of life and creativity and highlight the lead enjoyed by medium-size cities). Of course, only a subset of mid-size cities are potential winners, but those that exploit their location and strategically develop the assets that contribute to long-term prosperity can equal or exceed the innovation and productivity advantages of the most dynamic large cities.[30]

A city with an abundance of skills is better positioned to maintain industrial competitiveness, to move up the value chain by assimilating technologies and reinforcing catch-up with innovations, and to diversify into more profitable activities as existing ones enter the stage in their life cycle when commoditization lowers entry barriers, pares profit margins, and triggers migration to lower-cost locations. Glaeser (2011) singles out Boston as a skilled city that has flourished because its world-class universities and urban ambience have made it "sticky" for talented people (on stickiness, see Markusen 1996). The wide base of skills has nurtured entrepreneurs and led to the proliferation of firms offering jobs for skilled workers; with the universities generating so many ideas, Boston has recovered from downturns and bouts of deindustrialization by pursuing new technological opportunities using its unique labor pool and financing

these with the help of highly experienced, locally based venture capitalists. Boston is not alone. Other cities such as Bangalore, Beijing, Singapore,
and Taipei are adopting similar models of development to good effect.

The leading smart cities have not only deep pools of skills, but also
high-quality skills. Growth regressions are uncovering a robust relationship between the quality of schooling, as captured by test scores of middle
school students, and the increase in gross domestic product (GDP)
(Hanushek 2010; Hanushek and Woessman 2010). These have been
capped by related findings highlighting the significance of the numbers of
students in the upper tail of the distribution of test scores (see Pritchett
and Viarengo 2010). A country—or city—with many students with science and math scores in the highest percentiles has the strongest growth
prospects. Singapore, which is top-ranked by test scores, also has impres-
sive competitiveness and innovation capacity rankings. It has successfully
diversified and sustained an average growth rate of 5 percent since 1995.
Shanghai, which topped the 2009 Programme for International Student
Assessment results, is en route to becoming a smart metropolis the equal
of Seoul and Tokyo. Shanghai is a magnet for talent from throughout
China, and this inflow augments its own base of high-quality skills. As
traditional light manufacturing industries transfer to cities in Shanghai's
hinterland or to the interior, new and more skill-intensive activities are
enabling Shanghai to expand in fresh directions appropriate for a city with
per capita GDP that is five times the average for China. Mexico City and
São Paulo trail Shanghai's performance, and their prospects are less bright
because they have not set their sights on becoming smart cities with
human capabilities as the prime source of growth.

Governing the Metropolitan Center

A metropolis will struggle to accumulate and retain talent and create new
business lines if urban planning, management, and financing do not provide the necessary preconditions for development. That is, smart urban
governance complements other forms of urban intelligence. Suffice to say
that the selection and empowerment of city managers are one of the req-
uisites. Smart cities plan ahead, establish realistic monitorable targets, and
place a premium on rapid and efficient implementation of policies.[31]
Cities such as Seoul, Singapore, and Tokyo draw their governance capabilities from the quality of a well-paid municipal workforce and an institutional infrastructure that evolves with changing developmental
imperatives and is quick to incorporate IT as well as other technologies to

improve services delivery. The enduring characteristic of smart cities is the awareness of competition and the commitment to incremental progress through benchmarking and learning from other cities. Smart cities such as Singapore are not caught unawares by the hollowing out of traditional industries; instead, they seek to anticipate and avert or neutralize trends that can lead to the entrenching of slums and environmental decay— physical as well as social. Cape Town, Karachi, and Rio de Janeiro have sacrificed many of the advantages that could be derived from a concentration of skills because the environment in both cities is rendered perilous by widespread unemployment, serious security concerns, and the obtrusiveness of slums, whether in the core city areas or on the outskirts.

Being smart is all about defining ambitious but achievable development objectives, mobilizing resources using a frequently sharpened set of incentives to deliver results, thinking ahead so as to minimize the risk of being caught napping, and solving problems expeditiously. Smart cities can raise their game by making full use of technological opportunities as they arise and by inculcating a culture of innovation. However, high-tech and IT intensity is not the answer for most cities, or at best it is a partial answer. Smart urban development in Cairo and Karachi would be low-tech yet innovative at the outset, while aiming for longer-term growth based on skills and technological capabilities that would narrow the vast gaps in productivity between these cities and some of their competitors in East Asia.

The Resilience Imperative

A metropolis that is deemed smart and successful must also meet the test of sustainability and resilience. Metropolitan economies in low- and middle-income countries must strive after decades of growth in the 5 to 8 percent range to generate enough employment, raise living standards of the vast majority to socially acceptable levels, and find the resources to address legacy problems and upcoming challenges, not to mention environmental and economic shocks.

Both governance and skills directly impinge on sustainability. Governance affects development because it is a determinant of the urban business climate and the level of business activity. Skills likewise have a powerful bearing on development, as discussed above. The point to be noted is that the sustainability of a metropolitan economy is inseparable from growth. If growth stalls or goes into reverse, as happens when a key industrial or mining activity implodes—as has happened in Detroit, Pittsburgh, and some cities in Eastern Europe—sustainability is imperiled because industrial decline is followed by rising poverty and social unrest and by an exodus of capital and skills. Avoiding such a contingency is central to the notion of sustainability. A diversified metropolitan region is at lower risk than smaller specialized urban centers, but, as even New York discovered in the mid-1970s, a narrowing of the industrial base and excessive dependence on a few services subject to crisis-induced swings can become problematic. Both Seoul and Shanghai have industrial breadth, as do Karachi, Lagos, and Mumbai, but the plight of the latter three cities draws attention to two other facets of sustainability: urban finance and urban design.

Financing Urbanization

Urban development assumes the provision of an array of services for businesses and households. If these dip below minimum standards of adequacy, development is impeded and the urban economy begins to stall and unravel, as happens in conflict and immediate postconflict situations. Infrastructure services, public health services, education services, and policies are among the basics. Scarcity of water, for example, can seriously constrain urban development, and poor sewage, waste disposal, and sanitation severely compromise the health and living conditions of the majority.

Whether a metropolitan region can build and maintain physical infrastructure, finance basic services, supply affordable housing, and offer recreational amenities is ultimately a function of finances. Transfers from central and provincial governments (both general and specific) are the source of revenues, but sustainability requires that these constitute a relatively minor source of income and that the local tax base is the primary source of revenues. At least five criteria must be met for a city to be broadly self-sufficient with regard to revenue.

First, revenue generation is a function of the scale of economic activity and how this translates into earnings of residents, the distribution of incomes, and the value of taxable assets.

Second, the revenue actually raised depends on the degree of local tax autonomy and taxes assigned to local authorities. Other fees collected by municipalities supplement taxes, but income and real property taxes generally constitute the bulk of local revenues. To meet expenditure assignments, subnational governments often look to central governments to bridge any gaps, but a sustainable metropolis should, in principle, be self-sufficient.

Third, the selection and use of tax instruments need to be efficient and to derive the maximum advantage by maintaining incentives for businesses and households to remain in the jurisdiction (see Inman 2007). Moreover, local authorities need to be able to enforce and collect taxes, especially property and real estate taxes, and to assess properties and adjust rates regularly.

Fourth, a metropolis spanning multiple jurisdictions must be able to coordinate regional development so as to optimize the provision of infrastructure and internalize scale economies where these exist. Equally important is the coordination of tax instruments and rates so as to avoid distorting incentives and inducing tax arbitrage and Tiebout shopping.[32]

Fifth, fiscal responsibility laws can serve to underscore local responsibilities, minimize moral hazard, and induce fiscally prudent behavior.[33] Furthermore, the fiscal performance and service delivery of local governments can be bolstered by procedures for evaluating performance. Bangkok, much like other metropolitan centers in developing countries, relies on a mix of transfers and locally sourced revenues, but efficiency is compromised by the large number of local government organizations and an inability to analyze the data collected to improve monitoring and performance.

Tax revenues can partially finance infrastructure, but most long-lived capital-intensive facilities call for additional financing, which can come from development grants provided by the center or raised by issuing bonds that are guaranteed by the center or provincial governments.

Whether it is tax revenues or financing through public-private partnerships or the financial market, sustainability first and foremost assumes that industrial development is on track and that trends are pointing in the right direction. Where the development impetus is weak or failing, financial sustainability can prove elusive. Governance mechanisms—central and local—are an equally important determinant of sustainability, affecting not just corruption and malfeasance but also legislative log rolling, a common problem in U.S. cities, which is when legislators avoid the risk of policy gridlock by indiscriminately voting for all new initiatives.[34]

Designing for Sustainability

Today's metropolitan regions emerged in most instances with the minimum of planning and attention being given to resource constraints or long-term environmental considerations. Low energy prices, transport subsidies, cheap land, low property taxes, the lure of automotive mobility, and the emergence of powerful lobbies composed of real estate developers and auto manufacturers together led to horizontal, sprawling urban development. This process is continuing in industrializing economies such as China, Indonesia, Malaysia, Nigeria, and South Africa and also in North America, which provided the model of the sprawling metropolitan region.[35] This form of development, while it surely provides city-dwellers with more living space, requires costly investment in transport, water, sewage, and energy infrastructure and greatly increases dependence on private automobiles.[36] Sprawl also goes hand-in-hand with eating and exercise habits that are injurious to health (Frumkin, Frank, and Jackson 2004). The sprawling metropolis, with its low densities and emptiness,[37] poses a huge challenge for sustainable development. Sustainability is predicated on energy and resource conservation and on the building of robust and resilient infrastructures. The model of a resource-frugal city is compact and vertical, with high population densities that permit the efficient use of public transport.[38] This model, attractive to efficiency- and resource-conscious planners, may be coming into vogue, but it should not take the form of the "tower in the park" model so popular in China, which is much more energy intensive and isolating than the mixed-use neighborhoods it is displacing.

A doubling of urban populations demands a rethinking of how people can be accommodated, especially if there is a growing need to conserve both energy and fertile farmland adjacent to cities. The need to invest in facilities to protect the more vulnerable cities from the consequences of climate change is another factor that will be harder to realize given the declining trend in global savings linked to aging populations in the developed world as well as in some of the industrializing countries. The imminence and seriousness of each of these trends can be debated. Legacy housing, transport, and public utility infrastructure and the force of inertia are huge obstacles to changing the pattern of urban development, but they cannot be ignored, and retrofitting them is unavoidable. Resistance to an increase in energy and water prices, or the price of externalities arising from unchecked private automobile use,[39] reluctance to raise and collect real property taxes, and reluctance to modify zoning and floor area regulations affecting land use (Mumbai is a frequently cited example) are fierce in all countries.[40] The political economy of urban development in virtually all countries favors endless delay. This is because politicians have short time horizons and few incentives to champion radical policies, interest groups with a stake in the status quo forcefully oppose actions that would jeopardize the rents they gain from existing arrangements, and households reflexively oppose higher taxes and prices. Even severe fiscal crises, the threat of spiraling energy prices, and the increasing frequency of severe weather events seem unable to persuade metropolitan residents in advanced and developing countries that delay is fast becoming an unaffordable luxury.

The issue of urban sustainability is here to stay, and with each passing year it will only become more pressing. In different ways—sometimes obliquely, sometimes directly—it is being debated in crisis-ridden advanced countries in a state of political paralysis such as the United States, in industrializing countries currently with deep pockets where urbanization is approaching a midpoint, such as China, and in low-income countries in the crosshairs of climate change, such as Pakistan, that are struggling with acute resource scarcities, limited organizational capabilities, and dysfunctional governance. Reluctantly and later rather than sooner, the great metropolitan centers throughout the developing world will translate the concept of sustainable urbanization into practice through a physical redesign of cities and the widespread incorporation of green technologies and resource-frugal ways of living. Legacy infrastructure cannot be wished away overnight; however, through a process of deconstruction, retrofitting, adaptation, and new construction based on green templates, cities will have to be transformed if they are to remain livable and economically dynamic. It may be too late to contain carbon dioxide concentration to the desired 450 parts per million, but mankind will need to adapt to the 550 parts per million atmosphere toward which we are heading.

Metropolitan Futures

The terms smart and IT-enabled, compact, vertical, mixed use, green, and livable define the vision of the future for some, but no one knows quite how these terms can define a coherent and holistic long-term development plan for a Beijing, a Karachi, or a São Paulo, what kind of organizations could manage urbanization across several dimensions, what it would cost to implement, the amount of dislocation it would entail, and the viability of the eventual outcome in the world that future generations will inherit. The advantages—and also the drawbacks—of the compact city have been aired for many years. The technologies—hard and soft—that can make a city "greener" have been taking shape and are being tested piecemeal. No one of the tiny experimental green cities currently under construction has been put to the test and its carbon neutrality convincingly established.[41] The livability of compact and green cities and how they would accommodate diverse industrial activities are also not known. The technologies coming off the drawing boards and some being commercialized are perhaps decades away from widespread application once they have been debugged and made more affordable. However, building sustainability cannot wait. Cairo, Dhaka, Karachi, São Paulo, and Shenzhen are daily pouring more concrete into the ground, accommodating more people, and building more roads. Instead of becoming more dense, urban areas are becoming less dense. Bangkok's urbanized area grew sixteenfold between 1944 and 2002, and that of Accra grew 153 percent between 1985 and 2000. In spite of recurrent fiscal debacles, local politicians and city managers are unable to learn enduring lessons, and acres of literature on urban fiscal policies have failed to improve urban tax systems substantially worldwide. These are frightening trends and missed opportunities. Left unchecked they will make a rationalization of urban development far harder. Some economists are of the view that price adjustments reflecting energy and water scarcities, increased vulnerability of cities near rivers to flooding and coastal locations to rising sea levels,[42] and inland areas to droughts and firestorms will bring about the redistribution of the population, force a refashioning of the urban landscape, and demand the building of passive and active coastal defenses, as in the Netherlands. Economists rightly underscore the strength of the market mechanism but are apt to minimize its failings, as evidenced by the devastating financial crisis of 2008 and 2009 and the many real estate bubbles.

From the perspective of urban sustainability and green development, market-induced changes might be too slow, too myopic, and too piecemeal, and the market might not promote the kind of fast-paced innovation that is urgently needed or provide the insurance required by the inhabitants of vulnerable cities in developing countries.

On the current trajectories, Karachi and Lagos could become the world's two largest cities by mid-century, assuming that the availability of water permits such growth. A doubling of populations with no change in layout will lead to metropolitan regions that could be unsustainable and ungovernable over the longer term and forced to confront painful crises.

Advanced countries may have the resources to indulge in wasteful sprawling urban regions, and they may even endure deindustrialization for several decades by living off their accumulated fat. But industrializing countries need to learn quickly and avoid the costly decisions made when energy, land, and water were relatively cheap, green technologies were unknown, and global warming was a scientific curiosity. Low-income countries have even less room for maneuver because they are lacking the growth momentum of the leading middle-income nations, the technological capabilities, and the resources; in addition, they must cope with rapidly expanding populations.

With so much urbanization still lying ahead and the stakes rising, the design and implementation of forward-looking urban development strategies are taking on added importance. Whether countries make rapid strides on the economic front will depend on one or a small handful of metropolitan centers. And whether these are smart, sustainable, economically dynamic, and livable will also depend on how cities develop organizational and technical skills, assure revenue autonomy, create agile (soft and hard) infrastructure, and make the best use of evolving practical ideas and technologies to take existing and budding metropolitan regions boldly into an uncertain future.

Annex: City Rankings

Table 8A.1   Mercer Quality of Living Ranking of Cities Worldwide, 2010

City and country	Rank	Index
Vienna, Austria	1	108.6
Zurich, Switzerland	2	108.0
Geneva, Switzerland	3	107.9
Vancouver, Canada	4	107.4
Auckland, New Zealand	5	107.4
Dusseldorf, Germany	6	107.2
Frankfurt, Germany	7	107.0
Munich, Germany	7	107.0
Bern, Switzerland	9	106.5
Sydney, Australia	10	106.3
Copenhagen, Denmark	11	106.2
Amsterdam, Netherlands	12	105.7
Ottawa, Canada	13	105.5
Brussels, Belgium	14	105.4

Source: Mercer LLC, http://www.mercer.com/qualityof living.
Note: Index base city: New York, United States = 100.

Table 8A.2   Ranking of Creative Cities in the United States, by Arts Employees per Capita, 2008

City, State	Rank	Arts employees per 1,000 residents	Population
Atlanta, GA	1	47.7	537,958
San Francisco, CA	2	39.7	808,976
Seattle, WA	3	36.1	598,541
Washington, DC	4	34.4	591,833
Minneapolis, MN	5	33.5	382,605
Boston, MA	6	32.7	609.023
Los Angeles, CA	7	31.4	3,833,995
New York, NY	8	28.0	8,363,710
Portland, OR	9	27.5	557,706
Philadelphia, PA	10	27.4	1,447,395

Source: Americans for the Arts, http://www.artsusa.org; U.S. Census Bureau, http://www.census.gov.

Table 8A.3   Ranking of Innovative Cities in the United States, 2008

City and state	Rank	Population
Portland, OR	1	557,706
Chicago, IL	1	2,853,114
Seattle, WA	1	598,541
New York, NY	1	8,363,710
San Francisco, CA	1	808,976
Minneapolis, MN	6	382,605
Boston, MA	6	609,023
Los Angeles, CA	6	3,833,995
Baltimore, MD	9	636,919
Sacramento, CA	9	466,488
San Diego, CA	9	1,279,329
Dallas, TX	12	1,279,910

Source: SustainLane, http://www.sustainlane.com/us-city-rankings/categories/innovation; population statistics from the U.S. Census Bureau, http://www.census.gov.

Table 8A.4   Top 10 Innovation Cities in the World, 2010

City and country	Global rank
Boston, United States	1
Paris, France	2
Amsterdam, Netherlands	3
Vienna, Austria	4
New York, United States	5
Frankfurt, Germany	6
San Francisco, United States	7
Copenhagen, Denmark	8
Lyon, France	9
Hamburg, Germany	10

Source: 2thinknow Innovation TM Cities Program, www.innovation-cities.com.

Table 8A.5   Ranking of Innovation Cities in the Americas, 2010

City	Rank in the Americas	Global rank
Boston, MA	1	1
New York, NY	2	5
San Francisco, CA	3	7
Toronto, Canada	4	12
Washington, DC	5	23
Philadelphia, PA	6	30
Montreal, Canada	7	34
Seattle, WA	8	35
Austin, TX	9	44
Minneapolis–St. Paul, MN	10	45

Source: 2thinknow Innovation TM Cities Program, www.innovation-cities.com.

Notes

1. All those pouring into cities are looking for "good jobs," if not for themselves, then for their children. Banerjee and Duflo (2011, 228).

2. Firms test their competitiveness by selling in the domestic market, which is frequently sheltered by tariffs, transport costs, local regulations, cultural predispositions of consumers, and complexities of marketing and logistics that foreign firms have difficulty mastering. Lenovo, the Chinese manufacturer of personal computers, and Haier, the producer of white goods, have established and maintained a lead in the domestic market by catering more effectively to local preferences and using domestic marketing channels effectively.

3. See McGee et al. (2007) on the globally oriented industrialization of Dongguan; see Yusuf, Nabeshima, and Yamashita (2008) on the international experience with clusters.

4. Larger, more capital-intensive, and more productive firms are more likely to venture into the export market. See Bernard et al. (2007); Iacovone and Javorcik (2010). On the relationship between trade and growth, see the survey by Lopez (2005); Greenaway, Morgan, and Wright (1999).

5. Some evidence suggests that successful SMEs begin orienting toward global markets from the very outset. See the papers in Lloyd-Reason and Sear (2007).

6. Much depends on the availability of affordable accommodation for small firms and their employees. In cities such as London, New York, Paris, and the cities in Silicon Valley, such space is becoming hard to find, which is squeezing out the most dynamic elements of the urban economy.

7. See Heitzman (2004) on the development of Bangalore; see also http://www.nytimes.com/2006/03/20/business/worldbusiness/20bangalore.html?ex=1300510800&en=993a11e65908ab91&ei=5088.

8. With a population of almost 7 million in 2008, including nearly 5 million migrants, Dongguan is the fourth ranked Chinese city in terms of exports.

9. Now Chongqing is attempting to create a similar eco-system by inducing Foxconn and Hewlett Packard to establish production facilities in the city, with the promise that the city will work with them to attract suppliers to the inland metropolis. Together, the two companies will be investing US$3 billion. http://www.chinadaily.com.cn/business/2009-08/05/content_8528616.htm.

10. MNCs account for 87 percent of China's exports of electronic devices and 88 percent of the exports of telecommunications equipment (Moran 2011).

11. In spite of rising wages, new entry and export growth continued in the Pearl River Delta during 2009–10.

12. Government investment in port and highway infrastructure and incentives for developers contributed to the growth of these cities and the transfer of some of the automobile, electronic, machinery, and other industries from the core city areas. See Yusuf and Nabeshima (2010).

13. A software industry serves the domestic market, but it lacks the large firms that account for the performance of Indian IT centers. Cape Town is in a similar predicament: the software-IT industry caters mostly to the domestic finance and insurance industry, which constrains its growth prospects.

14. The discovery of huge offshore pre-salt oil deposits will increase the revenues accruing to the state, depending, of course, on the terms negotiated with the center.

15. Engineering industries are transferring some of their operations to Australia.

16. See the discussion of the product space and core-periphery issues in Hidalgo et al. (2007).

17. The U.S. Department of Commerce estimates that technological innovation is responsible for as much as three-fourths of U.S. growth since World War II (Ezell and Atkinson 2010). This is not necessarily inconsistent with the findings of Jorgenson, Ho, and Samuels (2010) because the contribution of capital is heavily determined by embodied technological advances.

18. http://www.economics.harvard.edu/faculty/jorgenson/files/Houston_productivity_DJA.pdf.

19. http://www.itif.org/.

20. See Farivar (2011); Lee (2005); http://www.itu.int/ITU-D/finance/work-cost-tariffs/events/tariff-seminars/kuala-lumpur-05/presentation-lee.PDF.

21. See http://www.portnet.com/WWWPublic/pdt_portnet.html on Singapore's Portnet IT-based business-to-business system.

22. São Paulo's Santos port has long been a bottleneck, even though the cost of its inefficiency and its roots are well known. See Doctor (2002).

23. Cities with major ports are coming to recognize the air and water pollution that is caused by shipping, but they have been slow to take remedial action, although some are preparing to offer power sources to run the systems of docked ships.

24. On the importance of air cargo services especially for high-value goods, see Leinbach and Bowen (2004).

25. This has given rise to Internet Alley in a four square mile area called Tyson's Corner, a short drive from Dulles airport. See Ceruzzi (2008).

26. http://www.songdo.com/songdo-international-business-district/the-city /master-plan.aspx.

27. Cisco, IBM, and Siemens are among the companies working to create smart networked cities where computer monitoring and control of activities will increase the efficiency of everything from transport systems to energy and water use. Cisco's Connected Urban Development approach and how it affects the workplace, transport, energy consumption, and businesses using IT are described by Villa and Mitchell (2009).

28. Many of these individuals are likely to be attracted by the presence of major universities. See Winters (2011).

29. Depending on the type of industry and environmental regulations, mid-size cities can be more or less polluted.

30. The relationship between size and innovation is analyzed by Carlino, Chatterjee, and Hunt (2007) and by Carlino and Hunt (2009).

31. The grave weaknesses of governments in industrializing countries are not so much in the making of policies as in their implementation. See Hallward-Driemeier, Khun-Jush, and Pritchett (2010).

32. Philadelphia has suffered from a lack of coordination on taxation, land use, and transport development among the 238 municipalities making up the greater metro area. See Pugh O'Mara (2002).

33. The bailouts of Rio de Janeiro and São Paulo highlight the problem of moral hazard. Discouraging cities from using long-term debt to finance current expenditures is a key objective. For a review of international experience with fiscal responsibility laws, see Liu and Webb (2011).

34. See Inman (2007), who cites a study showing that a doubling in the size of a city council results in a 20 percent increase in spending per city resident.

35. North America is the model of the sprawling industrial and science parks, which have also proliferated in developing countries (O'Mara 2007).

36. It also imposes a heavy burden on the poor living on the fringes of the city, who must engage in long and costly daily commutes, as, for instance, in Johannesburg and Rio de Janeiro.

37. The architect Rem Koolhaas remarks, "There are city centers around the world in which no one seems to be a full-time resident," quoted in Heathcote (2010, 4).

38. This point is strongly championed by Ed Glaeser (2011). Although Manhattan is compact and densely populated, the New York metro area covers 3,000 square miles (Greater London is 600 square miles, Paris is 1,000 square miles), and it is significantly less dense than Los Angeles—the supposed epitome of a sprawling metropolis (7,738 residents per square mile compared with 5,728 per square mile for New York). But for all its density, Los Angeles is not a walkable city (Rybczynski 2011). Metropolitan São Paulo covers 8,000 square kilometers, while the Cape Town City region spans 100 kilometers (UN-HABITAT 2010).

39. The vision of "mobility on demand" (see http://cities.medi.mit.edu/) offered by the MIT Media Lab is alluring, and bit by bit, some elements of this are taking shape. Whether it or something like it is a part of the metropolitan future, not just in a few enlightened cities but worldwide, remains to be seen.

40. For example, a recent World Bank (2009) report notes that in China, the fragmentation of land on the fringes of cities is growing worse, land use is not being coordinated with the development of urban transport, and floor area ratios are increasing much too slowly. In fact, the gross floor area ratios are far lower in Chinese cities than in Seoul or Tokyo and much lower than in Manhattan.

41. Some incredible specimens of the green city are taking shape in Abu Dhabi (Masdar), Seoul-Incheon, Shanghai, and Tianjin, but their economic and social viability and carbon neutrality have yet to be put to the test.

42. See also Kahn (2010). See Jha et al. (2011) on both the magnitude of the problems and remedial measures.

References

Banerjee, Abhijit V., and Esther Duflo. 2011. *Poor Economics: A Radical Rethinking of the Way to Fight Global Poverty.* New York, NY: Public Affairs.

Bernard, Andrew B., J. Bradford Jensen, Stephen J. Redding, and Peter K. Schott. 2007. "Firms in International Trade." *Journal of Economic Perspectives* 21 (3): 105–30.

Brynjolfsson, Erik, and Adam Saunders. 2010. *Wired for Innovation: How Information Technology Is Reshaping the Economy.* Cambridge, MA: MIT Press.

Carlino, Gerald A., Satyajit Chatterjee, and Robert M. Hunt. 2007. "Urban Density and the Rate of Invention." *Journal of Urban Economics* 61 (3): 389–419.

Carlino, Gerald A., and Robert M. Hunt. 2009. "What Explains the Quantity and Quality of Local Inventive Activity?" Working Paper 09-12, Federal Reserve Bank of Philadelphia, Philadelphia, PA.

Ceruzzi, Paul E. 2008. *Internet Alley: High Technology in Tysons Corner, 1945–2005.* Cambridge, MA: MIT Press.

Doctor, Mahrukh. 2002. "Business and Delays in Port Reform in Brazil." *Brazilian Journal of Political Economy* 22 (2): 79–101. http://www.rep.org.br/pdf /86-5.pdf.

Ezell, Stephen J., and Robert D. Atkinson. 2010. *The Good, The Bad, and the Ugly (and the Self-Destructive) of Innovation Policy: A Policymaker's Guide to Crafting Effective Innovation Policy.* Washington, DC: Information Technology and Innovation Foundation, October. http://www.itif.org/files/2010-good -bad-ugly.pdf.

Farivar, Cyrus. 2011. *The Internet of Elsewhere: The Emergent Effects of a Wired World.* Piscataway, NJ: Rutgers University Press.

Frumkin, Howard, Lawrence D. Frank, and Richard Jackson. 2004. *Urban Sprawl and Public Health: Designing, Planning, and Building for Healthy Communities.* Washington, DC: Island Press.

Glaeser, Edward L. 2011. *Triumph of the City: How Our Greatest Invention Makes Us Richer, Smarter, Greener, Healthier, and Happier.* New York: Penguin Press.

Greenaway, David, Wyn Morgan, and P. W. Wright. 1999. "Exports, Export Composition, and Growth." *Journal of International Trade and Economic Development* 8 (1): 41–52.

Hallward-Driemeier, Mary, Gita Khun-Jush, and Lant Pritchett. 2010. "Deals Versus Rules: Policy Implementation Uncertainty and Why Firms Hate It." NBER Working Paper 16001, National Bureau of Economic Research, Cambridge, MA.

Hanushek, Eric A. 2010. "The High Cost of Low Educational Performance: The Long-Run Impact of Improving PISA Outcomes." Programme for International Student Assessment, Organisation for Economic Co-operation and Development, Paris.

Hanushek, Eric A., and Ludger Woessmann. 2010. "Education and Economic Growth." In *Economics of Education*, ed. Dominic J. Brewer and Patrick J. McEwan, 60–67. Amsterdam: Elsevier. Reprinted in *International Encyclopedia of Education*, ed. Eva Baker, Barry McGaw, and Penelope Peterson, 245–52. Amsterdam: Elsevier.

Heathcote, Edwin. 2010. "Urban Evolution." *Financial Times*, September 8, 2010.

Heitzman, James. 2004. *Network City: Planning the Information Society in Bangalore.* New York: Oxford University Press.

Hidalgo, Cesar A., Bailey Klinger, Albert-László Barabási, and Ricardo. Hausmann. 2007. "The Product Space Conditions the Development of Nations." *Science* 317 (5837): 482–87.

Hopkins, Michael S. 2010. "The Four Ways IT Is Revolutionizing Innovation." *MIT Sloan Management Review*, May 21.

Iacovone, Leonardo, and Beata S. Javorcik. 2010. "Getting Ready: Preparation for Exporting." University of Oxford. http://www.economics.ox.ac.uk/members/beata.javorcik/Tequila.pdf.

Inman, Robert P. 2007. "Financing Cities." In *A Companion to Urban Economics*, ed. R. J. Arnott and D. P. McMillen. Oxford: Blackwell.

Jha, Abhas, Jessica Lamond, Robin Bloch, Namrata Bhattacharya, Ana Lopez, Nikolas Papachristodoulou, Alan Bird, David Proverbs, John Davies, and Robert Barker. 2011. "Five Feet High and Rising: Cities and Flooding in the 21st Century." Policy Research Working Paper 5648, World Bank, Washington, DC.

Jorgenson, Dale W., Mun S. Ho, and Jon D. Samuels. 2010. "Information Technology and the Productivity Expansion." Paper presented at the 2010 Sixth Biennial North American Productivity Workshop, Rice University, Houston, TX, June 2–5.

Jorgenson, Dale W., and M. Vu Khuong. 2009. "Information Technology and the World Economy." http://www.frbsf.org/economics/conferences/0511/6_ITAndWorldEconomy.pdf.

Kahn, Matthew. 2010. *Climatopolis: How Our Cities Will Thrive in the Hotter Future*. New York: Basic Books.

Komninos, Nicos. 2008. *Smart Cities and Globalization of Innovation Networks*. New York: Routledge.

Leamer, Edward E., and Michael Storper. 2001. "The Economic Geography of the Internet Age." NBER Working Paper 8450, National Bureau of Economic Research, Cambridge, MA.

Lee, Byoung Nam. 2005. "Korean Government-Driven ICT Policy: IT 839 Strategy." Paper presented at the Regional Seminar on Costs and Tariffs for the TAS Group Member Countries, Cyberjaya, Malaysia, May 31–June 3.

Leinbach, Thomas R., and John T. Bowen Jr. 2004. "Air Cargo Services and the Electronics Industry in Southeast Asia." *Journal of Economic Geography* 4 (3): 299–321.

Liu, Lili, and Steven B. Webb. 2011. "Laws for Fiscal Responsibility for Subnational Discipline." Policy Research Working Paper 5587, World Bank, Washington, DC.

Lloyd-Reason, Lester, and Leigh Sear. 2007. *Trading Places: SMEs in the Global Economy: A Critical Research Handbook*. Cheltenham, U.K.: Edward Elgar.

Lopez, Ricardo. 2005. "Trade and Growth: Reconciling the Macroeconomic and Microeconomic Evidence." *Journal of Economic Surveys* 19 (4): 623–48.

Markusen, Ann. 1996. "Sticky Placers in Slippery Space: A Typology of Industrial Districts." *Economic Geography* 72 (3, July): 293–313. http://www.jstor.org /stable/144402.

McGee, Terry, George C. S. Lin, Mark Wang, and Andrew Marton. 2007. *China's Urban Space: Development under Market Socialism.* Routledge Studies on China in Transition. London: Routledge.

Moran, Theodore. 2011. "Foreign Direct Investment and Development: Launching a Second Generation of Policy Research." Peterson Institute, Washington, DC.

O'Mara, Margaret. 2007. "Landscapes of Knowledge: History and the Evolving Geography of High Technology." In special issue on "The Future Metropolitan Landscape," ed. Peter Bosselman, *Places* 19 (1, Spring 2007).

Pritchett, Lant, and M. Viarengo. 2010. "In Brief … Producing Superstars for the Economic World Cup." CentrePiece Summer, London School of Economics, London. http://cep.lse.ac.uk/pubs/download/cp310.pdf.

Pugh O'Mara, Margaret. 2002. "Learning from History: How State and Local Policy Choices Have Shaped Philadelphia's Growth." *Greater Philadelphia Regional Review* (March).

Rybczynski, Witold. 2011. "Dense, Denser, Densest." *Wilson Quarterly* (Spring): 46–50.

UN-HABITAT. 2010. *State of the World's Cities 2010/2011: Cities for All; Bridging the Urban Divide.* Nairobi: UN-HABITAT.

van Pottelsberghe, Bruno. 2008. "Europe's R&D: Missing the Wrong Targets?" Bruegel Policy Brief 2008/03, Bruegel, Brussels, February.

Villa, Nicola, and Shane Mitchell. 2009. "Connecting Cities: Achieving Sustainability through Innovation." Paper presented at the Fifth Urban Research Symposium 2009, Connected Urban Development, Cisco Systems, Internet Business Solutions Group.

Winters, John V. 2011. "Why Are Smart Cities Growing? Who Moves and Who Stays." *Journal of Regional Science* 51 (2): 253–70.

World Bank. 2009. *World Development Report 2009: Reshaping Economic Geography.* Washington, DC: World Bank.

Yusuf, Shahid, and Kaoru Nabeshima. 2010. *Two Dragon Heads: Contrasting Development Paths for Beijing and Shanghai.* Washington, DC: World Bank.

Yusuf, Shahid, Kaoru Nabeshima, and Shoichi Yamashita. 2008. *Growing Industrial Clusters in Asia: Serendipity and Science.* Washington, DC: World Bank.

www.ingramcontent.com/pod-product-compliance
Lightning Source LLC
Chambersburg PA
CBHW061304220326
41599CB00026B/4724